Seasons of the Hunter

SEASONS OF THE HUNTER

An anthology edited by

Robert Elman and David Seybold

Foreword by Vance Bourjaily

Illustrations by Joseph Fornelli

Alfred A. Knopf   New York   1985

THIS IS A BORZOI BOOK
PUBLISHED BY ALFRED A. KNOPF, INC.

Library of Congress Cataloging-in-Publication Data

Main entry under title:
Seasons of the hunter.
1. Hunting stories.
2. Hunting—Addresses, essays, lectures.
3. Short stories, American.
I. Elman, Robert.
II. Seybold, David.
PS648.H86S43   1985   818'.5408'080355   85-40088
ISBN 0-394-54213-4

Manufactured in the United States of America
First Edition

To Ellen Elman,

Kathleen Fornelli,

and Laurie Seybold

ACKNOWLEDGMENTS

We would like to express our deep appreciation to Angus Cameron and Charles Gaines, whose support and suggestions were of great value in the planning of this book.

David Seybold and Robert Elman

CONTENTS

FOREWORD

There is something at stake in this new collection of hunting narratives, quite openly in some, in the background of others, something which is itself new: how can we write with grace about an activity that many decent people have come to find distasteful, repugnant, even appalling?

Especially for those of us who are in middle age or beyond, it is strange to know that a large fraction of the society which once accepted or even admired us now considers us monsters to hunt, cretins to flaunt it, and insensitive troglodytes to want to write about it. The younger contributors must have faced this from the start.

Yet it reflects no more than the emergence at large of a self-doubt that was always there, contained in an almost theological question: if we claim the godlike privilege of taking lives and, worse, of sometimes maiming creatures we profess to love, how can we justify the suffering that we inflict? Do not look for a satisfactory answer to the question in this foreword, or in any one of the articles and stories. It is a mundane version of the question children have asked forever of religion's gods, getting answers more tortuous than illuminating. To my mind, there is no answer, sacred or profane—only something to ponder, over and over.

How, then, shall we write with grace? The first part of grace is honesty, and the next is to avoid self-serving. You will not find any false or tendentious pieces in this book. (Perhaps a third part of grace was best explained by Vladimir Nabokov, in the opening of *Lolita:* "You can count on a murderer for a fancy prose style." It may not be true of every piece here, but isn't it symptomatic that the quality of the prose written about hunting has improved so in the past twenty years?)

Four of the pieces in the book are fiction, two are reportage; the other fourteen are (or seem to be) autobiographical. Let me make it fifteen, with a few paragraphs of recent autobiography of my own.

I pretty much gave up hunting for a time. Now I have started going out again a little, half-a-dozen times a season, after birds generally. But last fall, at the age of 62, and for the first time ever, I killed a whitetail buck. I was pleased about it and didn't try to hide it. Measure me for a monster suit, a cretin's hat—even a troglodyte's club—for here I am, writing about the subject again, something else I thought I'd given up.

When I did a good deal of such writing, twenty-five years ago, I could acknowledge that there were people who disapproved, but I felt at no real disadvantage taking a position opposed to theirs. At that time we needed no more profound defense than the environmental one. The American deer herd, we said then, is the largest it's ever been (today it's even larger). We follow scrupulously, we said, rules for the harvest of waterfowl, of big and upland game, rules laid down by professionals who study the populations and assign us, in the form of limits and seasons, not the surplus but only a portion of it. This we enjoy trying to harvest, while providing, through license fees, excise taxes, and donations, the funds to hire the professionals, along with others to enforce their rules. These funds are also used to develop and maintain habitat, which not only fosters the flocks and herds of game but harbors nongame creatures, too. So we said, and felt good enough about it.

So what, monsters? You like to kill things, isn't that the point? Whether they are few or many, whether you pay to increase their numbers, you still like to kill them. And so? We monsters used to reply: Your meat comes from a slaughterhouse. Is that humane? Oh, you're a vegetarian? All right, have you never squashed a squash bug in your vegetable garden? Never eaten an egg laid by a chicken treated as an expendable little piece of soft machinery? Game tastes good (we'd say), the exercise is healthful, the companionship . . . And these things we used to say miss the point as widely as an attempt to persuade a nonsmoker of the merits of a fine Havana cigar.

And so we have retreated from saying irrelevant things. We acknowledge there is wrong in wounding and killing. We must talk about why, in spite of that, we do it. If we can no longer ask for wider understanding, we must look inside ourselves more carefully, and try at least to understand ourselves and our kind.

Well, then, of the reasons I go hunting again, the most irresistible, whether or not it's much of an argument, is familial. My son grew up a hunter's son, in a community of farmers. Though a talented shot, he had no taste for the kill until he was in his early twenties. Then, to my surprise, he took up hunting quite passionately. I surmise that it had something to do with reading my old hunting stuff, but perhaps even more it was one way to use and be close to our farm which he loves, part of the connection with the land he was raised on and has returned to. In addition, it was a challenge: To hunt proficiently is a matter of both self-esteem and status in the community he has chosen, and his ability at it is by now very highly respected. If someone's wounded deer has disappeared, Philip finds it. He and his cousin, my brother's son, are the men you want backing you in the field around Iowa City, probably even leading the way.

When he wanted first my guidance, then my companionship, in learning this proficiency, I had no inclination to hold back, nor do I now, when his abilities exceed my own.

Next, I think I hunt from time to time these days, after the several years during which my gun was quiet, for one of the old values that formerly meant much less to me, which is companionship in general. Men who hunt—a few of them, for I confess myself three kinds of snob (manners, law, and safe-going)—seem to be my sort. Many are much younger than I, and it matters to me that I can still keep up—when I can—with younger legs and lungs, though I expect to be outshot, and often out-generaled as well. This is a change; once I quite preferred doing it all myself.

For a third, perhaps the least-becoming, kind of emotional urge, I'll admit to a touch of surly pride. When I set aside my shotgun, it was a decision slowly and independently arrived at. When I picked it up again, I suppose I was saying to society something like, look, my conscience is my own, my morals up to me. The growth in opposition to hunting isn't unrelated to my doing just a little of it now. It's human to meet disapproval not by giving in but by hardening up.

This psychological account I've given of myself is pretty simple. So are some of the accounts that follow, while others are more intricate psychologically, and even sometimes philosophical. That doesn't mean you'll find them in any way abstract. They are full of life, full of anecdotes and stories. If I have tried to pull a few ideas out, the best is still ahead for you to read.

In Thomas McGuane's "Sportsmen," the rationale for hunting is existential—you achieve identity by what you do: existence precedes essence, as the philosophers say. McGuane's characters, a couple of kids, see life as a choice between becoming hoods and becoming sportsmen. If they have some violence in them, as the hoods have, they will express it as duck-hunters, by the lake waters they love— that is the premise of a strange, surprising piece. Threaded into its fabric is an awareness of fear and love, friendship, compassion, the pain of maturing. It is, indeed, a surprising piece.

Brian Kahn, writing of a cowboy and his country "In Max's Mountains," expresses a very different reason for going into the world of game, a reason hunters know and others, perhaps, find hard to believe. Max, the appealing cowboy, is apologetic because their bow-and-arrow hunt for elk has been unsuccessful. "Max, it's good to *be* here," the hunter says, and this is much more than merely saying that it's always good to be outdoors. "Here" is the world of Max and the elk, to which simple admission is a privilege, whether an arrow ever leaves the bow or not.

In Geoffrey Norman's "Music on the Fringe," a new value appears: hunting can enhance other experience. "I shot well enough. But I don't remember the birds so much as learning to see the scene whole for the first time . . . what I am talking about when I tell disbelieving or nonhunting friends that the actual killing is not the whole thing, or even the best part . . ." The senses, he tells us, are not just sharpened but widened, too.

". . . the birds we kill fly on forever." That phrase, which might have done as a title for this book, is in the opening line of Robert F. Jones's "Everything Your Heart Desires." It turns out to be a robust piece about bird-shooting, one encounter with animals, and some modern dangers, during a safari in Africa. But in the opening paragraphs, Jones is musing on the way our experience of killing creates a pattern which will someday be completed by our individual deaths. It is something many hunters have felt, but I've never seen it said more memorably.

E. Annie Proulx's "The Unclouded Day" is fiction, and very deft fiction, too—a good, rich yarn, almost a tall tale, finally. There are serious enough themes, which have to do with hunting as natural in rural life, with what is genuine, what phony. The themes don't show obtrusively; Proulx is good fun to read.

In Robert Elman's "God Bless the Running Deer," we are shown the hunt as capable of producing a magical healing in the hunter, not all that far removed from the healing a religious experience may bring to a mystic. For this narrator, a whole life has gone into a slump, of which missed shots and a run of bad luck in the field are all too symbolic. To make perfectly what, for him normally, would be an impossible shot on a running deer—one he usually wouldn't even try—is to be back in charge, to renew that sense of identity lost in the days of uncertainty.

Earlier, in connection with Brian Kahn's story, I mentioned the deeply felt privilege of admission to someone else's world of land and game. There is a related matter which has to do with making such a world for oneself. One of the things going on in Craig Woods's "The Endless Cover" happens to those of us fortunate enough to be able to hunt the same land through many seasons. We start to belong to it and, as Woods says, get energy from it—"it seems stupid to think that a piece of land can fill some of the void left by the recklessness of human relationships—but it can . . ."

The idea of voids is, oddly enough, very much present in Anthony Acerrano's "Pictures of Ourselves and Other Strangers"— voids and the existential (again) choices that we make to fill the voids. This is a brooding, darkly engaging piece, counterpointing moments from the hunt with others in the company of men who raise animals to sell for meat. Hunting becomes part of the search for meaning.

Probably the most comprehensive answer to my opening question can be found in Charles Gaines's "Tokens from a Dream," in which I am both mentioned and quoted, for which I thank my old friend. Part of his complex answer—Charles is a man who can think subtly and boldly at the same time—comments in a different way than Robert Jones on the endurance of experience. "I've stayed with bird-shooting long enough . . . to possess much of the time I've spent doing it. Really possess it, not in the mind but in the senses, where it stays . . . most of my days, perhaps like many of yours, are lost in a general blur. . . ."

That we can choose to leave our technology-dominated lives for days that are primitive and physical is a strong part of the appeal of hunting in these times. Lionel Atwill celebrates it in "The Fourth Day," a second account of bow-hunting for elk. And in this piece yet another point is made: when one member of the party has shot a fine bull, it is enough for all of them. Lacking an opportunity to equal or surpass, the others pass up shots at lesser trophies, yet are oddly content. There is meat enough for all.

"My Chukars" is as close to being a how-to piece as any in this collection, but it, too, finds still another, different satisfaction in hunting. With his elegant, well-used British side-by-side double in hand, Charles Waterman feels himself part of sporting tradition; by bringing this gun to a situation where method and manners are not yet established, he feels himself not only upholding tradition but helping to create it. It makes him an eager instructor.

David Seybold's "A Natural Notion" is fiction, but it confronts our question quite directly. In fields and forests, to be killed by a hunter who shares the land is a natural death for an animal, no less so than falling victim to disease, starvation, or predation. This is as acceptable to Nancy, the wife, who feels all suffering very keenly, as it is to Leon, the hunter, who brings venison to their table when it is legal to do so. What is unnatural is not just that a deer has been fatally injured on the highway, but that the hit-and-run driver lacked the compassion to try to succor the creature. It has been killed by the changing times.

Guy de la Valdene, in "Little Lover of the Bogs, Little Queen of the Woods," reminds us that there are simple, hedonistic reasons for hunting. "Given the choice of eating pork chops or wild fowl, my regret shifts to the cellophane wrapper," he says; he hunts the ridges, woods, and marshes because "that's where I'd rather be." That is where his malaise lifts, his spirits rise, and if he can sometimes be saddened by the beauty of nature, because it makes him vulnerable to other sorrows, it is also the right place to feel those other sorrows.

In Angus Cameron's "A Hunt with the Innuit," we have the first of the two reporting pieces. This one chronicles the courage and exuberance of the Eskimo, who will challenge a polar bear at arm's length with a .22. The story points out how this reckless joy in the hunt has been lost in a new generation of town Eskimos who work for the Navy, but nostalgia is not the chief point. Mostly, it is a loving observation of a people to whom hunting was not just a way of life, but one of life's delights.

The third piece of fiction in the collection is Richard Ford's "Communist," about which I had the following exchange with my young friend Dave Wilson, another contributor:

"I'm not sure I follow the politics in the piece," I said. "Why does Ford make Glen a communist? How does that connect with Glen's shooting the crippled goose with a handgun?"

"Because Glen is the crippled goose," Dave said, rather more promptly than I thought he needed to. "Glen's a disillusioned CIA man, back from Vietnam. He'd rather be in Russia. He's the cripple. Shooting the goose is a kind of suicide."

That sounded like a pretty good reading to me.

From John Randolph's "Hawk Who Walks Hunting," a reporting piece about a celebrated hunter, we can infer another reason why men still hunt. It is because the combination of skill, strength, and knowledge required to be outstanding is rarely found in one man, and the possessor of that combination is no less compelled to exercise his genius than any other first-rate outdoorsman—hiker, climber, explorer. The piece observes and listens to such a man, and there's a good deal to be learned from it.

A wry resignation can be the best—or only—response to some aspects of life, and it is a response expressed by more than one of these writers. Dick Wentz, yet another old friend, needs all the wryness he can summon in his piece, "The Candy Jar." There's a little anger and a lot of regret in the piece, as well. The narrator has moved beyond the need to find reason or justification for hunting. He just yearns for it. The land and the times have changed for Dick—as they have for others in the book, but more drastically for him. There just isn't any hunting out there any more. Perhaps this will be the solution to the whole controversy eventually—mooted, because the open land is gone.

Dave Wilson's contribution to this book is a short story called "The Great Shot," from which you will learn about another curious experience hunters have sometimes: Everything may be properly arranged, you may be where you like to hunt, with game available, and time—yet still find something missing, something in yourself, holding you back. It can happen in nonhunting situations, too, and perhaps it's hunting that teaches us to handle it in the kind of way Dave's character does.

Much of the time, Thomas McIntyre's "Across the Line" is a comic memoir, about mishaps and missed shots, on an Alaskan big-game trek for caribou. But his people are less inept than they call themselves. Actually, they solve things pretty well, and meantime the pleasures and problems, sights and sounds, of the place and the kind of chase it provides, are made ours to enjoy. It's only the narrator, really, whose luck is bad. The resignation with which he takes it, in the end, is a fine example of the saving grace of wryness which hunting has to teach.

In placing Gene Hill's "When No One Is Looking" at the end of their collection, the editors have made of one more reason why men hunt the last word on the subject here. We hunt because there is a testing of the self involved, not, in this case, a test of strength or skill, but one of character. There are rules of behavior we have for ourselves, far stricter than any law could be, and to adhere to them is a private matter, and a satisfaction of fundamental importance.

There are twenty pieces in *Seasons of the Hunter*, all of them specially written for this book. I like and respect them all a good deal. I think their total something more than the sum of the parts, because of the variety of thought, sometimes overlapping, always reaching out, never trying to evade the change in the hunter's situation today. To confront may not be to solve, but it's the way to start—and it's produced some marvelous reading here.

Vance Bourjaily

Seasons of the Hunter

SPORTSMEN

Thomas McGuane

We kept the perch in a stone pool in front of the living-room window. An elm shaded the pool, and when the heavy drapes of the living room were drawn, so that my mother could see the sheet music on the piano, the window reflected the barred shapes of the fish in the pool.

We caught them from the rocks on the edge of the lake, rocks that were submerged when the wakes of passing freighters hit the shore. From a distance, the freighters pushed a big swell in front of them without themselves seeming to move on the great flatness of the lake. My friend that year was a boy named Jimmy Meade and he was learning to identify the vessel stacks of the freighters. We liked the Bob-Lo Line, Cleveland Cliffs, and Wyandotte Transportation with the red Indian tall on the sides of the stack. We looked for whalebacks and tankers and the laden ore ships and listened to the moaning signals from the horns as they carried over the water. The wakes of those freighters moved slowly toward the land along the unmoving surface of water. The wakes were the biggest feature out there, bigger than Canada behind them, which lay low and thin like the horizon itself.

Jimmy Meade and I were thirteen then. He had moved up from lower Ohio the previous winter and I was fascinated by his almost southern accent. His father had an old pickup truck in a town which drove mostly sedans, and they had a big loose-limbed hound that seemed to stand for a distant, unpopulated place.

Hoods were beginning to appear in the school, beginning to grow drastic haircuts, wear Flagg Flyer shoes, and sing Gene Vincent songs. They hung inside their cars from the wind vanes and stared at the girls I had grown up with, revealing an aspect of violence I had not known. They wolf-whistled. They laughed with their mouths wide open and their eyes glittering, and when they got into fights, they used their feet. They spent their weekends at the drags in Flat Rock. Jimmy and I loved the water, but when the hoods came near it, all they saw were the rubbers. We were downright afraid of the hoods, of how they acted, of the steel taps on their shoes, of the way they saw things, making us feel we would be crazy to ever cross them. We were sportsmen.

But then, we were lost in our plans. We wanted to refurbish a Civil War rifle Jimmy's father owned. We were going to make an ice boat, a duck blind, and a fishing shanty. We were going to dig up an Indian mound, sell the artifacts, and buy a racing hydroplane that would throw a rooster tail five times its own length. But above all, we wanted to be duck hunters.

That August we were diving off the pilings near the entrance to the Thoroughfare Canal. We were talking about salvaging boats from the Black Friday storm of 1916 when the Bob-Lo steamer passed. The wash came in and sucked the water down around the pilings. Jimmy dove from the tallest one, arcing down the length of the creosoted spar into the green, clear water. And then he didn't come up. Not to begin with. When he did, the first thing that surfaced was the curve of his back, white and Ohio-looking in its oval of lake water. It was a back that was never to widen with muscle or stoop with worry because Jimmy had just then broken his neck. I remember getting him out on the gravel shore. He was wide awake and his eyes poured tears. His body shuddered continuously and I recall his fingers fluttered on the stones with a kind of purpose. I had never heard sounds like that from his mouth in the thousands of hours we had talked. I learned from a neighbor that my screams brought help and, similarly, I can't imagine what I would sound like screaming. Perhaps no one can.

My father decided that month that I was a worthless boy who blamed his troubles on outside events. He had quite a long theory about all of this, and hanging around on the lake or in the flat woods hunting rabbits with our .22s substantiated that theory. I forget how.

He found me a job over in Burr Oak cleaning die-cast aluminum molds with acid and a wire brush. That was the first time I had been around the country people who work in small factories across the nation. Once you get the gist of their ways, you can get along anyplace you go, because they are everywhere and they are good people.

When I tried to call Jimmy Meade from Burr Oak, his father said that he was unable to speak on the telephone. He said Jimmy was out of the hospital and he would always be paralyzed. In his father's voice, with its almost-southern Ohio accent, I could feel myself being made to know that though I had not done this to Jimmy, I had been there, and that there was villainy, somehow, in my escape.

I really don't think I could have gotten out of the factory job without crossing my own father worse than I then dared. But it's true, I missed the early hospitalization of Jimmy and of course I had missed having that accident happen to me in the first place. I still couldn't picture Jimmy not being able to move anything, being kind of frozen where we left off.

I finished up in August and stayed in Sturgis for a couple of days, in a boardinghouse run by an old woman and her sixty-year-old spinster daughter. I was so comfortable with them that I found myself sitting in the front hall watching the street for prospective customers. I told them I was just a duck hunter. Like the factory people, they had once had a farm. After that, I went home to see Jimmy.

He lived in a small house on Macomb Street about a half-mile from the hardware. There was a layout duck boat in the yard and quite a few cars parked around, hot rods mostly. What could have explained this attendance? Was it popularity? A strange feeling shot through me.

I went in the screen door at the side of the house, propped ajar with a brick. There were eight or ten people inside, boys and girls our own age. My first feeling, that I had come back from a factory job in another town with tales to tell, vanished and I was suddenly afraid of the people in the room, who were faster, tougher kids than Jimmy and I had known. There were open beer bottles on the table and the radio played hits.

Jimmy was in the corner where the light came through the screens from two directions. He was in a wheelchair and his arms and legs had been neatly folded within the sides of the contraption. He had a ducktail haircut and a girl held a beer to his lips, then replaced it with a Camel in a fake pearl-and-ebony cigarette holder. His weight had halved and there were copper-colored shadows under his eyes. He looked like a modernized station of the cross.

When he began to talk, his Ohio accent was gone. How did that happen? Insurance was going to buy him a flathead Ford. "I'm going to chop and channel it," he said, "kick the frame, french the headlights, bullnose the hood, and lead the trunk." He stopped and twisted his face away to draw on the cigarette. "There's this hillbilly in Taylor Township who can roll and pleat the interior."

I didn't get the feeling he was particularly glad to see me. But what I did was just sit there and tough it out until the room got tense and people just began to pick up and go. That took no time at all: The boys crumpled beer cans in their fists conclusively. The girls smiled with their mouths open and snapped their eyes. Everyone knew something was fishy. They hadn't seen me around since the accident, and the question was: What was I doing there now?

"I seen a bunch of ducks moving," Jimmy said.

"I did too."

"Seen them from the house." Jimmy sucked on his cigarette. "Remember how old Minnow Milton used to shoot out of his boathouse when there was ducks?" Minnow Milton had lived in a floating house that had a trap attached to it from which he sold shiners for bait. The floating house was at the foot of Jimmy's road.

"I remember him."

"Well, Minnow's no longer with us. And the old boat is just setting there doing nothing."

The next morning before daybreak, Jimmy and I were in Minnow Milton's living room with the lake slapping underneath and the sash thrown up. There were still old photographs of the Milton family on the walls. Minnow was a bachelor and no one had come for them. I had my father's 12-gauge pump gun propped on the windowsill and I could see the blocks, the old Mason decoys, all canvasbacks, that I had set out beneath the window, thirty of them bobbing, wooden beaks to the wind, like steamboats seen from a mile up. I really couldn't see Jimmy. I had wheeled him in terror down the gangplank and into the dark. I set the blocks in the dark, and when I lit his cigarette, he stared down the length of the holder, intently, so I couldn't tell what he was thinking. I said, "What fun is there if you can't shoot?"

"Shoot," he said.

"I'm gonna shoot. I was just asking."

"You ain't got no ducks anyways."

To my relief, that was true. But it didn't last. A cold wind came with daylight. A slight snow spit across the dark gray water, touching and scattering down into the whitecaps. I saw a flight of mallards rocket over and disappear behind us. Then they reappeared and did the same thing again right across the roof over our heads. When they came the third time, they set their wings and reached their feet through hundreds of feet of cold air toward the decoys. I killed two and let the wind blow them up against the floating house. Jimmy grinned from ear to ear.

I built a fire in Minnow Milton's old stove and cooked those ducks on a stick. I had to feed Jimmy off the point of my Barlow knife, but we ate two big ducks for breakfast and lunch at once. I stood the pump gun in the corner.

Tall columns of snow advanced toward us across the lake, and among them, right in among them, were ducks, some of everything, including the big canvasbacks that stirred us like old music. Buffle-heads raced along the surface.

"Fork me some of that there duck meat," said Jimmy Meade in his Ohio voice.

We stare down from our house window as our decoys fill with ducks. The weather gets so bad the ducks swim among the decoys without caring. After half a day we don't know which is real and which is not. I wrap Jimmy's blanket up under his chin.

"I hope those ducks keep on coming," he says. And they do. We are in a vast raft of ducks. We don't leave until the earth has turned clean around and it is dark again.

IN MAX'S MOUNTAINS

Brian Kahn

We met across a summer campfire. Lillian, teacher-turned-cowgirl, introduced us, Max coming from the darkness after a hard day pushing cows and calves. I remembered the name.

Fifteen years earlier, a summer and fall before law school, I'd worked for Frank Brady, Max's neighbor on the summer range. Brady was getting old, even then. Too much rough riding and rough drinking had crippled him, and he lived in the bedroom and kitchen of the main house, reading cheap novels and watching the destruction of his world.

Brady grew up on the ranch homesteaded by his father in 1912. He'd been a good horseman and a fair guide. To hear him tell it, he'd been a crack shot, great elk hunter, top bronc rider, and one tough guy. He probably was. But he'd grown old and fat, living in his bathrobe, only his mind remaining sharp. And he fed on bile as his ways of living and ranching died, horses giving way to trucks, cowboys to businessmen.

His voice cracked as the young, rich bull breeder who leased Brady's land pulled up to the corral on a lathered mare. "That man's hard on horses."

Brady respected Max. "He's a fair hand," he said. Max did things right. He cared for his horses, knew the faces of his cows. Each October, when he pushed his herd across Brady land, beginning the sixty-mile cattle drive down the Madison to the winter range, Brady brightened for a time, dressed, tied on a black silk scarf, and hobbled out of the house under his silver belly Stetson, heading for the horse barn. Breathing hard, he saddled his favorite horse, the Shadow mare, and, climbing on an apple box, stepped into the stirrup. He and Max worked the herd, Max pushing, Brady cutting out the strays. Shadow pranced under Frank's heavy body, certain of him and herself, proud, even haughty in her work. Brady rode in silence until the work was done. Then he joined Max at the corral gate, where they sat in the saddle, side by side, looking at the milling herd. And Brady would say, "That's one more time we got 'em clean."

In the intervening years I'd worked in many jobs, from boxing coach to politician. The jobs had one thing in common—the need to know people, making contact and at the same time keeping distance, to see what was inside. And so I watched Max, watched as he followed the conversation of Lillian's young, urban friends, a cup of red wine cradled in heavy, work-hardened hands.

The conversation drifted with the smoke—politics, environment, the world. When Max talked, one instinctively listened. It wasn't the force of his voice or its tone, but rather the pace at which he talked, and the frequency. He spoke rarely, with a deliberateness pregnant with forethought. The sentences were short, delivered under dark brown eyes which focused on the listener.

His face was somber and spoke of reflection. The nose was long and slightly flattened in the middle, making the evenly proportioned face seem longer than it was. The hair, thinning now and flecked with gray, still shone black against the red-brown of his skin, colored and lined by fifty summers and winters on the range. The face changed when he laughed, the drawn mouth and slim lips curling catlike while lines broke around the face and the eyes sparkled. A laugh one remembered seeing, not hearing.

Max and I talked across the fire, yellow flames lighting our faces, each of us sensing the other was a maverick in his field, knowing our lives differed, understanding there was truth in both.

It grew late and I rose to leave. Max stood too.

"It was good meeting you," I said.

"We'll have to get you up to the cow camp for a meal," he said. "I'd enjoy the company."

We had that meal, and many more. He took to Sandra, my wife and a painter. Another truth, another world. Short-handed that summer, he used our help, cutting cows, mending pipe, checking on the herd.

He owned nothing new. Everything purchased was instantly

transformed, as though by the force of its surroundings. That summer he bought a vinyl gun case. It emerged from the forty-mile ranch-to-cow-camp truck ride a grizzled veteran, dust-covered and scarred by the assorted tools, wire, and gear which occupied Max's cab. The truck itself appeared to be either the survivor or the victim of a demolition derby. One did not notice scratches, dings, or dents, but gouges, smashes, crushed and twisted steel. The essentials—doors and drive train—worked. Mulling the prospect of a new truck, Max smiled slowly. "I probably won't get much in trade."

Max cared more for his horses than for his machinery. "I just expect my equipment to work," he said. "It wouldn't be ranching without horses." He owned, perhaps, twenty-five. Colors and conformation varied, though most carried the large head and spotted blanket of Appaloosa blood, sleek and round-hammed, rolling muscles dominant under thin coats of summer. His horses had to be versatile: Each must cut, rope, hunt, and pack. "In the mountains, a man depends on his horses."

One morning a young roan had balked when approached with a pack saddle. He reared wild-eyed against the lead rope, twelve hundred pounds of fear and jarring violence. Max swore softly, retrieved the oats bucket, and gave the roan an added portion. The young horse stood, still breathing hard and chewing oats, while the offending sawbuck was slipped over his back.

"Some use whips, but I oat-train my horses," said Max. "Whip-trained, they come when they have to. In the mountains, they don't have to."

Evenings at the cow camp we retrieved jug wine from the spring and talked on benches in the old trapper's cabin. And from the talk, sitting across the narrow table, testing the words and eyes for truth and conviction, ties were made. Unlike childhoods, unlike lives, unlike generations had led to common ground. We both had come to know that the land was worth more than money, and people more than profit, and that basic truths of life and death and time could be found silently, alone, on a windy ridge amidst aspens and tall grass.

We knew also that we differed. And in the knowing each understood he could learn—learn things of value—from the other.

We spoke of many things, but not, in the beginning, of hunting. It was odd, for both of us. In the West, hunting is conversation in every bar and gas station. Men talk hunting as they talk weather, casually over coffee or leaning against pickups.

Then one night Max said he had hunters due that fall.

"You guide?"

"When I need to," said Max. "When beef prices are down we need the money." Then he grinned, his laugh soft. "Seems like I'm guiding all the time."

"Sounds as though it's not your favorite pastime."

Max was serious again."Oh, it's not so bad. I've had some good hunters . . ." He fell to thinking. "Some bad ones too." He smiled again. "Problem is, you can't choose your company." He thought some more. "Funny bunch," he said. "Not many shoot that well. Oh, they're death on targets. But when they get into game they go all to pieces. Hell, when you see game, that's the time to settle down!"

I thought of the times I'd made the stalk, feeling the tension rise, fighting to stay calm as I moved in close, close to the wild animal.

"And there's the pressure. Makes business out of pleasure." He spoke slowly, each word distinct. "People don't understand elk. They figure they've paid their money, so they're going to just walk out and shoot one." He shook his head. "They don't understand."

One day he saw my bow. "You hunt with that?"

"Mule deer." I felt the high basins, the big bucks, lying close, blinking in the shade. "It's a different hunt."

"I've often thought to try that," Max said. "That would be real sport." He paused. "Come up next fall and we'll try to bugle up an elk. I think you'll like the mountains."

More than once I tried to pay. Each time he had a different way of saying no. "You'll help me a little with the cows." "I've got to go in anyway to set up my hunting camp." "It's my vacation."

This would not be business. We would hunt as friends.

The pack train came to a grassy park amid the pines. Watkins Creek tumbled noisily past on the east side of the meadow, just beyond the weathered railroad ties half buried in lush grass.

"The trapper cabin set there before we had the cow camp," said Max, turning in the saddle. "We ran sheep out of here for eleven years. A big grizzly killed eight of our sheep. Then one night he came here to the cabin."

I remembered the cabin's window screen: two one-inch holes, side by side.

The grizzly had died ten years before, but these were still wild mountains.

In July a renegade bear had killed a man, and now, in September, I packed a heavy pistol as we rode toward elk camp.

The trail led up a long canyon and disappeared in heavy timber. We rode west, toward gray stone peaks.

We reached the timber, and the world changed. The trail, dry in the meadows, became soft and dark. A world of shadows wedged between thin uprights of close-pressed pines. The earth was littered with blowdowns, graying skeletons of trees, and held the near-round tracks of elk, heading higher.

We crisscrossed Watkins Creek, the horses stepping cautiously, easing in broad muzzles to drink the live water.

The trail climbed north, the horses grunting at its pitch. Max rode in silence, straight and lean, left arm high and to his chest, holding a light rein. His right hand, stiff and down, gripped the pack rope. The three-horse string followed, halter ropes sheepshanked to tails. Sandra and I rode behind, exchanging glances at the beauty of the land and the steepness of the trail.

Another hour, and Max cut off the main track, across an open side hill, up and over a narrow ridge into blowdowns. The trail vanished in the maze, Max picking his way, using his heels when his young mount paused, questioning his judgment.

"Been a while since this trail's been cleared."

A half-hour on, Max turned from the trail, crossed a tiny stream, and rode into a long, narrow meadow, lush in mountain grass. He rode to the meadow's head, reined in the mare, and stepped down. We were in camp.

The horses tied, we unloaded the manty-covered packs—tent, sheepherder's stove, sleeping bags, and duffel. Plywood panniers held precious cargo: canned goods, fresh meat, eggs, and wine.

An hour later the white of the wall tent stood full and square against the pines, braced by lodgepoles from last year's camp. Blue-gray smoke boiled from the jutting stovepipe, thinning and slowing as it rose. Heavy down bags lay on thick foam pads and a pot of potatoes bubbled slowly on the stove.

We stood near the tent and practiced with the bows, driving

arrows into rich meadow soil. Max shot the way he spoke, deliberately. "I still feel green with this thing," he said, absorbed in the ritual, nocking, drawing, holding, and releasing the glowing shafts, then standing, retracing with his mind their hissing flight. Satisfied, he turned and smiled. "It lets us be kids again, for a little while."

Night fell. The horses ate lazily in the meadow, snorting softly as they pulled their drags. Max, hair slicked down and face washed for supper, bent over the low-set stove, slowly stirring milk gravy while the steaks sizzled and muffins browned.

Conversation flowed with the red wine. We sat on sawed stumps and Max spoke of past hunts and sheep and early snows. He talked of elk and deer and horses. And he spoke of the land and its new users, of bureaucrats and subdividers and tax-dodge ranchers. And of the mountains' past, of Nez Percé pursued by phalanxed troops in blue, struggling north through Targhee's snow, desperate warriors on spotted horses, fighting for families and freedom.

"They were right," Max said.

The slow dying of the lantern signaled the end of talk, and we slipped through tent flaps to dip our cups in the stream, savoring pure water under low stars.

We scouted in the morning, moving silently along broad game trails in the trees. Max walked in the same western boots in which he rode ("My feet are too old to change," he said, smiling), kneeling, looking close at round, split-hoof prints in soft earth. This was the rutting season and we listened for the shrill, braying challenges of mating bulls. The only sound was wind. We found rubbed trees, thin bark shredded by heavy antlers, and elk wallows, gray-brown pools of mud at the head of springs, rank with musky sweetness.

"We're in their living room," said Max.

In the afternoon we stalked grouse as they clucked among the trees. In close, we straightened against the pull of our bows, and sent blunt-tipped arrows at the birds. Two fell, nourishment for hunters, the rest rattling through branches to set broad wings and sail toward sheltering pines.

Back at the horses, he turned to me. "Sorry we haven't seen game."

I looked at his eyes, knowing the guide had surfaced in his mind. "Max, it's good to *be* here."

The red-brown face turned slowly to a smile, eyes shining. "Yeah."

We rode to camp under black rolling clouds, a hissing wind pressing at our backs. Night came, clear and still, but the illusion of fall had fled, leaving the stark awareness of winter, closing.

We were back next day and this time armed, our arrows tipped with razored heads. The difference, though, was more than in the weapons. Now we felt the elemental tension of the hunt.

We walked spiny ridges above gaping canyons solid in virgin trees. On northern slopes, the trees stacked close to form a wall of green and black; on southern slopes, fewer trees, growing singly or in small groves amid gray rock and green meadows.

We blew hard into black-tubed elk "bugles," squealing shrill challenges to unseen bulls below, then knelt in silence, waiting. Throughout the day, the trees swallowed up our sounds, returning nothing.

Stopping at a spring, we dipped handfuls of clear water and sat chewing sinewy strips of jerky, the long-stored energy of a buck deer, once sleek and fat and far away.

The day ending, sharp light moving into gray, we sat above a timbered saddle, waiting. A camp robber flapped past in labored, noisy flight. Above us on the slope a dusky grouse picked his way among the trees, the high-headed, low-tailed strut simultaneously pompous and frightened. A movement below: a coyote in full coat, reddish brown. He froze, crouched, then pounced, vanishing as he had come, unaware he shared the mountain with other hunters.

Again we bugled. The long, high note vanished down the canyon, replaced by silence. A hint of wind. Then, from the blue-black depths of the forest, a faint, low sound, shifting, before it was fully grasped, to something high and thin and urgent, gripping and primeval, rolling back centuries, cutting through boots and clothes, piercing to the center.

MUSIC ON THE FRINGE

Geoffrey Norman

We turned off the blacktop and drove down a dirt road with shallow ditches on either side. The ditches were full of blackberry vines, bare of both leaves and fruit in November. You could see the thorns. You could almost feel them. One thing about quail hunting in south Alabama—you have to get used to briars.

We turned up a small drive and parked in front of a little frame farmhouse. It was painted white, with a small, well-tended lawn, azalea bushes, and a few tall pines planted around it to soften the way it stood out in the middle of the plowed fields and fenced pastures. We got out of the car and walked up to the front door of the house. Uncle Robert knocked.

This part always made me uncomfortable. I was a kid and I didn't know anything. I didn't live among these people—came over for the weekend from the city a hundred miles away—and I just assumed that the people would say no when you asked if it would be all right to run dogs through their fields and shoot any quail the dogs found. But Uncle Robert didn't seem to mind. In fact, he actually seemed to enjoy it. Of course, I thought, he lived here and he knew these people. The few he didn't actually know—well, he knew someone close to them. Knew their kin. So it was never a completely cold introduction for him, the way it would be for, say, somebody selling soap.

"Morning," Uncle Robert said when the screen door opened.

"How you?" a man in overalls said back.

He and Robert shook hands. Then Robert explained who he was and how he happened to know this man's father. "I bought some saw logs from him . . . oh, must be six or eight months ago."

The man nodded.

"By the way," Robert said, "this is my nephew." He introduced me and I managed to shake the man's hand. I wanted to be gone from there in the worst way.

"We're looking for some birds to hunt this morning," Robert went on, "and we thought we'd stop and see if we could hunt over your land. We'd be obliged."

"Waaaal," the man said, looking off toward the fields as if he were thinking it over, weighing the issue. He had a lean face full of creases that a lifetime of farming had put there. It wasn't a mean face, necessarily. But it was proud and private. I hoped he would merely say no and leave it at that.

He pulled at his unshaven chin and finally said, "Go on and hunt. Lemme see can I remember where I last saw some birds. There's been a few."

He paused again.

"Lessee. Probably the best place is gone to be down by that bean patch. There's bicolor along the edge and I just combined the beans a week ago. Ought to be plenty still on the ground."

I felt enormously relieved and figured that would do it. We could leave this stranger's porch and get on with what we'd come to do. But Robert seemed to want to stay and talk.

"You have a good crop?" he said. "Dry as it's been?"

"Pretty good. This is only my third year of beans and I'll tell you . . . it would have to get a whole lot worse before it would be as bad as cotton in a *good* year."

Robert said something sympathetic and they talked for what seemed like an awful long time about fertilizer and pesticides and other things I didn't think anyone except a farmer would know about. Finally the farmer shook our hands again and said "Good luck" and we left for the freshly combined bean field, which we could see against a line of pine trees maybe half a mile away.

We found birds that morning. Found them right where the farmer had said we'd find them. There was lespedeza along the edge of his bean patch, just as he'd said. There were also lots of blackberry briars, which he had neglected to mention. But we had a tough old pointer that year. Named Doc or something like that. He didn't mind briars. In fact, he didn't seem to mind anything, not even a beating now and then for running off and chasing a rabbit. When he was through, he would just come on in, calm and matter-of-fact, and take his whipping. When it was over, he'd dive back into the blackberry briars and go back to work.

About twenty minutes after we got started, Doc locked into this hard quivering point with his nose about six inches off the ground and his tail stuck up in the air like a lightning rod.

"My, my," Robert said. "Look at that. Isn't it *pretty?*"

"Sure is," I whispered. I was already getting nervous. I was a new young bird hunter and I still went all to pieces on a covey rise.

"I'd call that a stylish point," Uncle Robert went on calmly, as though he were admiring a painting and not a flesh-and-blood dog. "No matter what the field trial boys say."

We were easing up on Doc now. My heart was thudding in my ears and I had a white-knuckled grip on the stock of my 20-gauge. "Just one bird," I said to myself. "Just one bird. Pick one out and shoot."

As we passed Doc, the covey erupted from the grass twenty steps in front of us. The birds came up at the same time, like a football team coming off the ball all at once on the quarterback's count. Then every bird did something different but each was part of this play. And the noise was overpowering. I went all to pieces again, threw my gun to my shoulder, and shot in the general direction of the noise where the covey was becoming twenty separate birds, each flying its own desperate, hasty pattern.

My shot missed, of course, but I did see a bird drop cleanly when Robert shot beside me. Then, while I was looking for a shot and trying to make the muzzle of my gun go where my eyes were looking, he shot again and another bird fell. I got my second shot off, finally, but it was too late. I was actually shooting at a single bird, instead of at the whole covey, but that one bird was woefully out of range.

After the startling whirring noise of the birds taking wing and the four shotgun blasts, everything seemed very quiet for several seconds. I could hear my heart beating again.

Robert broke open his gun at the breech and said, "Fetch, Doc." The dog trotted out to where the birds had fallen.

"You get one?" Robert said.

"No," I said, disappointed and mad at myself. I'd done it again. Fallen apart when a few birds got up in front of me.

"Don't worry," Robert said gently. "It takes time."

I nodded and watched, full of envy, as he took his bird from Doc's mouth and sent him back out to find the other.

He looked the bird over, then put it in the game pouch of his vest. There were streaks of dried brown blood around the mouth of the game pouch. I wanted mine to look that way someday. I'd had it for a year and it was still very clean.

While I was waiting impatiently for Doc to retrieve the other bird, I noticed something. It came to me first as a sound. The steady drone of a motor. Then something caught my eye. It was a tractor, moving back and forth in the field adjacent to the one where we were hunting. It was over a half mile away—well out of shotgun range—but it was still part of the scene, along with the dogs, the broomweed, the briars, and the two still-warm birds in Robert's game pouch.

I could look over my shoulder and see the little house where we had stopped and asked for permission to hunt. It came to me then that these birds lived close up against land that people used. That we were a long way from hunting the wilderness.

That was a little disappointing to a callow boy. Hard as it was for me to hit them, I began thinking of bobwhites as a sort of domesticated bird and, for that reason, one that was less worthy. I imagined myself out in the river bottoms, where you hunted deer and turkey in the big hardwoods. Thought, too, about the mountains that I'd only read about, where you hunted elk and sheep. This bird hunting seemed more and more like hunting in your yard.

So I continued to shoot lamely as Doc worked the singles that had put down short of a cypress pond that filled the low ground between two fields. Every bird I flushed went straight for that bottom with my pattern of eights chasing but missing, by wider and wider margins. The briars and the sound of the tractor and my miserable shooting were all factors that worked on my morale and made me, after a couple of hours of it, one miserable boy.

Robert gave me a word or two of encouragement and then, wisely, left it alone. I trudged along, behind the dog, through the briars, with the sound of the tractor a kind of dirge in my ears.

Sometime around noon we quit for lunch.

"How about a seafood platter?" Robert said cheerfully when we got back to the car. He had six birds in his pouch.

"Uh . . . sure," I said. I hadn't realized there was a restaurant within forty miles. Certainly not one that served seafood platters. Pork chops, black-eyed peas, and turnips would be about right.

We drove back to the blacktop and, ten miles down the road, parked in front of a general store. It was the kind with steel Nehi and Dr Pepper signs nailed to the walls, rusting around the corners and where the nails had gone through and nicked the paint.

Robert knew the men who were sitting on the porch, leaning back in their chairs, chewing tobacco. He spoke to all of them. They asked if he'd shot any birds and he said, "Scared 'em mostly, boys."

"Hit's them damned Mexican quail," one of the men said. "They won't hold still for a point. They're the ruin of quail hunting, you want my opinion."

"What's a Mexican quail?" I asked when we were inside.

"Damned if I know," Robert said happily. "I've never seen a quail wearing a sombrero. But anything you want to talk about with those fellows, they'll be happy to explain to you why it ain't like it used to be."

It turned out that a seafood platter consisted of a can of tuna fish, a can of salmon, a can of sardines, a box of soda crackers, the soft drink of your choice, and pickled pig's feet for dessert. It was a fine lunch. We ate it on the porch and listened while the men in the chairs explained why the country at large was going the way of quail hunting.

They were a conservative bunch and they usually concluded that it was the guv'ment behind whatever it was that had gone wrong with things that were once so good. Probably it was the guv'ment that had brought in those infernal Mexican quail that wouldn't stand to a point and were crossbreeding with our stately little bobwhite so that he wouldn't either.

Robert and I listened gravely to everything these philosophers had to say. He was still young enough—in his thirties—to make a point of deferring to his elders. When we'd finished our lunch and were leaving, he said to one of them, "Well, cap'n, I suppose you're right. But tell me one thing. What is it that you think the guv'ment *ought* to be doing?"

The man gave it a second or two of deep thought, leaned forward in his chair, spat a load of Red Man, and said, "The guv'ment ought to guard the coast, tote the mail, and stay the hell out of everything else."

I remembered that line often, especially in political science classes, where no one could manage a definition so succinctly.

From the store, we drove on to another farm, where once again we asked for permission to hunt and, just like before, received it almost ritually. Also like before, Robert talked a while with the farmer about the weather and his crops. Then we drove to the field where we would be hunting and slept for an hour in the shade of a live oak tree.

Fifteen minutes after we woke up, Doc hit a point at the corner of a bean patch and Robert said, "I believe this is the one. It just has that look."

I was still feeling slightly stunned from the heavy lunch and the long nap, stiffened up a little from the walking we'd done that morning, so I went in on the dog in a kind of distracted fog, not tense and determined the way I had been all morning.

The covey flushed when we were a step or two beyond Doc. The sudden noise and the confusion of brown fragments angling desperately away from us, toward another cypress bog, still rattled me but not the way it had in the morning. I seemed cooler at the core and, perhaps for that reason, the birds flew a little more predictably and the gun barrel came up quickly and smoothly. My stupefied senses were in control. I moved the muzzle of the gun as if it were the point of a pencil I was using to mark the correct answer on one of my school tests. I covered a bird, touched the trigger, and knew right away that I had hit. I saw the bird crumple and drop, already lifeless as a stone. I was much too excited to even try for a second shot.

"Good man," Robert said, "you just had to find your groove. Now you got it . . . there's no stopping you."

Doc brought my bird in and dropped it at my feet and I saw the retriever through new eyes. I picked the little cock bird up and held it in my hand. It was barely ruffled, except for two little spots of blood that seeped from its back feathers. I admired the bird for a moment, feeling the trace of regret that you always feel. Then I put the bird in my game pouch, being careful to smear some of the blood on the fabric as I did it.

We walked up the singles that hadn't made it to the cypress swamp. It went better for me now. I still missed but, knowing that I could do it, I didn't expect to miss. I was genuinely surprised when I did. I took my time and I killed some birds.

And as I began to succeed, the setting became agreeable. It seemed right to be hunting on the fringes of human settlement, among the patch farms and the little stands of pine that were notched for turpentine. The sound of a tractor seemed appropriate background music, just as the occasional steer grazing in a field we'd wanted to hunt seemed like an obstacle to be taken in stride.

We found another covey or two that afternoon. And I shot well enough. But I don't remember the birds so much as I remember learning to see the scene whole for the first time. As I've hunted birds, more and more to the exclusion of other things, this is what I see most clearly and what I remember . . . what I am talking about when I tell disbelieving non-hunting friends that the actual killing is not the whole point or even the best part of hunting birds.

I have come across all sorts of things hunting birds. Things that make you think about what a long, touch-and-go struggle it is to clear and cultivate a piece of ground. Of how eagerly the land will stage a comeback if it is given the chance. In the South, there are the old outbuildings from farms that have perished or gone to some kind of centralized, single-crop system. You might even run across a building made of rough-ripped pine boards, roofed with tin and raised off the ground on squares of brick. Even though the building is crumbling and matted with kudzu, you can tell that it was once home to a family. A sharecropper's place, more than likely. A man had once built this place, then lived in it while he tried to support his family on a few acres of poor ground and an endless string of backbreaking days in the field. Probably he failed and left the land and his home to the insects, elements, and vines that will eventually finish it off.

In Vermont, I have come across the remains of several sugaring operations. The buckets and taps and pans rusty and half covered with leaves. I would pause on my way out of a grouse covert and wonder about all that galvanized steel going to junk. There was tragedy in it, because no Vermonter would simply pick up and leave all that perfectly good equipment to rust in the woods. He'd have a reason. Too old or sick to sugar another season, maybe. Or even dead.

I've found old cast-iron hand pumps almost everywhere I've hunted. One in North Carolina stuck up from an overgrown hillside like an aiming stake. There was no other sign of anything human around. It was as if some ghost artillery had set up here, fired a few rounds, and, as the flow of battle changed, moved on to another position. My best guess was that the well had been sunk by the crew that logged the area. It was probably easier than bringing water up from the river. There was an old whiskey jar on the ground next to the pipe. It was full of some fairly evil-looking water, which I used to prime the pump. A few strokes on the handle cleared the rust, and the water ran clear and cold. It tasted great. I refilled the whiskey bottle for the next thirsty hunter.

I've run across countless sawdust piles left over from traveling peckerwood operations. The remains of a couple of old brick kilns. The railbed where a narrow-gage once ran, hauling timber out of the deep woods. And recently, a small but intensively cultivated marijuana patch.

And small plots, dozens of them, where the people who had once farmed the land are now buried. In Vermont I have come upon a couple that are neatly fenced and carefully tended and where the dates on the stones are all earlier than 1800. In one plot, the dates on half of the stones are all within five or six days of each other. Some epidemic, no doubt. A curse that no one can even recall these days. One of the victims was only two. There is a fragment of Scripture carved into the face of each stone. "Suffer the little children to come unto me," the words on the two-year-old's marker read, "for theirs is the kingdom of God."

This plot is on the high slope of a hill that is grown up into big hardwoods, mostly beech. It is cool there, a good place to rest in the early season, when there are still leaves on the trees and the shade feels good after a couple of hours in the heat and the briars.

So the dog and the birds and the shotgun are still important to me, all these years after that first good day, the one with Robert, when I finally learned to kill birds on the covey rise. But the background has become even more important to me. Perhaps because it is the one part of the mix that is most threatened. Every year, everywhere, more and more good bird-hunting country is lost to posting or to development. The land that remains becomes more and more the same kind of land, with holdings growing larger and with farmers and foresters both turning to monoculture under the pressures of the economy. Patch farming and small woodlots are a thing of the barely gone but very dead past.

The dogs are still great performers; the birds are even more abundant now than they were when I started. I have learned to handle the gun a little better now that I don't feel so much riding on every shot. But the background for it has shrunk and I find that regrettable, even though it probably makes me sound like the fellows back on that porch, chewing and rocking and bitching about how the Mexican quail has been going around mongrelizing the bobwhite and ruining everything.

There is still good bird country, I suppose, but it isn't the same. How could it be? How could anything be as good as the evening when I had quit and was coming out of the fields on an old logging trace to the place where I thought I had left my car. The dog was up ahead, somewhere in the gloom. I couldn't see him but that was all right. It was almost suppertime and this particular dog never missed a meal. My gun was over my shoulder and I was taking my time. Enjoying the fragrance of pine that seems keener at dusk than any other time. I had half a dozen birds in my pouch, which was at last sufficiently bloody so that I didn't think about it anymore.

For some reason the dog came back to walk at my side. It was impossible that he'd learned to heel. That, I knew, would never happen. Something had chased him back to me. Maybe there were some coon hunters, I thought, setting up ahead of us. Then I heard a sound that carried through the woods like the wind before a storm.

The noise rose. Then stopped. The dog moaned. I walked on but my legs felt suddenly lighter. Then the noise began again—low and soft but with the power to carry through the dark and the trees.

I made out a shape. A farmhouse, I thought, or a barn. Something with the angles and symmetry that let you know it was man-made. There were lights in the windows.

It was, I saw when I was a hundred steps from the building, a church. A backwoods, pine-board church, and the light that came through its windows was a lantern light.

The sound I'd heard was the sound of singing. Fifty or sixty black voices—men, women, and children—singing songs of Jesus' mercy and God's glory in their little church in the woods. In the last light of day, it was a sound sweet enough to break your heart.

I listened for fifteen minutes or so. Then I began to feel like some kind of intruder. I walked on down the trace with the music falling more and more faintly behind me until it was gone. I believe I felt redeemed.

EVERYTHING YOUR HEART DESIRES

Robert F. Jones

In some strange way the birds we kill fly on forever. Perhaps it's the broken arc, the interrupted parabola, the high zig through the alders that never quite made it to zag—all those incompletions crying out to be consummated. But something there is that keeps them airborne if only in our hearts, their wings forever roaring at the base of our trigger fingers. The partridge that puffs to the shot string this morning at the edge of some frost-crisp apple orchard in the hills of Vermont is the selfsame bird—but totally different, of course—as the very first dove we ever knocked down, a lifetime ago, over a midwestern cornfield. And watched in disbelief the pale feathers spill slowly from a saffron sky.

Sometimes, drunk or dreaming, I see the world crisscrossed in a webwork of avian force fields, the flight paths of ghost birds winging on out as if they'd never been hit. In the end, of course, they will weave our own rough winding sheets . . .

June 1974: The big Bedford lorries had arrived the day before, so by the time we wheeled into the campsite along the Ewaso Nyiro River the tents were up—taut, green, smelling of hot canvas and spicy East African dust. It was a sandy country, red and tan, and the river rolled silently but strong, dark almost as blood, under a fringe of scrawny-trunked doum palms and tall, timeworn boulders. Sand rivers cut the main watercourse at right angles, and the country rolled away to the north and west in a shimmer of pale tan haze. The fire was pale and the kettle whistled a merry welcome.

This was to be the last camp of a month-long shooting safari through Kenya's bone-dry Northern Frontier Province, a hunt that had begun three weeks earlier at Naibor Keju in the Samburu country near Maralal, then swung northward through the lands of the Rendile and Turkana tribes to Lake Rudolf, and back down across the Chalbi and Kaisut deserts past Marsabit Mountain to the Ewaso Nyiro.

"Welcome to E.D.B.," said Bill Winter as we climbed down out of the green Toyota safari wagon. "Elephant Dung Beach. The first time I camped here the lads had to shovel it aside before we could pitch the tents, it was that thick."

Not anymore. On the way in from Archer's Post, Bill had pointed out the picked skeleton of an elephant killed by poachers, and not long since, judging by the lingering smell. We'd stopped to look it over—vertebrae big around as pistons, ribs fit for a whaleboat, the broad skull still crawling with ants, and two splintered, gaping holes where the ivory had been hacked out.

"Probably *shifta*," he'd said, and when we got into camp the safari crew confirmed his diagnosis. *Shifta* are the plague of northeastern Kenya, raiders from neighboring Somalia who feel, perhaps with some justification, that the whole upper right-hand quadrant of Kenya rightly belongs to them. When the colonial powers divided Africa among themselves, they all too often drew arbitrary boundaries regardless of tribal traditions. The Somalis—a handsome, fiercely Islamic people related to the Berbers of northwest Africa and the ancient Egyptians (theirs was the Pharaonic "Land of Punt")—are nomads for the most part, and boundaries mean as little to them as they do to migrating waterfowl. But these migrants, armed with Russian AKs and plastic explosives, have blood in their eyes. They poach ivory and rhino horn, shoot up *manyattas* (villages) and police posts, mine the roads and blow up trucks or buses with no compunction. Sergeant Nganya, a lean old Meru in starch-stiff Empire Builders and a faded beret, led us over to a luggah near the riverbank. In the bottom were the charred, cracked leg bones of a giraffe, scraps of rotting hide, the remains of a cook fire, and an empty 7.62-mm shell case stamped *Cartridge, M1943* in Cyrillic letters. Nganya, who had been with Winter since their days together in the Kenya game department, handed the cartridge over without a word. The Russian lettering said it all.

"I'm sure they'll leave us alone," Bill said as we drank our *chai* under the cool fly of the mess tent. "They know we're armed, and the lads will keep a sharp lookout around the *kampi.* Just to ensure sweet dreams for one and all, I'll post guards at night. Not to worry."

Of course not, but we worried nonetheless.

Actually, when it came to facing the Perils of the Dark Continent, we were as safe in Winter's charge as we might have been in the hands of Trader Horn or Allan Quatermain. A short, muscular Englishman with a leonine blond mane and a movie-star grin bright enough to grace an Aquafresh commercial, William Henry Winter had been a Kenya police inspector during the Mau Mau "Emergency" and then a game warden before turning professional hunter after *Uhuru.* Prior to that he had fought in Korea and served in Malaya in the grim, bloody counterinsurgency that, unlike our own involvement in Vietnam, had successfully thwarted a Communist takeover. He had hunted men as well as beasts. For all that, he was bright, witty, and literate, a nonstop punster and spur-of-the-moment limerickist whose raunchy doggerel would make Gershon Legman's anthologies of obscene verse read like the Book of Common Prayer. His knowledge of wildlife was encyclopedic, as befitted his profession, but he could also bandy literary quotes with the best of them: John Donne and William Blake were as familiar to him as such legendary African adventurers as Frederick Courtney Selous and Richard Meinertzhagen. And he faced everything with a jolly irony that made him the brightest part of any day.

On the other side, though, were the *shifta* . . .

That evening we went out for buffalo. I still had one on my license, having killed a decent bull on the Tinga Plateau near Naibor Keju—killed it in heavy cover at the edge of a brush-choked *donga* after a day of cold rain, the sun breaking through as we stalked the big *mbogo* where he lay up with his companion bulls, him standing suddenly when we were within thirty yards, big and black in silhouette, the light almost blue on his bulging shoulder, upturned shiny black horn tips above a muddy boss, him chuffing with puzzlement, staring at us, and then—pow!—socking him at the point of his shoulder with a .375 solid as he lurched forward, crashing through the shrubbery like a black runaway boulder leading an avalanche, saplings swaying, snapping as he ran straight toward us, then suddenly fell, with a loud anguished blaaaaah! And died. Later, when the boys were carrying hunks of him up to the truck, I noticed that the tin cup full of warm scotch in my right hand was quivering. A boy was lugging one of the *mbogo*'s feet, destined to become a bookend. As he climbed the slope he surreptitiously dipped marrow from the bone with a twig, then slurped it down like guacamole. In the high odd light of that Tinga sunset, the marrow looked green. I swallowed the scotch and poured another.

Tonight's sunset was as gaudy as that one: a skyful of purples and mauves and lavenders shot through with ribbons of dying fire. Walking down the riverbank through those pyrotechnics was like strolling through a gallery of bad picture postcards. There were crocodiles along the bank, big ones that slithered off into the dark fast water with a speed that belied their mechanical bulk; baboons yapped and farted in the bush across the way. Big abrupt knobs of dark red rock thrust up through the trees and we scanned them as we walked, keeping our eyes skinned for *shifta*. And suddenly one was standing there—tall and skinny against the light, heart-stopping in his instant emergence from nothingness. Then I saw that it was Lambat, our head tracker, a handsome, skinny Ndorobo who only a minute earlier had been right behind me. He must have scampered up the hundred-foot Kopje like a klipspringer.

"Ah," said Bill, following my gaze. "His Lordship's having a *shufti*—a bit of a look-see, as you'd say in Amurrican. Aha—and he sees something!"

Lambat had squatted and was peering intently upriver. It was almost too melodramatic, like a scene from a John Ford Western where the intrepid Indian scout on the rimrock suddenly spots Cochise's band. But this was real life and there *was* that high intensity about Lambat: slow, quiet, loose-jointed as a dead snake during times of inaction, he literally "lit up" when he spotted game, his dull dark skin suddenly glowing like polished mahogany, his muscles showing like well-wrapped cables under his hide, eyes bright as a gundog's on point. Now he raised his hands, palms forward, fingers spread. Ten. Then folded them, and opened them again. And again and again . . .

"Christ," sighed Bill, "he says forty, fifty. Shite—sixty or more."

"*Shifta?*"

"No," Bill laughed. "Buffalo. At least I hope that's what he means."

The herd was feeding a quarter of a mile ahead of us, along the riverbank. We could smell them before we saw them, that sweet-sour stench of the barnyard that put me in mind of boyhood summers in northern Wisconsin, trout streams and roast-chicken suppers in the big comfortable lakeside kitchen after the evening chores were done and the herd milked, while bats flew over the flowering honeysuckle. But this was savage Africa; milkmen of doom, we bellied up to deliver death to the wild bovines.

"That one on the right," Bill whispered beside me in the thorn-bush. "With its head down right now, near that group of cows, now he's lifting his head up, chewing, chewing, now looking toward us. Shaking off the flies."

"I see him."

"He'll go well over forty inches," Bill said. "He's the best of the lot. Hold on bone, bwana, right on the shoulder. We want to break him down. But don't shoot unless you're really ready. Are you ready?"

"Yes."

"Sure you can take him?"

"Yes."

"We don't want to be going in after him now. Not in this light."

Pa-wham!

The bull dropped to the shot. The herd broke and stampeded, bulls, cows, and calves erupting like a mortar burst, as the dead bull hit the ground.

"Oh, shite! Look at that!" Bill was beside himself with frustration. Out of the thick bush to the far right stepped a bull buffalo that looked, in the dying red light, to be half again as big as the one I'd dropped. "Oh, look at that big sod! He must have been crossed with a Texas Longhorn. He's one for the book, bwana, but we can't shoot him now, can we?"

The big buffalo and two smaller ones went over to the dead bull and hooked at him gently, grunting and lowing.

"Crikey," Bill said, "aren't they bloody marvelous? Look at them, all scabby and thick and covered in shit, mean as a half-ton hemorrhoid. I've killed them by their hundreds, over the years, but if

I had my way I'd put them all back on their feet. Knee deep in candy."

His eyes shone noonday blue in the gathering darkness.

So blood can pall. The buffalo was the last of the big, warm, dangerous animals for that safari, and we would finish out the week at E.D.B. with bird shooting. It was a welcome relief, a slow, leisurely cooling-out from the high tension and dark tragedy of big game, and for me doubly so, since bird hunting has always been my first love among the shooting sports. But it was a different kind of hunting: I'd grown up on ruffed grouse, woodcock, sharptails, and pheasants in the upper Middle West, and that kind of gunning meant cold mornings, iron skies, crisp wild apples, the crunch of bright leaves under muddy boots. It was all tamaracks and muskegs, old pine slashings, glacial moraines and ink-black ponds, peopled with tough little Finns and potato-faced Germans. In the one-horse logging towns we whiled away the evenings on draft beer, bratwurst, and snooker. The great unspoken fear in that land of Green Bay Packer worship was not *shifta* but something far more fearsome: the Chicago Bears.

The contrast between American and African bird shooting comes quickly clear. The morning after the buffalo hunt we are up before dawn—even this coolest part of the day is tee-shirt weather; hyenas giggle downriver and a great fish eagle winnows the air overhead as we sip strong Kenya coffee at first light. My safari companions, Dan and Virginia Gerber, find lion tracks outside their tent, great bold pug marks that circled them twice during the night. But the guards, a wry Turkana named Otiego and the big, slab-faced Samburu we call Red Blanket, report no signs of *shifta* during their watches.

Not far from the river is a hot spring, a *maji moto* in Swahili, and we walk in quietly through a low ground fog, armed only with 20-gauge shotguns. Soon the sandgrouse will be flying. Lambat leads the way, peering intently into the mist. He raises a hand: halt. We hear a huffing sound in the fog, then dimly make out two dark bulky shapes. "*Kifaro,*" hisses Lambat. "*Mama na mtoto.*" Either the fog thins or our adrenaline sharpens our vision, for suddenly they come into focus: a big female rhino and her calf. The mother whuffs again, aware that something is wrong but unable with her weak eyes and the absence of wind to zero in on the threat. She shakes a head shaped like a Mexican saddle and shuffles off into the haze, followed by her hornless offspring, which looks at this distance like an outsized China hog. I'd often jumped deer while bird hunting in the U.S., and once a moose got up and moved out of an alder swale I was pushing for woodcock near Greenville, Maine. But rhino are different. If only for the heightened pucker factor.

The sun bulges over the horizon, a giant blood-orange, and the fog is gone, sucked up by the dry heat of day. But then it returns, in the whistling, whizzing form of a million sandgrouse, chunky tan birds as quick and elusive as their distant relatives, the doves. These are chestnut-bellied sandgrouse, *Pterocles exustus*, the most common of some six species that inhabit the dry thorn scrub or *nyika* of East and Central Africa. They flight to water each morning, hitting the water holes for about an hour soon after dawn, fluttering over the surface to land, drink, and soak up water in their throat feathers for their nestlings during season.

Gerber and I promptly began to miss them, overwhelmed and wild-eyed at their sky-blackening abundance. Then we settled down as the awe receded and began knocking down singles and doubles at a smart clip. It was fast, neck-wrenching shooting with the birds angling in from every direction. A chiropractor's heaven. We stood under the cover of acacias, surrounded by shell husks, the barrels hot enough to raise blisters, shooting until our shoulders were numb. Bill Winter stood near us, calling the shots and laughing raucously at our misses.

"Quick, behind you, bwana!"

I spun around to see a double slashing in overhead, mounted the gun with my feet still crossed, folded the lead bird, and then leaned farther back to take the trailer directly above me—pow! The recoil, in my unbalanced, leg-crossed stance, dropped me on my tail. But the bird fell too.

"Splendid," said Bill. "The Classic Twisting, Turning, High-Overhead, Passing, Fall-on-Your-Arse Double. Never seen it done better, I do declare!"

Then it was over. They disappeared as quickly as they had begun; the trackers began to pick up the dead and locate any "runners." There were few wounded birds. We'd been shooting sixes, the high-brass loads we'd used earlier in the safari for vulturine and helmeted guinea fowl. The heavy shot killed cleanly when we connected. I suppose you could use No. 8 shot, perhaps even nines on these lightly feathered, thin-skinned birds and increase the bag a bit, but there is really no need to. By using heavier shot, you ensure swifter kills, and there is never a dearth of birds.

Or so I was thinking. Just then one of the birds—a cripple, far out near the white-scaled salt of the hot spring's rim—scuttled away, trailing a shattered wing. Lambat stooped like a shortstop for a line drive, slung the stone sidearm, and knocked the bird dead at twenty yards. He picked it up and brought it to me, walking long and limber, dead casual, a look of near-pity, almost contempt, on his face as he placed it in my hand. Ah, the sorry, weak *Muzungu* with his costly firestick, blasting holes in the firmament with those expensive shells, when there were rocks right there for the picking. "His Lordship," indeed. Bill Winter's eye for human foibles is every bit as keen as his eye for game.

As Lambat handed me the bird, I felt an eerie sense of déjà vu. I'd been here before—but no, that was in Mexico. Shooting whitewings in the hills back of San José del Cabo. The country and the heat were just the same, the flight patterns of the birds just as wild and erratic. The same explosion of feathers, deeply satisfying, when you'd centered them; the same gratifying thump as they bounced stone dead on the hard red earth. And the same eager spring when the human retrievers—lanky brown kids in stained sombreros, down there in Baja—ran out to pick up the birds. The International Brotherhood of Bird-Busters, worldwide in scope, the only requirements for membership a pocketful of shells, a smooth-bored steel tube, and an eminently human desire—the *need*, perhaps—to see them puff and fall.

The camp was in an uproar when we returned. *Shifta*—four of them, scruffy little men with dirty shirts and heads wrapped in hand towels, accompanied by even scruffier dogs—had approached the camp. Ganya had driven them away with warning gunfire. No, they hadn't shot back, merely eased themselves into cover and out of range. They had faded southward, into the tangled vegetation along the riverbank. Everyone was excited. Even the old *mpishi*, the safari cook, was rattled, muttering and shaking his head as he poked viciously at his perpetual fire. Normally the *mpishi* was Mr. Imperturbable. I remember one night on another safari, camped beside a clear spring not far from our present spot but on the opposite side of the Ewaso Nyiro, when a herd of no fewer than eighty elephants ran through camp. They'd been drinking at the spring, unaware of our presence, then suddenly tipped to it. I'd been lying in my tent, reading Tolstoy's Caucasian war stories, and wondering what that strange grumbling sound was that I could hear not far from the flimsy tent wall, a sound like a cement mixer or perhaps a five-hundred-gallon Cuisinart chopping coleslaw, when suddenly it dawned on me: elephants' stomachs make that noise when they're angry or confused. Or even when they're contented. A moment later they began to trumpet—the sound track from an old Tarzan movie when Johnny Weissmuller yelled "*Umgawa!*"—and then they stampeded. I ran to the verandah of the tent and saw them crashing by, great wrinkled dark hides, legs like tree trunks, clouds of night-black dust with the moonlight reddening it around the edges. Trunks writhing like serpents above the dust cloud. Bill Winter was out of his tent too, watching them go and grinning gleefully. Two tents away, surrounded by gaping safari boys, the *mpishi* stood, nodding and grinning. He loved it, as we all did. But not this, not the business of the *shifta*. He was more frightened of men than skittish elephants: the Wisdom of the Ancients.

After a lunch of oxtail soup (courtesy of the previous day's *mbogo*) and grilled sandgrouse breasts, we drove up the track to Merti, the last town downriver before the Ewaso Nyiro makes its big bend and loses itself in the Lorian Swamp, hard by the Hothori and Sabena deserts. There is a police post at Merti and Bill wanted to check in, letting them know we were in the area. Along the way we kept seeing wrecked vehicles beside the twisting, twin-rutted sand road—fully half a dozen of them in the course of a thirty-five-mile drive. Some were badly rusted and nearly buried with blown sand, but others seemed more recent. We stopped to examine one. The frame was bent like a steel pretzel, the hood ripped as if by a giant's can opener. Even the wheel rims were warped. The vehicle was barely recognizable as an ancient Land-Rover, one no doubt that had seen noble service as a safari wagon in the 1960s but then was supplanted by the cheaper, sturdier, more readily repairable Toyotas that came into Kenya with a rush in the early 1970s. But what the hell could have torn the truck up so badly? On this barely traveled road, it could hardly have been a multi-truck collision.

"Plastic," said Bill. "C-4 or the Russian or Egyptian equivalent. A land mine did this work—the *shifta* use them all over the N.F.D."

"Command-detonated?"

"I doubt it. They don't use vehicles themselves as a rule, so why should they wait around to blow up a specific target when they can just plant a mine on a rarely used track and go about their nefarious business? They don't seem to care who they blow up. Whoever comes along will be a Kenyan official, or so they hope."

Merti, when we got there, had the look and feel of a besieged "strategic hamlet" in Vietnam. The police post was strewn ten feet high with rusting barbed wire, two corners guarded by machine-gun towers. The town itself resembled the old, grainy sepia-tone photographs of laagers during the Boer War, and you almost expected to see wide-hatted, leathery men hung with bandoliers lounging outside the *duka* drinking beer, waiting for the order from Smuts or Botha that would send their commando back into the field. But the Kenya police were definitely on the defensive in this undeclared war. "Oh yes indeed, sah," the sergeant in charge said, smiling widely. "There are *shifta* about. Perhaps a hundred of them. Bad men, yes. *Mbaya sana.*" He nodded wisely, grinning. But clearly he wasn't doing anything about it. And rightly so. If he sortied from the town, the *shifta* might lure him and his men deeper into the waterless thorn-scrub while another contingent swung back to loot the *dukas* and make off with whatever supplies and weapons it could lay hands on.

"Well," Bill told him, "we're upriver in Block Seven near Kittermaster's Camp, hunting, and I'm sure they won't bother us."

"Oh no, sah." The sergeant smiled. "Of course not. Not with the police so near at hand." They both laughed heartily.

We stopped at the *duka* and drank a warm Tusker beer. The dusty, cool shop was pleasant but poorly stocked. "I came off safari once, years ago, into a little *duka* like this," Bill recalled. "Back in my Anti-Stock-theft days. I'd been chasing Turkana cattle thieves all

over hell and gone. God, it was hot. What I wanted more than anything was a good, clean shave, and I'd run out of razor blades days
before. I came into the *duka* and asked the owner what he had. A big,
happy, smiling chap he was, like that police sergeant we were just
talking to. 'Oh, bwana,' he said, 'everything your heart desires!' He
gestured around at his shelves. 'Do you have a razor blade?' '*Hakuna*.
We have none.' " Bill laughed uproariously. "Everything your heart
desires.' Don't you love it, bwana?"

In the evenings I was reading myself to sleep with a book from
Bill's copious collection of Africana: a 1910 edition of *In the Grip of
the Nyika* by Lieut. Col. J. H. Patterson, D.S.O. Bill called it *In the
Grip of the Knickers*. Patterson, of course, had made his name by
killing "the man-eaters of Tsavo," those voracious lions that virtually
stopped the construction of the Mombasa-to-Uganda railway early in
this century by scoffing the Indian coolies who were laying the rails.
The good colonel recounted those adventures in a book of that title,
but this volume was about a safari he'd made along the Ewaso Nyiro,
surveying the boundaries of the Northern Frontier District in company with an old pal of his, whom he called "B." in the coy manner of
early-twentieth-century writers. With them was the brave, lovely
"Mrs. B." Somewhere near the place we were now camped, B. fell ill
and without warning allegedly blew his brains out with a pistol. Patterson buried his buddy and got on with the surveying. Later, he too
came down with fever and was nursed back from the brink of death
by the brave, lovely Mrs. B. "Makes you wonder, doesn't it?" Bill
would chuckle. "Maybe a little postprandial slap-and-tickle between
the handsome White Hunter and his brave, lovely little Clientess? In
the dank heat of the night, don't you know, with lions coughing and
hyenas cackling in the dark, that sort of thing, and poor old B. under
his mozzie net out of his head with fever. Then, a shot! Kind of a
'Short Happy Life of Francis Macomber' in embryo, wouldn't you
say?"

But the book was fascinating and I would slope off into dreams
of blood and illicit love, hearing the hyenas whoop, the crunch of
their jaws on fragile bone, and see looming up through the river mists
the vague menacing shape of . . . Abdul the Abominable, the Power

Shifta. He was lying there in ambush for us, to pay us for our sins. Never mind that the sins were undefined, we all had plenty behind us. Images of slow bright knives, me staked out covered with honey in the track of the *siafi*, the safari ants. Abdul standing there in the dark, cackling at our helplessness like a foul-breathed, rot-eating *Fisi* . . .

"I think I'll go out this afternoon with the shotgun," I told Bill at lunch on our last day at E.D.B. "See what I can walk up. There must be plenty of birds right around camp."

"Sure," Bill said. "Take along Lambat and Otiego to push them out for you. There's no end of *ndeges* around here. I hear them calling in the morning—guineas, francolin, yellow-necked spur fowl, maybe even some button quail. You can have a good rough-shoot, I'm sure. *Ndege mingi sana*—birds galore."

And *shifta* as well, but we left that unspoken. It was too beautiful a day to worry about them, at least out loud. This was the last day afield, maybe the last chance I would ever have to hunt in Kenya. And the bird shooting had been an alien form so far—I'd shot driven guineas with Bill a few years back, in an old coffee shamba that once belonged to Karen Blixen, a.k.a. Isak Dinesen, and it had been good shooting but too formal, too much like an English driven pheasant shoot for my rough-and-ready American taste. The boys had formed a line at the top of a long, brushy slope and pushed the birds down to us where we stood above the jungly banks of the Tana River near where it rises beyond Thika, the guineas lurching into the air well above us, big dark birds heavier than pheasants, but just as fast as they poured past, cackling, and we shot fast and furious, folding some nicely but seeing others slant down, heavy-hit, legs trailing, to land in the riverside tangle. When we went in to finish them we found fresh buffalo sign: steaming mounds of shiny dung, trampled shrubbery, the sweet stench (again) of the cattle barn. "What do we do if they come?" I asked Bill, hefting the 20-gauge pitifully in my hands. "Climb," Bill laughed. "*Panda juu.* There's plenty of trees all around us." "I don't know if I'm still that arboreal," I said doubtfully. "You will be, bwana," he said. "Don't worry about it. I was in a situation like this with a fat old English nobleman once. He scampered up a thorn tree like a bloody *nugu*—just as agile as a monkey, he was. Never let out a yelp."

We'd gone in then and collected our birds, and the buffalo left us alone. Just as the *shifta* would leave me alone today. I hoped. Yet deep down it was because of the *shifta*—the chance of their being there—that I was doing this. Every bird hunter knows the creepy, neck-itching feeling that crawls up from your kidneys when you go into a good cover. As if something deadly were waiting there, stone-silent in the mottled green dark. What's waiting, though, is nothing deadlier than humiliation if you fluff the shot. Yet when the bird goes up with a rattle and a roar, it's as if some bogey man suddenly leapt out at you, heart-stopping, remorseless, Abdul the Objectionable in his final, fatal pounce. The adrenaline rush is beyond compare. This would be even better.

The country upstream from camp was thick with wait-a-bit thorn and elephant grass, tough going as we pushed into it. Behind us the sounds of camp life—clanking pots, happy conversation in English and Swahili—quickly faded; ahead the doum palms and borassus swayed, their shadows shifting back on the bright, blinding grass. A heavy silence descended, broken only by the buzz of flies and bees, the rusty creak of nooning birds. Otiego swung wide and slapped his spear at the edge of a low thorn thicket. A bird got up with the forever-startling feathery whirr—a long brown bird, big as a pheasant—and I centered it, pow! Then another, and three more. I didn't hear my second barrel fire, but there were two birds down. Feathers still falling through the hot, hard light. Otiego brought them back—yellow-necked spur fowl, their throats pale orange, conspicuously bare, the wet dead eyes rimmed with bare skin, pebbly red. We could hear others ahead of us calling back and forth, *graark, grak, grak.* They ran ahead of us as we approached, we could see them scuttling gray-brown through the scrub. Then from the left a different bird got up—darker, chunkier—and Lambat fell flat as he saw me swing past him, then shoot. The bird fell down. Its white throat, pale legs, and mottled belly proclaimed it a Shelley's francolin, Africa's counterpart of the sharp-tailed grouse of my boyhood. In the denser forest back of the riverbank, another variety abounded—Heuglin's francolin, dark-feathered and plump as a partridge. They got up like ruffed grouse, with a great spooking thunder of wings, in there under the confining forest canopy, and had the same maddening habit of waiting until you were past, then lining out with a tree trunk between them and the gun barrel. In the open, with the pheasant-like spur fowl and the tight-holding, sharptail-like Shelley's francolin, I couldn't seem to miss; now it was hard to score a hit. Otiego grinned wickedly and clucked his mock disapproval.

Back out in the open, we jumped a small covey of buff-colored, round-winged birds that buzzed off like outsized bumblebees. Button quail. I dropped two before they pitched in less than a hundred yards ahead. Lambat scooped them up on the run, but when we got to where the survivors landed we couldn't trigger a single reflush. Yet there had been at least eight, perhaps ten birds—slow fliers at best—that landed in the tall grass. We could hear them scuttling, hear their frog-like "whoo-whoo-whoo" as they ran. We didn't see them again. The dead birds in hand looked like quail all right, but there was something odd about their feet. They lacked the hind toes of true quail. It certainly didn't seem to hinder their speed afoot.

For three hours we zigzagged through that wild, thorn-fanged riverside bush, a game-bird heaven, the trackers working like clever gundogs, spotting each possible hiding place, circling beyond it, then pushing through to put the birds out toward the gun. On some I shot nicely, on others I might as well have thrown the shotgun at them. But it was a Time Machine—no, a Time-and-Place Machine. At one moment I was back in a southern Wisconsin pheasant field, swinging on a fast-moving rooster with the corn tassels crunching underfoot; in the next I was kicking the soybean stubble for Georgia quail. Then I was up in Minnesota working the shortgrass prairie for sharptails, and in the next step jumping a pa'tridge out of alder edges in Maine. Yet at the same time I was aware that this was Africa: there could be a surly old bull buffalo just under the bank to my left, very angry at having his midday snooze disrupted; or a lion behind the next bush, sleeping off his midnight gluttony but not too lazy to get up and chomp a *Muzungu*. And above all, there was Abdul & Company, with automatic rifles, plastic land mines, and a total lack of compunction when it came to killing unwary travelers. By the time we swung back into camp, Lambat and Otiego had ten birds dangling from their hands and I a couple more slapping my hip, their heads forced through my belt loops, their shot-loose feathers sticking to my legs with a glue of dried blood, both theirs and mine, thanks to the hungry thorns. The three of us were laughing as we came out of the *nyika*.

Bill, Dan, and Ginny, sitting over their tea, looked up with puzzled smiles. But there was no way to tell them about it. The joke was too simple: we were back. Things that good are supposed to kill you; and for me, as always, the ghosts of those birds, the spirit of those dangers, would indeed fly on forever. For a few fine hours I'd had it all. I'd been, as Bill would put it, knee deep in candy.

"I take it you had a decent shoot, bwana?"

"Everything your heart desires."

THE UNCLOUDED DAY

E. Annie Proulx

I t was a rare thing, a dry, warm spring that swelled into summer so ripe and full that gleaming seed bent the grass low a month before its time; a good year for grouse. When the season opened halfway through September, the heat of summer still held, dust lay like yellow flour on the roads, and a perfume of decay came from the thorned mazes where blackberries fell and rotted on the ground. Grouse were in the briars, along the watercourses, and, drunk on fermenting autumn juices, they flew recklessly, their wings cleaving the shimmering heat of the day.

Santee did not care to hunt birds in such high-colored weather. Salty sweat stung the whipped-branch welts on his neck and arms, the dog worked badly, and the birds spoiled in an hour. In their sour, hot intestines he smelled imminent putrefaction. The feathers stuck to his hands, for Earl would not gut them. Noah, the dog, lay panting in the pulsating shade.

The heat wave wouldn't break. Santee longed for the cold weather and unclouded days that lay somewhere ahead, for the sharp chill of spruce shadow, icy rime thickening osier twigs, and a hard autumnal sky cut by the parabolic flights of birds in the same way pond ice was cut by skaters. Ah goddamn, thought Santee, there were better things to do than hunt partridge with a fool in these burning days.

Earl had come to Santee the year before and begged him to teach him how to hunt birds. He had a good gun, he said, a Tobias Hume. Santee thought it overrated and overpriced, but it was a finer instrument than his field-grade Jorken with the cracked stock he'd meant to replace for years. (The rough walnut blank lay on the workbench out in the barn, cans of motor oil and paint standing on it, and the kids had ruined the checkering files by picking out butternut meats with them.) Santee's gun, like its owner, was inelegant and long in the tooth, but it worked well.

Earl had come driving up through the woods to Santee's place, overlooking the mess in the yard, nodding to Verna, and he had flattered Santee right out of his mind.

"Santee," he said, measuring him, seeing in which certain ways he was inclined, "I've talked to people around and they say you're very good. I want to learn how to hunt birds. I want you to teach me. I'll pay you to teach me everything about them."

Santee could see that Earl had money. He wore nice boots, rich corduroy trousers in a golden syrup color, his hands were as well shaped as doves, and his voice rolled out of his throat like sweet batter. He was not more than thirty, Santee thought, looking at the firm cheek slabs and thick yellow hair.

"I usually hunt by myself," Santee said, giving each word its fair measure of weight. "Me'n the dog." Noah, lying on the porch under the rusty glider, raised his head at the sound of the words "hunt" and "birds" and "dog" and watched them.

"Nice dog," said Earl in his confectionery voice. Santee folded his arms across his chest rather than let them hang by his sides. Hands in the pockets was even worse, a wastrel's posture. Earl's hands were in his pockets.

Earl oiled Santee with his voice. "All I ask, Santee, is that you try it two or three times, and if you don't want to continue, why then ... I'll pay for your time." He gave Santee a smile, the leaf-colored eyes under the gleaming, swollen lids shifting from Santee to the warped screen door, to the scabby paint on the clapboards, to the run-down yard. Santee looked off to the side as though the muscles in his own eyes were weak, and said, "Maybe give it a try. Rather go out on a weekday than a weekend. You get away on Monday?" Earl could get away any day Santee wanted. He worked at home.

"What doin'?" asked Santee, letting his arms hang down.

"Consulting. I analyze stock and economic trends." Santee saw that Earl was younger than his own oldest son, Derwin, whose teeth were entirely gone and who worked up at the veneer mill in Potumsic Falls breathing fumes and tending a machine with whirling, curved

blades. Santee said he would go out with Earl on Monday. He didn't
know how to say no.

The first morning was a good one, a solid bright day with a spicy
taste to the air. Noah was on his mettle, eager to find birds and showing off a little for the stranger. Santee set Earl some distance away on
his right until he could see how he shot.

Noah worked close. He stiffened two yards away from birds in
front, he pointed birds to the left, the right. A step from Santee or
Earl sent partridge bursting out of the cover and into straightaway
flight. He pinned them in trees and bushes, scented them feeding on
fallen fruit or dusting in powdery bowls of fine earth, marked them as
they pattered through wood sorrel. He worked like two dogs, his
white sides gliding through the grass, his points so rigid he might
have been a glass animal, and the grouse tore up the air, the shotguns
bellowed. Earl, Santee saw, didn't know enough to say "Nice dog"
when it counted.

Santee held himself back in order to let his pupil learn, but Earl
was a very slow, poor shot. The bird would be fifty yards out and
darting through safe holes in the air when Earl finally got the gun
around and pulled the trigger. Sometimes a nervous second bird
would go up before Earl fired at the first one. He couldn't seem to
catch the rhythm, and had excuses for each miss.

"Caught the butt end in my shirt-pocket flap," he'd say, laughing a little, and "My fingers are stiff from carrying the gun," and
"Oh, that one was gone before I could get the bead on him."

Santee tried over and over again to show him that you didn't aim
at the bird, that you just . . . threw up the gun and fired in the right
place.

"You have to shoot where they're goin', not where they are." He
made Earl watch him on the next one, how the gun notched into
place on his shoulder, how his right elbow lifted smoothly as his eyes
bent toward the empty air the bird would enter in a second. *Done!*
went the shotgun, and the bird fell like a nut.

"Now you do it," said Santee.

But when a grouse blustered out of the wild rose haws, Earl only
got the gun to his hip, then twisted his body in an odd backward
contortion as he fired. The train of shot cut a hole in the side of a tamarack and the bird melted away through the trees.

"I'n see you need a lot of practice," said Santee.

"What I need *is* practice," agreed Earl, "and that is what I am paying for."

"Try movin' the stock up to your shoulder," said Santee, thinking his kids had shot better when they were eight years old.

They worked through the morning, Santee illustrating swift reaction and tidy speed, and Earl sweating and jerking like an old Vitagraph film, trying to line up the shotgun with the bird. Santee shot seven grouse and gave four to Earl, who had missed every one. Earl gave Santee a hundred dollars and said he wanted to do it again.

"I can practice all the rest of this week," he said, making it sound like a piano lesson.

The next three Mondays were the same. They went out and worked birds. Earl kept shooting from the hip. With his legs spraddled out he looked like an old-time gangster spraying the rival mob with lead.

"Listen here," said Santee, "there are six more weeks left in the season, which means we go out six more times. Now, I am not after more money, but you might want to think about goin' out a little more often." Earl was eager and said he'd pay.

"Three times a week. I can go Monday, Wednesday, and Friday." They tried it that way. Then they tried Monday, Tuesday, and Wednesday for the continuity. Earl was paying Santee three hundred dollars a week and he hadn't shot a single bird.

"How's about this?" said Santee, feeling more and more like a cheating old whore every time they went out. "How's about I come over to your place on the weekend with a box of clay pigeons and you practice shootin' them up? No charge! Just to sort of get your eye in, and the gun up on your shoulder."

"Yes, but I'm not upset about missing the birds, you know," said Earl, looking in the trees. "I've read the books and I know it takes years before you develop that fluid, almost instinctive response to the grouse's rising thunder. I know, believe me, how difficult a target those elusive fast fliers really are, and I'm willing to work on it, even if it takes years."

Santee had not heard shooting birds was that hard, but he knew Earl was no good; he had the reflexes of a snowman. He said to Verna, "That Earl has got to get it together or I can't keep takin' his money. I feel like I'm goin' to the salt mines every time we go out. I don't have the heart to hunt anymore on my own, out of fear I'll bust up a bunch of birds he needs for practice. Dammit, all the fun is goin' out of it."

"The money is good," said Verna, giving the porch floor a shove that set the glider squeaking. Her apron was folded across her lap, her arms folded elbow over elbow with her hands on her shoulders, her ankles crossed against the coolness of the night. She wore the blue acrylic fur slippers Santee had given her for Mother's Day.

"I just wonder how I got into it," he said, closing his eyes and gliding.

He bought a box of a hundred clay pigeons and drove up to Earl's house on a Sunday afternoon. It was the kind of day people went for a ride.

"I wish I hadn't come now," said Verna, looking through the cloudy windshield at Earl's house, an enormous Swiss chalet with windows like tan bubbles in the roof and molded polystyrene pillars holding up a portico roof. She wouldn't get out of the truck, but sat for two hours with the window ground up. Santee knew how she felt, but he had to go. He was hired to teach Earl how to hunt birds.

There was a big porch, and on it was Earl's wife, as thin as a folded dollar bill, her hand as narrow and cold as a trout. A baby crawled around inside a green plastic-mesh pen playing with a to-mato. Earl told them to watch.

"Watch Daddy shoot the birdy!" he said.

"Beady!" said the baby.

"Knock those beadies dead, Earl," said the wife in a sarcastic voice, drawing her fingernail through a drop of moisture from her drink, fallen on the chair arm, until it resembled a trailing comet, a streaking tear, a rivulet of rain on the windshield.

Santee cocked his arm back again and again and sent the pigeons flying out over a garden of dark shrubs. His ears rang. The baby screamed every time the gun went off, but Earl wouldn't let the woman take him inside.

"Watch!" he cried. "Dammit, watch Daddy shoot the beady!" He would get the gun to his hip and bend his back into the strange posture he had made his trademark. Him and Al Capone, thought

Santee, saying "Put it to your shoulder" like a broken record. "It won't backfire."

He looked to see if Earl shut his eyes behind the yellow spectacles when he pulled the trigger, but couldn't tell. After a long time a clay round flew into three black pieces and Earl shrieked "I got it!" as if it were a woolly mammoth. It was the first object he had hit since Santee had met him.

"Pretty good," he lied, "*now* you're doin' it."

Verna called all the kids home for dinner a week later. There was home-cured ham basted with Santee's hard cider, baked Hubbard squash, mashed potato with thick Jersey cream spattered over each mound, and a platter of roast partridge glazed with chokecherry jelly. Before they sat down at the table Verna got them to clean up the yard. Derwin had borrowed the dump truck from the veneer mill. They all counted one-two-three and heaved the carcass of Santee's 1952 Chevrolet in with the torn chicken wire, rotted fence posts, and dimpled oil cans. Derwin drove the load to the dump after dinner and brought back a new lawn mower Verna had told him to get.

Another day she spent the morning wading the brook, feeling for spherical stones of a certain size with her feet. Santee carried them up to the house in a grain bag. When they had dried on the porch she painted them snow white and set them in a line along the driveway. Santee saw the beauty of it—the green shorn grass, the gleaming white stones. It all had something to do with teaching Earl how to hunt birds, but aside from the money he didn't know what.

After a while he did know what. It was that she wouldn't let him quit. She would go out into the yard at the earliest light of hunting days—Santee had come to think of them as working days—walking in the wet grass and squinting at the sky to interpret the character of the new day. She got back in bed and put her cold feet on Santee's calves.

"It's cloudy," she would say. "Rain by noon." Santee would groan, because Earl did not like to get his gun wet.

"Won't it hurt it?" he always asked, as though he knew it would.

"Don't be no summer soldier," said Santee. "Wipe it down when you get back home and put some WD-40 to it, all good as new." It took him a while to understand that it wasn't the gun. Earl didn't like to get rain down his neck or onto his shooting glasses with the yellow lenses, didn't care to feel the cold drops trace narrow trails down his back and forearms, or to taste the salty stuff that trickled from his hatband to the corners of his mouth.

They were walking through deep wet grass, the rain drumming hard enough to make the curved blades bounce up and down. Earl's wet twill pants were plastered to him like blistered skin. Something in the way he pulled at the sodden cloth with an arched finger and thumb told Santee the man was angry at the rain, at him, maybe mad enough to quit giving Santee three hundred dollars a week for no birds and a wet nature walk. Good, thought Santee.

But the rain stopped and a watery sun warmed their backs. Noah found tendrils of rich hot grouse scent lying on the moist air as solidly as cucumber vines on the garden earth. He locked into his catatonic point again and again, and they sent the birds flying in arcs of shaken raindrops. Earl didn't connect, but he said he knew it took years before shooters got the hang of it.

The only thing he shot that season was the clay pigeon, and the year ended with no birds for Earl, money in Santee's bank account, and a row of white stones under the drifting snow. Santee thought it was all over, a bad year to be buried in the memory with other bad years.

He never thought of Earl through the next spring and summer without a shudder. The droughty grouse summer held into September. Santee bored the replacement stock for the Jorken. He bought a new checkering file and sat on the porch after dinner making a good job of it and waiting for the heat to break, thinking about going out by himself in the chill October days as the woods and fields faded to neutral grays and browns and the clods of earth froze hard. He hunched to the west on the steps, catching the last of the good light; the days were getting shorter, in spite of the lingering heat from the baked earth. Verna fanned her damp neck with a sale flier that had come in the mail.

"Car's comin'," she said. Santee stopped rasping and listened.

"It's that Earl again," said Verna.

He was a little slicker in his talk, and wore an expensive game vest with a rubber pocket in the back where the birds would lie, their dark blood seeping into the seams.

"My wife gave me this," he said, and he showed them the new

leather case for his shotgun, stamped with his initials and a design of three flying grouse.

"No," Santee tried to say, "I've taught you all I can. I don't want to take your money anymore." But Earl wasn't going to let him go. He wanted something more than a teacher this time. He wanted a companion with a dog, and Santee was it, with no pay.

"After all, we got to know each other very well last year. We're a good team—friends," Earl said, looking at the fresh paint on the clapboards. "Nice job," he said.

Santee went because he was guilty. He had taken Earl's money the last season, and until the fool shot a bird on his own or gave up, Santee was obliged to keep going out with him. The thought that Earl might ruin every fall for the rest of his life made Santee sick.

"I've come to hate partridge huntin'," he told Verna in the sultry night. "I hate those white stones too." She knew what he was talking about.

Derwin heard Earl bragging down at the store, some clam dip and a box of Triscuits on the counter near his hand. Earl's new game vest hung open casually, his yellow shooting glasses hung outside the breast pocket, one earpiece tucked in through the buttonhole.

"Yes," he said, "we did quite well today. Limited out. I hunt with Santee, you know—grand old fellow."

"He didn't know who I was," raged Derwin, who had wanted to say something deadly but hadn't found any words until he drove up home and sat on the edge of the porch. "Whyn't you tell him where to head in, Daddy? At least quit givin' him birds he makes like he shot himself."

"I wish I could," groaned Santee. "If he would just get one bird I could cut loose, or if he decided to go in for somethin' else and quit comin' around. But I feel like I owe him part of a bargain. I took a lot of his money and all he got out of it was a clay pigeon."

"You don't owe him nothin'," said Derwin, but without conviction.

Earl came up again the next morning. He parked his Saab in the shade and beeped the horn in Santee's truck until he came out on the porch.

"Where you want to hit today?" called Earl. It wasn't a question. "Might as well take your truck, it's already scratched up." In some way he had gotten an advantage and Santee just followed along.

"I thought we'd go to the Africa covert and then hit White Birch Heaven." Earl had given fanciful names to the different places they hunted. "Africa" because there was long yellow grass on the edge of a field Earl said looked like the veldt. "White Birch Heaven" because Noah had pointed six birds in twenty minutes. Santee had taken two, leaving the rest for seed after Earl shot the tops out of the birches. They were gray birches, but Santee had not cared enough to say so, any more than he pointed out that the place had been called "Ayer's high pasture" for generations.

It was breathlessly close as they climbed toward the upper fields of the old farm. The sky was a slick, pearly-white color heated bubbling hot by the hidden sun. Noah lagged, the dust filling his hot nose. Santee's shirt was wet with a sweat patch in the shape of Uganda, and he could feel thunder in the ground, the storm that had been building for weeks of drumming heat and endless cicada whine that went on and on, but was now failing and falling away like rain moving on to another part of the country. Deerflies and gnats bit furiously at their ears and necks. The leaves hung limp and yellowed, the soil crumbled under their feet.

"Gonna be a hell of a storm," said Santee.

Nothing moved. They might have been in a painted field, walking slowly across the fixed landscape where no bird could ever fly, nor tree fall.

"You won't put no birds up in this weather," said Santee.

"What?" asked Earl, the yellow glasses shining on his turned face like insect eyes.

"I said it's gonna be a corker of a storm. See there?" Santee dropped his arm toward the west, where a dark humped line illuminated by veins of lightning lay across the horizon. "Comin' right for us like a house on fire. Time to go home and try another day."

He started back down, paying no attention to Earl's remarks that the storm was a long way off and there were birds up there. He was dogged enough, thought Santee sourly.

As they went down the hill, slipping on the drought-polished grass, the light thickened to a dirty ocher. Little puffs of wind raised dust and started the poplars vibrating.

"You might be right," said Earl, passing Santee. "It's coming along pretty fast. I just felt a drop." Santee looked back over his shoulder and saw the black wall of veined cloud had swollen high into the sky. Bursts of wind came ripping across the slope, and the rolling grind of thunder shook the earth. Noah scampered fearfully, his tail clamped between his legs, his eyes seeking Santee's again and again.

"We're goin', boy," said Santee encouragingly.

The first raindrops hit like bird shot, rattling down on them and striking the trees with flat smacks. White hail pellets bounced and stung where they hit flesh. They came into a belt of spruce at a half-run. There was a narrow opening in the trees like a bowling alley, and halfway down its length a panicky grouse flew straight away from them. It was at least eighty yards out, an impossible distance, when Earl heaved his shotgun onto his hip and fired. At the moment he pulled the trigger, lightning struck a spruce behind them. The grouse dropped low and skimmed away, but Earl believed he had hit it. He had not even heard the lightning strike, buried in the sound of his crashing gun.

"Get it!" he shouted at Noah, who had pasted himself to Santee's legs when the lightning cracked the tree. "Make your dog get it!" yelled Earl, pointing in the direction the grouse had flown. The rain roared down on them. Earl ran for a spruce shelter in the direction his bird had vanished, still pointing through the bursting rain. "Fetch! Fetch! Oh, you damn thing, fetch my bird!"

Santee, trusting the principle that lightning never strikes twice in the same place, sheltered under the smoking spruce. The bolt had entered the pith and exploded the heartwood in a column of live steam. White wood welled out of the riven bark. Almost at his feet, lying where they had fallen from the needled canopy of the top branches, were three dead grouse. They steamed gently in the cold rain. The hard drops struck the breast feathers like irregular heart-beats. Santee picked them up and looked at them. He turned them around and upside down. As soon as the rain slackened he pulled his shirt up over his head and made a run for Earl's tree.

"You don't need to yell at my dog. Here's your birds. Three in one shot, mister man, is somethin' I never seen before. You have sure learned how to shoot." He shook his head.

Earl's eyes were hidden behind the rain-streaked yellow shooting glasses. His thick cheeks were wet and his lips flapped silently, then he gabbled, "Something felt right," seizing the birds in his hands. "I knew something was going to happen today. I guess I was finally ready for the breakthrough."

He talked all the way back to Santee's truck, and as they drove up through the woods, the windshield wipers beating, the damp air in the cab redolent of wet dog, explained how he'd felt the birds were there, how he'd felt the gun fall into line on them, how he saw the feathers fountain up.

"I saw right where they went down," he said. Santee thought he probably believed he had. "But that dog of yours wouldn't retrieve. He's not my idea of an impartial dog."

Santee pulled up in his yard beside Earl's Saab and set the hand brake. The rain flowed over the windshield in sheets. Santee cleared his throat.

"This is the parting of our ways," he said. "I can take a good deal, but I won't have my dog called down."

Earl smirked; he knew Santee was jealous. "That's okay with me," he said, and ran through the hammering rain to his car, squeezing the grouse in his arms.

Santee woke before dawn, jammed up against Verna's body heat. He could see the pale mist of breath floating from her nostrils. Icy air flowed through an inch of open window. He slipped out of bed to close it, saw the storm had cleared the weather. Stars glinted like chips of mica in the paling sky, hoarfrost coated the fields and the row of stones along the drive. The puddles in the driveway were frozen solid. It was going to be a cold, unclouded day. He laughed to himself as he got back into the warm bed, wondering what Earl had said when he plucked three partridges that were already cooked.

GOD BLESS THE RUNNING DEER

Robert Elman

Only once have I shot a running deer, and it was a most important running deer. Having been forced to grow comfortable with my limitations—in much the same way that I have acquired a fond tolerance for the limitations of my neighbors, at least in small doses—I don't ordinarily shoot at wild-flushing pheasants or ducks that flare too wide of the blind. There are those who say the kill doesn't matter. They are fools or liars. I can laugh at misses, pass up easy shots when there is reason, and come home skunked but happy. All of that doesn't matter. The kill matters. And the manner of the kill matters. All else is trivial, for nothing else is final.

I have killed deer as they walked or trotted or started up from a last bed. I have killed a buck as it chewed its cud and another as it raised its head, curled its lips, flicked its tongue to savor every wafting molecule of estruating doe musk—flehmening, the biologists call it. Lusting, I say, as it died. But only once have I shot a running deer.

The summer when I was almost nine years old, my name was Running Deer. My parents had sent me to a summer camp where, sometimes, I forgot my fat and inability to hit a ball while discovering that I could tell oak from maple leaves, squirrel tracks from raccoon tracks. As often as two or three times a day I secretly molted out of my dog-day cicada self, remaining outwardly a bulbous insect husk but inwardly transformed into a fleet Sioux brave tracking fearsome bears and fearful enemies. How intoxicating was the pungency of wet, moldering acorns and punk wood, and I signed my postcards to my mother: "Love, Running Deer."

Almost half a century later I stood over a young buck mule deer that lay on its right side, stone dead but with its motor reflexes whirring feebly like the prop of an old outboard motor that has just been turned off. The final sputter is disconcerting. The deer's forelegs, horizontal, touching only air, continued to rotate, feebly running as the deer lay still.

My wife and children and I long ago consumed the last morsel of that deer's flesh, and I took delight in sucking the marrow from a femur. All the same, the running deer will run in my mind forever. I would have it no other way. Its being is joined to mine for eternity. Remorse is not regret, and sympathy is something else entirely—as is remembrance, vital remembrance. I wonder if only the hunter can understand the compassion of the eater for the eaten. I wonder if only the hunter understands the apology and prayer offered by gracefully primitive tribes to the caribou or walrus before they joyfully spear it. Therein lies the sole metaphysical difference between me and the lion tearing out the paunch of a gazelle. Possibly there are additional differences between me and the more civilized gnawers of tender choplets sawn a month or two beforehand from a lamb's carcass hanging in a refrigerated abattoir. I can only wish them and myself *bon appétit.*

On the other hand, I'm not sufficiently analytical to make absolute statements about the need to hunt, or my other need—to tell stories about it. I can only say that this one needs telling because I suspect (my remembrance of the incidents being very clear) that it may touch the ghosts that run in the hunter's mind.

If this need of mine did not begin with the escape from myself when I tracked gray squirrels and made Camp Greylock's baseball diamonds disappear, then it must have begun a year or two later, when my family moved from New York City to a town called Summit, an up-and-coming bedroom community that kept itself very busy in those Second World War days by fighting valiantly to save the world for democracy while devising ways to keep more Jews and Italians from moving into town.

When our neighbors realized that their citadel had been infiltrated, that only their country club and their children's dance classes were legally off limits to us and they could not oust the enemy, they sent two missionaries to convert us. One was a Presbyterian minister who invited us to his church and gave me a tract about the joy of conversion. The second was a frail, white-haired lady who had served for years at her older brother's mission somewhere in China. Her dress reached to her calves: white with a pink and robin's-egg print of flowers and bluebirds. The print made me feel sad and guilty. I had split a bluebird's skull with a slingshot, and I wanted to confess to her and ask forgiveness. She arrived at our house on my birthday—I never found out how she knew it was my birthday—and said she had a gift for me. It was a Bible.

I thanked her. She asked me to promise I would read some Psalms. I said I would. Then she explained to me, gently, hesitantly, that my older brother Jacky was burning in hell because he had not been baptized. It was hard to look at her—poor kind missionary lady, almost in tears, feeling so sorry for me. I was still grieving for Jacky, but I didn't cry in front of the lady. That night I struggled through the 96th Psalm before reading the last few pages of Jack London's *The Call of the Wild*. If my brother was burning in hell, he somehow managed an occasional furlough to visit me during the half-dreaming, half-awake interlude before the alarm clock rang in the morning.

"Been fishing?"

"No," I told him. "I'm a hunter now."

"Tigers?"

"Some. Mostly bears."

I was bursting with Jack London, Theodore Roosevelt, Zane Grey, Albert Payson Terhune. My dream life was composed of wilderness adventure and dogs. Not even sexual fantasies would supplant that fare for another couple of years.

I daydreamed my way through the sixth grade. Sometimes I saw myself running through the woods, accompanied by several deer. Sometimes I conjured up my brother Jacky when he didn't appear of his own accord, and once I tried to visualize my forebears and all of the world's other heathen stacked like corded firewood. About once every couple of weeks, Red or Charley—the school's best athletes— would be waiting on the school steps for me to come out and get whipped; and afterward I would walk way off beyond the golf course to the woods.

Not all the kids were Reds or Charleys. There were some who made friends despite their fathers' misgivings and their own. I haven't been in touch with any of them since my second year in high school, when we moved to another town. Some of them probably died in Korea. Losing touch with them was easy. I liked being alone;

alone in the woods, with no one to laugh at what I knew was laugh-
able, I could once again be Running Deer.

The summer after the sixth grade, my father gave me a BB gun,
and once, pretending to be a great hunter, I actually sneaked up close
enough to a woodchuck to kill it. It must have been a sick or injured
woodchuck, but no matter. The first shot only stunned the animal. I
wasn't upset. I put more BBs into its head until it was dead. Little
boys perceive no agony but their own. Grown-ups contain the ghosts
of agony inflicted, and those who kill may begin to understand about
the manner of the kill. The understanding of parents is of a very different kind; I wanted to cook and eat the woodchuck, but they
wouldn't hear of it. Afterward, I stopped hunting for a while because
dead animals do nothing interesting. I had become preoccupied with
the grace of garter snakes, the luxuriance of skunk cabbage, the
quickness and music of pale green frogs.

I might have forgotten about hunting if I hadn't met a kid named
Bobby Marvin, who wanted a friend like me and had nothing to
lose—frail, freckled, asthmatic Bobby, the son of a schoolteacher but
not what other teachers would call a good boy. More than once we
skipped school together. He raised garter snakes (he liked them because they bore live young) and he gigged frogs, fished, ran a trapline
for muskrats, and hunted squirrels with a loose-jointed old single-
shot .22 rifle. A misfit, like me. He took me into the woods and taught
me important things like how to examine bugs, skip stones on water,
forget to be home on time.

My father gave me a Benjamin air rifle that was a lot more powerful than my BB gun. Eight strokes of its pump handle forced
enough air into its compression chamber to send a pellet deep into a
squirrel. I became good with it, shooting it in our yard, where I
couldn't use Bobby's .22. I could stand under a tree and hit the head
of a squirrel forty feet overhead. So could Bobby. I hope he still can,
wherever he is. It was about then that a black man named George
Jelks, who worked for my father, taught me how to cook squirrel and
rabbit and raccoon, and showed me how a dog should hunt. I don't
know whether he knew I loved him, and I don't believe I ever
thanked him.

There were farms just outside of town then. One morning I sat
alone at the edge of a woodlot bordering a cornfield, watching chip-

munks load up their cheek pouches and dart home into crevices in a low stone fence. After a while I realized that all the chipmunks had disappeared. Then I saw a weasel working its way along the top of the stones like a rippling ribbon. Its long, thin body arched and then it pounced into a crevice. It was the first weasel I'd ever seen in the wild, and I was astonished that it was active after daylight. I sat for a long time but it never reappeared. Then I slowly realized that something else was moving close to me at the edge of the corn. I guess I must have heard a scratching. It was a hen pheasant pecking and poking like a barnyard chicken. Slowly, silently, I tugged a half-eaten sandwich of salami and rat cheese from my jacket pocket and took a bite. The hen paid no attention. She had settled down between rows of stubble and was sunning herself. I crumbled my bread and tossed crumbs in her direction.

She had to have seen me, smelled me, heard me, but she showed no interest and no fear. After a few minutes she stood up and pecked about, gradually working her way toward me. She was picking corn kernels, grit, and invisible specks of things off the moist earth. I never saw her pick a crumb of the bread. Why should she? Yet I told myself I had befriended a wild bird and was feeding her, that I was such a miraculous woodsman that wild creatures did not fear me. At any moment she would fly up to perch on my shoulder. When she was about six or eight feet from me, she turned, ran toward a row of stubble, nearly collided with a cornstalk, and bustled into the air with a great flapping of wings and venting of whitish excrement.

I still saw her as a wild creature I had befriended, but now she was also an elusive wild creature, my quarry, the woodchuck I had sneaked up on and the bear I had tracked in my dreams. That winter I set a Number 1 Victor Jump Trap very amateurishly on the sandy bank of a nearby creek, baited it for muskrat with a piece of apple, and caught one toe of a hen pheasant instead of a muskrat's foot. As I approached, the hen stood on her free leg, digging into the sand, trying to yank her other leg free. Abruptly she stopped pulling and just stood on her one leg, a bizarre statuette, her head cocked to the side, staring at me in terror with the eye that faced me, her wings slightly spread. Her long tail jabbed into the sand, the longest feather broken. There was no reason to think this was the same pheasant I had tried to feed, but I was sure it was. I was sure I recognized her. I tossed my jacket over her and tried to hug it down while stepping hard on the trap spring. It was my leather aviator's jacket, my best birthday present, but I didn't care if I tore it. I had to free her. She struggled frantically, throwing off the jacket, flapping her wings mightily, pecking at my face, trying to tear me with the talons of her free leg while thrashing about on her side. Then the trap opened just a little and I lost my balance and sat in the sand, showering myself with grit. She was gone. I laughed and waved. I had grit in my left eye, and just below it one of her scratches stung from lower lid to lower cheek. I was cold and muddy, but I would reach home before my parents did, and I would change my clothes. The scratches? Why tell them the story, not knowing how grown-ups would react? I could say I had tripped in some briars. I put on my jacket. With my sleeve I rubbed blood and mud from my cheek, and although I never could carry a tune I began whistling.

Years later, in British Columbia, I watched a grouse feign injury, hobbling across a logging road, dragging one wing piteously, to distract my attention from her chicks hiding in the brush. Another time, in New York, I saw a hen turkey fly off her nest at the base of a big pine, her wings thundering, when a fox came too close. Miraculously, I thought, the fox paid no attention to bird or nest. The fox was mousing and very soon went on its way, and the turkey came down out of the trees to settle again on her sixteen—*sixteen*—great buffy freckled eggs. Neither the fox nor the turkey knew I was there. Pheasant, grouse, turkey, fox, turkey eggs, I felt the same bond with them, they had become part of me and I had become part of their private universe: life, death, and joy hiding in the sand and brush. Who was it that wrote "Hope is the thing with feathers / that flutters in the soul . . ."? A fine poem. Emily Dickinson, I think. Does it matter? Is the immortality in the writer or the writing? Here in the woods it is not in the actor but in the act.

I suppose every pilgrim's progress hides a Slough of Despond, periods in every life when things go all awry. A period like that began for me one winter and lasted three years. That first winter I was living in a pleasant town, working for myself, and had no one but myself to blame. I decided I had better get me to the woods. St. Hubert, patron of huntsmen, tried it in 683 and was rewarded with a vision: in the Forest of Freyr he saw a mighty stag with a glowing crucifix between its antlers. Why, then, has God neglected to write out an ironclad guarantee that all such retreats will succeed? This one didn't for me.

One day I hunted grouse and moved not a bird, though my dog worked well. The woods are often full of sound, but not a squirrel crackled the leaves, not a catbird mewed nor a woodpecker rapped, and no breeze ruffled the boughs or creaked the trunks. That afternoon it rained. I like rain, but I didn't then, and the drops clung to my glasses and trickled down the back of my neck like slowly melting ice pellets.

A couple of nights later the temperature dropped and in the morning snow covered the ground. With Bob Stoutenburgh—a chortling prankster when caged in a house, a quiet friend in the woods—I went to kill a deer amid the gray hardwoods and green-black conifers of Pike County's Poconos. In the dark I found my stand at the base of a double-trunked tree, not bothering to clear away the leaves and twigs, as there would be no noise if I shifted my feet in the snow; just sitting on my day pack, leaning against the tree, warm enough in my down and wool, drowsing until daylight. I was awakened by a shot, off to my right and up the ridge, where Bob had his stand. Ordinarily I wouldn't have moved, but in the silencing snow I could get there fast. I found him dressing out a small buck with six-inch spike antlers. He wanted no help, and there was no need to drag the deer out to the road until later. He wiped his knife, washed his hands in the snow, sat down with me, and shared his coffee, which should have been therapy enough.

The little angers at an out-of-joint world should have loosened like caked snow sliding off spruce boughs in the sun. Instead the angers clung—not melting snow but wingless bugs probing the edges of concentration, crawling, tickling my scalp from inside, nibbling at my nerves. A wet, heavy snow began to fall. The flakes melted on my glasses and spattered on the objective lens of my riflescope. Naturally, goddamnit, I told myself, naturally I've got no lens caps.

Down below in the basin, hunters were moving deer. Even in the muffling snow we could hear a startled animal blundering through the woods toward us. It appeared abruptly—a fine, thick-necked, wide-antlered, blue-gray buck, walking straight toward me, then veering slightly, then pausing just behind a tree that blocked my view so that all I could see was a tree trunk with an antler jutting from each side of it: St. Hubert's crucifix grown monstrous. The buck moved clear of the tree and stopped again. Having seen or heard something alien to its world, it stood turning its head one way and then another, snow flecking its back with white, steam rising from its flanks. Nervously the deer raked the snow with its right forefoot. I am not a panicky hunter; I do not go catatonic with buck fever. But I cheeked the rifle and saw only a foggy blur through the wet scope. The deer wasn't forty yards away. I could have killed it with a shotgun. Sighting over the scope, I squeezed the trigger, and in the same instant the deer was gone and Bob howled in anguish. "Sweet Jeeeeeesus! You clipped bark three feet over his back." And—to hell with the details—that was the end of the hunt.

I leave superstition to the religious, and joke about jinxes. I felt the beginning of a long one coming on. We had some meat in the freezer, my wife and I, and enough income to get us through the winter, but I felt this jinx. I've read that ballplayers invariably, sooner or later, suffer from long slumps. I hope so.

The jinx brought on a lot of childhood memories, and mostly the sour kind. It was almost like being back in junior high or high school. We're told from infancy on about our sacred duty to fit in, to be team players—not misfits like Bobby Marvin and me. Bobby and me hunting frogs and squirrels: those memories were far from sour, yet they did not relieve the slump that I now recognized unequivocally as my jinx. Self-employment didn't require me to be much of a team player, but the achievements seemed trivial and the money came in erratically while the bills arrived in an unrelenting torrent. I accepted a job in Oklahoma and moved my family there. It didn't take long for everyone in the Oklahoma company to see that I might be capable but was not a team player. Funny thing about northeastern Oklahoma: no one was ever born there; they all come from Summit. Who says you can't go home again?

My new boss invited me on a deer hunt. He and I and several others met before daylight and drove to the woods. By the time we split up to take our stands I was feeling nervous and resentful, convinced that I was playing a command performance. I knew the boss didn't mean to do that to me, it just happened. Somehow he had given himself the impression that I was a Hunting Wizard. The Official Company Wizard of the Woods, I thought, shoved onstage to demonstrate. Demonstrate what? How to listen to a woodpecker's drumwork? How to watch a striped skunk waddle and undulate over a rocky ridge in the dawn light? How to go to sleep on stand or miss a buck at forty yards as I had the year before?

Alone on stand, I had the office with me, and the demons of my mind were in fine jeering form that day: "Hey, Hunting Wizard, they expect you to come out dragging a deer. How about that? Some smart-ass woodsman you turned out to be—an impresser of bosses, a fat-ass deskbound bumbler who gets lost in the woods, you simple turd, you wouldn't know a buck's snort from a wet-lunch snort. Christ."

At ten to five—time to leave—a fat, wide-antlered buck appeared out of nowhere and stood before me like an apparition. I was on one leg, leaning over, lifting my day pack off the ground and running its strap up my arm, getting ready to head out. My rifle leaned against a tree. I had a pipe in my mouth. The buck stared. I waited for the beast to turn its head, look the other way. I wondered how long I could hold my off-balance position without moving. I began to tremble and was sure the buck would flag its tail and get the hell out of there. A whitetail deer can see a man blink at forty yards or more. This one stood at forty yards or less. Finally the animal began to turn and I rushed my move. As I brought the rifle up, the stock slammed the pipe out of my mouth, showering ash over my eyeglasses. I couldn't find the deer in the scope. Sighting over the scope, I let off a shot. I needed no companion to say it this time, I said it myself. "Sweet Jeeeeeesus! You clipped bark three feet over his back."

It was getting dark; time for the Official Wizard to emerge from the woods as the Court Buffoon. The others must have heard the shot, and I would have to tell them the story or come up with a better one. To hell with making up stories. Halfway out of the woods, I saw a fat possum swaying in a spindly sapling. All right, if they want a Court Buffoon they'll have a Court Buffoon. I walked onto the road swinging a dead possum by its tail. And I loathe possum meat.

*   *   *

The jinx deepened. I was a company man now and I had to shave every morning, and one morning I spat at my face in the mirror. That night I shouted at my son, and when my wife gently laid her hand on my arm I snarled, "Quit your damn nagging." I would have to leave soon, if only for a little while. I would have to go somewhere, even knowing that the jinx would crawl into my luggage, would be with me until something helped me beat it. Something like reaching the bottom of this depression and not caring anymore. Letting the caring go, the way compressed air sighs and fizzes out of a release valve.

I numbed myself with work while waiting for Wyoming's deer and antelope seasons to open. The night before I left, I worked until well past midnight, then drove home and packed. I locked the gun case and crammed the last items of gear into a duffel bag, slept for a couple of hours, and caught my plane for Cheyenne. I knew the jinx flew with me, and I began to believe it would take some tangible form. I even hoped so, for then, I felt, it could be exorcised. Somewhere below me in the plane, dozing and waiting as I dozed and waited, my jinx must be bulging my duffel or my gun case. I did not know that, in a sense, it had already taken form, that it did not ride in the bag or case because it was a silly little thing I had forgotten to pack—the removable clip that was so nicely constructed to hold a second, third, and fourth shot in my battered old bolt-action rifle.

Unpacking in Cheyenne, I discovered its absence and almost as quickly discovered that a clip of the right model and caliber was not to be found in Wyoming. To obtain a replacement or have the original shipped from home would cost me a day of hunting. That was unthinkable. Strangely, I felt no anger at myself—only amusement and relief. My jinx had metamorphosed, and in its new manifestation had, indeed, assumed a tangible, ridiculous form—a missing clip, not some vague social alienation, no pressure inside the mind, just a simple goddamn handicap. Something easy. Something real, a handicap to be ignored, like the temptation to join the team or quit smoking. Screw the clip. Without it I had a single-shot rifle, I would be making one of those famous one-shot hunts, though involuntarily. Miss the first time and you lose. You get no second chance unless by some astonishing quirk of good fortune. Beautiful. Let's do it.

My partner on the first leg of the hunt—a quest for a good antelope—was a friend named Merritt Benson, and on the first day and night we would be accompanied by his sweetheart, his future bride Margaret. Ma*gee*, he called her fondly. I like people like Merritt: lean, young, sandy, serious, apt to be a bit weathered-looking toward the end of the season. Undecayed youth with an adult mustache. He can talk or listen. Earnest youth. It was our first hunt together, but I knew we'd get along. And Magee too: big eyes; the soft angularity of pretty young girls; a good voice, a good laugh. The quiet type, I suppose, but not self-effacing like some of the quiet ones. Resilient enough to like people. Merritt had taught her to shoot and was teaching her to hunt.

The first day out was Magee's, because she had to get back to town by the next evening to teach a Bible class or some such thing. I spent the day exploring and glassing the plains, liking the muted tones, the size of the rolling prairie, the rough irregularity of the terrain that looked so smooth in the hazy distance. I thought of the sea. I liked the sight and smell of the sage, and the numbers of jack-in-the-box jackrabbits, and the single lumbering sage grouse I saw, and the numbers and incredible fleetness of the pronghorn antelope, which made me think no more of the sea but of African plains game.

We were about an hour out of Medicine Bow, at a campsite overlooking a wide, shallow basin of amber and greenish-gray prairie. Sprinkled over the basin like wildflowers—as small as golden sage blossoms seen through the wrong end of a telescope—were loose clusters of russet and white dots, bands of pronghorn antelope against the distant hillocks. A few of them grazed their way closer, and every so often I saw one flash a burst of white, flaring the rosette of its rump patch, an alarm signal twinkling like a heliograph. Almost invariably, that animal and those nearby would then run, sometimes a short way, sometimes beyond the far screening hillocks. They streamed along, not bobbing like mule deer but with their backs nearly level, their bursts of speed effortless, a perfection of nature. I spotted a couple of hunters on the prairie, but could not tell what it was that sent any given band of animals into flight. I had the distinct impression that some of them were running just for the sheer hell of it.

Alert though the animals were, Magee could have rested her rifle over the hood of the slaty-blue pickup truck and killed one at, say, three hundred yards or so. She had learned to shoot, she carried a rifle that could do the job, and pronghorns are easier to approach in a vehicle than on foot—as most plains animals are. But that was not the way of our hunt. She was on foot, as I would be the next day. She would walk and glass and walk some more until she found an animal she wanted, and then she would get within range by slithering on her elbows and belly, rubbing her forearms raw and bruised as she inched forward, using every clump of sage, every rock, every knoll and gully for cover. There is something gratifying about sweating for one's meat.

No such gratification was to be hers that day. Back in camp that evening, she slumped to the ground, bedraggled. No wonder, I thought—it couldn't have been any cinch keeping up with that colt-ish lope of Merritt's all day. But her eyes shone in a way I'd seen before in others—the glow of a hard day of stalking without blunder or calamity, with all the easy assurance of having left the manufactured world to rejoin the real world and work the senses and muscles and be just another predatory animal, an integral part of the vast organic whole.

We made a cooking fire and lay on the pebbly ground, elbow-propped like Romans at an ancient feast, chewing venison chops and thick bread and salad and washing it down with a sharp, almost meaty Bordeaux. We used no tent, just sleeping bags, and the stars that night were so brilliant, so profuse that their light awakened me sometime after midnight. Behind us, behind a couple of game poles, were pale, spindly aspens on a gentle slope, and beyond them black conifers, blacker than the horizon under the stars. Hunters used the game poles to hang their "goats," as antelope are called out there, and skin them and remove the lower legs and put the final touches to the dressing-out, and slip protective cheesecloth game bags over the carcasses and let them hang there, cooling. The scraps of bone and ragged meat, sinew, and hide were lugged up the slope and tossed on the other side, where nature would quickly begin the recycling process.

Maybe it wasn't the stars that woke me. Maybe it was the coyotes, yelping and howling on the other side of the slope, less than a couple of hundred yards away. The recycling had begun. The howling told of something, I wondered what. Just hunger sated, perhaps, and an impulse to comment on a fine meal. Glee and a full belly. The fellowship of a good full group howl. I wished I had thought to howl when I had mopped up the juice with a final chunk of bread and downed the last swallow of Bordeaux. I clambered out of the sleeping bag, walked off a little way to relieve my suddenly strained bladder, thought about strolling out on the prairie under the stars, and immediately changed my mind as the cold penetrated my long underwear.

"Unsilent night, holy night ... every night is holy and there is peace on earth where the stars sing, the coyotes sing, the grateful earth rejoices, and the mind hears carols in October or July." At the moment I didn't need the comfort of my atheism, and I fell asleep recalling bits and phrases from a Psalm: *"Sing ... all the earth. . . . Let the heavens rejoice, and let the earth be glad. . . . Let the field be joyful, and all that is therein ... all the trees of the wood rejoice."*

The next morning Magee killed her antelope, a small buck, so small when she knelt beside its body that the remorse hit her harder than it should have. Watching her, I felt a sudden irrational guilt and wondered if somehow I had jinxed Magee as well as myself. Distant size is hard to judge on the open plains. All she said was, "It was a young one, wasn't it?" In an instant she had come to know about the human hunter's sympathy, empathy in fact, for that which breathed and ate and will be eaten. Then she left, to teach her evening Bible class.

We watched her rumble down a dirt road in her little beetle of a car. We raised a glass of beer in her honor, and went hunting.

We had walked less than a mile when Merritt spied a fine head in a band of about two dozen pronghorns atop a hill, silhouetted against the now graying sky and gazing in our direction as if taunting us, daring us to attempt an approach. After a few seconds they disappeared, slowly, nonchalantly, over the brow of the hill. We followed them up and down hills and rock-strewn ravines until my thighs ached, and always the herd faded back and away, drawing us. The next hill was steep and jagged with eroded gullies and rubble. Merritt's steady, loping walk took him up the hill faster than I could follow and I had to stop for a minute, rest, and get my wind back. I called to him that I would come when I could. He called back that he would top the rise, glass the herd again, and wait. I regretted the beer and my last five cigars as I went after him—not after the antelope anymore, really, but after him, taking my time.

He was sitting, slowly scanning the hills with his binocular. He waved toward the horizon and shrugged. "They were gone when I got up here. Damned if I know where." Yes, I thought, still jinxed, and then had a contradictory, unexpected thought: I wasn't unhappy. I was very happy. I was panting and coughing and my legs hurt and I was happy. Jinxed, hell. Except for the moment when I had feared that Magee might cry, I had felt right ever since the coyotes had howled in the night. It was just possible that the exorcism had begun.

We walked back to the truck. It wasn't as long a hike as I thought it would be. We got in and drove across the prairie, scouting. Merritt had a spotting scope affixed to the left window, and I had my binocular, and we made frequent stops.

In midafternoon we spotted a big band of antelope, actually two clusters feeding together, totaling perhaps three dozen animals. In the smaller cluster was a good buck, its black horns jutting high and wide above its ears. The two groups seemed to be drifting apart, the larger cluster moving over the hills to the right, the smaller cluster heading toward a shallow ravine on the left. Merritt pointed and I nodded. Taking care not to slam the doors, we got out and walked to the ravine, keeping the low hills between us and the herd. If we crouched and moved quietly, we should be able to walk the ravine, come up over its rim, and intercept the pronghorns. Merritt led the way. I was panting as we climbed the side of the ravine where Merritt thought I would have a shot. I was puzzled. I was sure we hadn't walked far enough, we'd still be hundreds of yards from the animals. I had been watching Merritt hunt, though, and decided to put more trust in his judgment than in mine. As I climbed to him, he pointed ahead and gestured to me to keep low and come on silently. Finally I was almost next to him, my head level with his upper back, and I peered over a skeletal tangle of ancient sage. Forty yards away my buck stood like a statue, almost facing me, its great dark left eye fixed precisely in my direction. I knew it didn't see me. Perhaps it had heard a rustle. Perhaps it was just keeping a lookout.

The roof of my mouth was dry and my breath rasped in my throat. I could feel my chest heaving. My hands, which never shake, were shaking. The short climb had winded me, but it was more than that. I have said I don't get buck fever, meaning I have never been too numbed by excitement to fire at a deer. But I have, many times, felt my wrists weaken when the morning's first geese came in over the decoys, and I knew at those times that I would miss my first shot and then settle down, and I was used to that, I wouldn't mind. Staring at the antelope, that feeling returned. I had a cartridge in the rifle's chamber. At this range there should be no need for a clip to hold a second, third, and fourth in reserve. Still, there was that feeling. I dug another cartridge from the shell holder in my pocket and stuck it between two fingers so that I could chamber a second round quickly. There was my antelope, standing forty yards from me, and I expected to miss. The hunter must control the kill, not let the kill control him. I felt as if the world had stopped, awaiting that pivotal instant that pales all other events, yet I was not in control.

"Can you shoot from the kneel?" Merritt whispered. Despite the breeze in our faces, I was surprised I could hear him and the antelope could not. I nodded, but I did not lower my haunch onto one solidly placed ankle and raise the opposite knee for support in a proper shooting kneel. Unaware of what I was doing, with all experience vanquished by this new quintessential experience, I knelt on both knees as if praying before my quarry in this open cathedral of prairie. I was on my knees, shooting offhand, an idiot's gambit. I missed the antelope at forty yards, the shot going just over the shoulder as the rifle wavered.

In that instant, I became calm. I had surpassed all the blunders of my hunting life, the crucial moment could not be retrieved, there was nothing more to lose, and I was calm again, even confident. The band of antelope ran, but not in a single direction as a herd normally does. They could not tell the direction of the sound, the source of alarm. Some of them scattered. Others, my buck among them, ran rearward and to my left for a short distance and then slowed to a nervous walk, milling about. I had the second chance, the rare second chance. My buck stood still, broadside but shielded by two does. Merritt tapped his left shoulder with his right hand. I knelt and rested my forward arm on his shoulder. It was a rock-solid shooting position. The two does moved. I did not hear my shot. I merely watched my buck collapse, as abruptly as if the animal had been slammed flat by a lightning bolt. Striking the ground, its body sent up a cloud of dust.

In my elation, I chambered another round, fired an offhand shot at a jackrabbit that had sat through this entire spectacle of disruption, and knew I'd missed the rabbit before the trigger was fully pressed. I laughed. Merritt went back for the truck while I began dressing out the buck. It was my first antelope. I lifted its head and examined its thick black horns and its dark buck's snout and cheek patches and the brown and white stripes on the upper neck. "God. How beautiful you are. Were and are." I stroked its coarse coat and then set to work with my knife, hesitantly, in awe of what had been created and destroyed. "Come on, you damn fool," I told myself, "it's no different from dressing a small deer," and my confidence came back with a tactile familiarity as my hands felt the hot paunch and blood.

It always surprises me how hot a newly killed animal is inside. Its machinery and mortality and mine—no difference of any consequence. And then I begin the job and grow comfortable with it, accepting it. Bob Stoutenburgh has killed more deer than I ever will, and evisceration still makes him queasy. I understand, but I raised Belgian hares and hunted cottontails when I was a little boy, and was too curious to merely slit them and spill their entrails on the grass as older people did. I dissected them. They felt nothing and I wondered how like them I might be inside. That impervious curiosity must be what the surgeon feels, and feels good feeling that way.

How odd that I could not look at a "benign" tumor a surgeon took out of my mother. "The size of a grapefruit," my father said, shaking his head and weeping. I didn't believe him. She was too forgiving, too loving to contain a horror. The surgeon, however, is all mechanic and pagan priest, and afterward dines heartily. Why should it be different for me, I thought, taking apart what I will eat? I have a compassion the lion lacks, but I am a predatory animal and content with what I am. I have good canine teeth and once I had a gallbladder, the gallbladder of a meat eater, unlike my poor herbivorous prey. . . . By God, what a fine thick ham that little antelope has!

That evening, Merritt and I ate diced antelope heart simmered with onions in a wine sauce while we watched a wall of cloud and snow blow toward us from the horizon, and then we broke camp.

I left Medicine Bow unjinxed, very unjinxed, and went west almost to the Utah line to hunt mule deer with another friend,

Jim Zumbo, a hairy, rough-hewn log of a man with a bushy black moustache and sometimes, on a hunt, an equally bushy beard, and forever loving, gleaming, carnivorous eyes and a toothy grin and a hat that must have been dragged through prickly pear. "Uncle Bob!" he bellowed, and threw his arms around me. I hugged him and planted a wet kiss on his porcupine cheek and asked if he'd been treating Lois right. He laughed and asked me for a cigar and I asked him if he had any dago red or schnapps in his gear. He did. We each took a great swallow of almost syrupy, throat-heating schnapps.

"Here we go," he said. "You ready to find the biggest-racked old Roman-nosed mossy-backed buck in the mountains?"

"Damn right. The Dago and the Sheeny strike again!"

"Can't beat that team," he said, and we clinked our cups together.

"Bobby Marvin with black whiskers."

"Huh?"

"Never mind. Just thinking about an old friend. Haven't seen him for years."

"Hey, listen, don't be killing any puny fork-horns, we've got some big deer in the mountains, *good* antlers, we don't need to settle for anything less than a four-point hat rack on each side."

There were others on the hunt, good people and important to me and others but not to the final part of what I have to tell now. We got into the mountains, and it snowed the first morning. Jim is a hard walker. I once watched him walk up a mountain while way off to my right eight or ten wild horses walked up the same slope. Jim reached the top first. He would slow down for me, of course, but he and I both like to hunt alone sometimes, so on that first morning he went his way and I went mine.

I climbed a great bald dome. At the top I found that a wide portion of it was as level and bare and long as a football field. On the far side was an overhanging ledge just behind some junipers, a nice place to take a stand and not get blanketed with snow. I started toward it, then stopped when I heard a muffled sound, like stones kicked loose and rolling. Over a hump strode two does, and behind them a fat fork-horned young buck. They had no notion that another creature shared their pasture. With the snow and no wind, they couldn't see or scent me. I centered the crosshairs on the buck's shoulder and watched him come closer. *"Don't be killing any puny fork-horns."*

"Who needs to?" I asked myself. "And for Christ's sake, who needs to play God, aiming and rejecting like the governor giving the condemned a last-minute reprieve? To hell with that." I lowered the rifle and just watched the deer coming nearer. The leading doe stopped and looked at me, trying to make out what I could possibly be. I waved and shouted. I don't recall the words. All three deer turned and bounded out of sight the way they had come.

"See any?" Jim asked when we met for lunch out at the road's end.

"Yeah. I passed up a fork-horn."

"You *what?*"

For three days Jim worried that I would go home without deer meat just because I'd taken his advice literally. After breakfast one morning, he chewed one of my cigars in half, and that evening, when I brought in no deer, he finished off the schnapps and started on the dago red. I was beginning to relish this business. If I played it right and didn't overdo it, I could needle him at least twice a day, before and after the hunt. Good banter, nothing serious. And as long as we hunted hard, gave ourselves and our world every chance, I didn't care about scoring.

The weather warmed, each day was prettier than the previous one, and the mountains here were different from the antelope prairies to the east. They were splotched with green—pinyon pine and juniper and such, and low tangles of mountain mahogany and plants I didn't know, and grasses. The land looked greener each day, as if spring had come.

"How're things going back home?" he asked on the third day.

"About the same," I said, "but just now, walking around the hills here, I decided it's time for a change." I hadn't known until I spoke that I had decided anything at all, or even thought about anything.

"What kind of change?"

"I'm gonna quit the job, go back to free-lancing. I guess this is the only team I'm fit to play on."

"I'll be go to hell."

"Yeah. Well, now let's hunt."

I was hunting harder. Evidently I'd also decided I wanted a deer, and the one bullet in the rifle no longer worried me. With the second shot at the antelope I had recaptured some power of concentration that I didn't understand but accepted with gratitude.

I thought of a story I'd once read, an account by John Muir about a very dangerous exploration of a glacier. Accompanied by a small dog, he had set out that morning despite an oncoming storm. The snow came, and Muir discovered that to reach safety he would have to cross a narrow ice bridge over a deep crevasse. He was concerned for his own life and the dog's, but there was no choice. As he chopped tocholds with a small ice ax, he realized he had risen to a new degree of concentration. I couldn't remember Muir's exact words until later, when I looked them up: "At such times one's whole body is eye, and common skill and fortitude are replaced by power beyond our call or knowledge."

I had trouble remembering the words, but I felt their meaning. My being out there, unconsciously sorting things out, had somehow replaced what little skill I possessed with another kind of power. My deer would come. I needed only one bullet in the rifle. When the time came, my whole body would be eye.

But on the fourth day, the last day, I was troubled. The members of the party had voted unanimously to come in early and drive like mad for town to have dinner at a restaurant with the Zumbo family. Here I was in my little wilderness, once again a make-believe wilderness, back to being little Running Deer, with steam heat and restaurants two hours away. Resentment was coming up as sour as bile. Maybe I'd find my deer that morning, maybe I wouldn't. If not, I was supposed to meet Zumbo and these three other clowns out at the road, at a designated spot, at three-for-Christ's-sake-thirty in the afternoon, with an hour and a half of good hunting time left.

High on a pine and juniper ridge at two o'clock, however, my resentment evaporated in the warm sun. I knew again that Zumbo was my friend. No clown, that one. The others were my friends too. How beautiful the woods smelled. It was public land, Bureau of Land Management range, and out where the ridge widened into an open flat, cattle were grazing. Intruders in my natural world, the domestic impinging on the wild, yet the day was too soft for resentment, and I found myself liking all of it, even the odor of their dung.

I was watching for deer, and it was a fine spot for a stand. The junipers were high and luxuriant. I'd picked pocketfuls of the berries to take home for meat seasoning. The ridge was splashed with greens and browns, purplish-gray rusty juniper berries with a chalky patina like that on dark grapes, black loam, gray and orange rocks. My spot overlooked a grassy basin, a bowl rimmed with ridges like mine. The sky was turquoise over and around snow-white cotton-candy cumulus clouds. The basin was gold and green, the ridges dappled with sun and shadow.

When I looked at my watch, it was time to start for the road. Damn! But now the twinge of resentment was mild. I felt that I would still, after all, get my deer on this last day, unlikely though it might seem if likelihood must be measured by logic. I gazed one last time at the green basin and bright sky before turning back into the woods. Again I thought of that story by Muir, of a passage describing a storm. My day was balmy, but the great white cumulus clouds reminded me of snow, and the ridge was a vast cathedral, as the prairie had been, though I was not kneeling now. "What a psalm the storm was singing," Muir wrote, "and how fresh the smell of the washed earth and leaves, and how sweet the small voices . . ."

Here was the church, here only, the church where God was allowed to give the orders and decide, where God was allowed to be God because there was no congregation around to stop such nonsense. Where God was allowed to be worshipped by people in out-of-style hunting clothes, and prayers were silent utterances of awe and love and gratitude, not bids for handouts. Where God was allowed to be worshipped by Catholics or Hindus or Jews or Presbyterians or Pentecostal Pantheists or even, by God, by atheists like me. Surely, surely, what a psalm the wilderness sings. What a hymn of the unrepentant.

Rejoice, rejoice. Emmanuel shall come to thee, O Israel.

I headed out through the woods, reaching the road before the appointed time, and a couple of hundred yards down the shoulder there was the whole crew, lounging around the truck, with the big chow box open, everyone eating, guns stowed, everyone sipping wine. "Peabrains," I muttered. "Some hunters. I bet they've been here half an hour getting tanked."

Seeing me, they called and waved. I didn't respond. I still had five minutes—and it wouldn't matter a damn anyway if I was an *hour* late. I crossed to the woods on the other side and heard a sound ahead of me and didn't think it was steers. I went forward crouched, very slowly, becoming aware that I was on the wooded rim of another open basin. Trying to move like a cougar, I inched forward and peered over the rim, and all of my body was eye.

Two bucks were just coming off the wooded rim a hundred yards to my left, a big-bodied fork-horn in the lead, followed by a fine four-point buck. They saw me and I saw them in the same instant. The four-pointer wheeled, and I knew as my rifle came up that he would be back in the woods before the stock touched my cheek. The fork-horn, having left the woods first, was farther out in the open—too far to turn tail, his instincts must have told him—and he was halfway down the slope at a dead-out run as my rifle came up and swung ahead of him. The old rifle, sometimes so heavy and awkward, moved like an integral part of my body, my eye, my arms sweeping ahead of the running deer.

Again I did not hear the shot. The recoil made me lose sight of the target, so that the deer vanished as the rifle went off. In other circumstances, I would have looked down the slope, trying to find the deer, to verify whether I had hit it. But I knew. I ran straight down to the boulder and clump of juniper that hid the buck where it had fallen. There it lay, on its side, dead, with its forelegs horizontal and still running, hooves tracing circles in the air. I had to stop that motor-reflex spasm of life after death. I couldn't watch it. I rammed another cartridge into the chamber and delivered a superfluous coup de grace, disrupting the equally superfluous electric charges coursing through a beast's dead nerves.

I haven't shot another running deer. I don't know whether I will. How can limitations—mine, Red's, Charley's, Bobby Marvin's, anyone's—be foretold out there amid the psalm singing and the running deer?

Seeing me, they called and waved. I didn't respond. I still had five minutes—and it wouldn't matter a damn anyway if I was an *hour* late. I crossed to the woods on the other side and heard a sound ahead of me and didn't think it was steers. I went forward crouched, very slowly, becoming aware that I was on the wooded rim of another open basin. Trying to move like a cougar, I inched forward and peered over the rim, and all of my body was eye.

Two bucks were just coming off the wooded rim a hundred yards to my left, a big-bodied fork-horn in the lead, followed by a fine four-point buck. They saw me and I saw them in the same instant. The four-pointer wheeled, and I knew as my rifle came up that he would be back in the woods before the stock touched my cheek. The fork-horn, having left the woods first, was farther out in the open—too far to turn tail, his instincts must have told him—and he was halfway down the slope at a dead-out run as my rifle came up and swung ahead of him. The old rifle, sometimes so heavy and awkward, moved like an integral part of my body, my eye, my arms sweeping ahead of the running deer.

Again I did not hear the shot. The recoil made me lose sight of the target, so that the deer vanished as the rifle went off. In other circumstances, I would have looked down the slope, trying to find the deer, to verify whether I had hit it. But I knew. I ran straight down to the boulder and clump of juniper that hid the buck where it had fallen. There it lay, on its side, dead, with its forelegs horizontal and still running, hooves tracing circles in the air. I had to stop that motor-reflex spasm of life after death. I couldn't watch it. I rammed another cartridge into the chamber and delivered a superfluous coup de grace, disrupting the equally superfluous electric charges coursing through a beast's dead nerves.

I haven't shot another running deer. I don't know whether I will. How can limitations—mine, Red's, Charley's, Bobby Marvin's, anyone's—be foretold out there amid the psalm singing and the running deer?

birds. Finally the pointer came up and held steady on a woodcock between Don and me, and when the bird flushed, flying straight up in front of us, we fired simultaneously. The bird fell. There was a moment of silence. Then Don said, "Nice shot."

I did not start calling the place the Endless Cover until a year or two after Don and his wife and children moved to North Carolina. Then I hunted the alders alone, and since I was not locked into entertaining Don's exclusive interest in woodcock, I began to scout the land farther up the ridges for grouse. I still haven't found the true boundaries of the cover, as I have never run out of good land to hunt.

A pattern for hunting the cover developed naturally. The slough along the road is dense with alders on either side. Away from the alders and the small creek that drains this crotch of land, the ground slowly rises and you begin to get into grouse cover: dry ground, chokecherry, apples. You begin by hunting the woodcock alders, making one complete circle (the road bisects the circle), ending up at your point of departure. This takes about an hour. When you have closed this circle, you continue in ever-widening circles, moving farther and farther up the ridges.

I have run into another hunter in the Endless Cover but once in seven years. It was midseason in a year that saw many grouse on the periphery of the woodcock alders, and I knew someone else had been hunting the cover because of the empty green Remington 12-gauge shells he left behind. My dog and I put up a large gray bird right in front of us. I fired twice, the second time just as the grouse was flying into a tall, thick pine. The shot and the bird hit the pine boughs together, creating a commotion, and I said to my dog, "I think I got it, Katie girl. Get up here. Hunt that bird. Dead bird." I was hoping.

"You missed." The voice was almost at my shoulder. The man had obviously been hunting through the cover from the other side, and here we had met halfway through.

"Flew out th'other side."

"You sure?" I asked.

"Yep."

I saw the tail feathers of a grouse sticking from the side pocket of his heavy work pants, but quickly calculated that he could not have picked up my bird. The man looked to be about fifty, and he carried a 12-gauge side-by-side. I decided I would trust him, I think mainly because the gun he carried was a side-by-side and not an automatic or something akin.

He looked down reluctantly to his bulging pocket.

"I forgot my hunting vest. Got here, and I forgot it."

"Just one bird?" I asked.

"Uh-huh."

Then we looked long at each other and I know we each thought the same thing: *So here's the guy who's been hunting my cover.*

Snow comes early to the Endless Cover, since the land is at a relatively high elevation. There were eight inches of snow there late one November, and deer season would be open for another week. But I wanted desperately to hunt birds. In the late season the grouse tend to come down from the ridges into the alders, probably because the stream and the damp ground offer more food than the ridges when winter takes hold of the land. I thought I would hunt the alders quickly, hoping not to be shot or have my dog Kate shot by a deer hunter. And I wouldn't hunt if I saw any signs of deer hunters near the slough. I had never seen a deer stand in the cover anyway.

Kate knew where we were going and why. She had heard her bell ring and the shells rattle in the pocket of my hunting vest as I took it from the hook near the door, and she saw the boots and gun and smelled the gun oil. But on the way in, things did not look good. Two pickup trucks were parked within a mile of the alder thicket, and there were all kinds of tire tracks on the snow-covered back road.

But having come this far, I thought we should make the quick circle in the alders and hope to move out maybe two birds. I chose to park in a spot where I hadn't parked before, put the bell on Kate's collar, and began the circle through the cover at what was usually the midpoint of the hunt.

It was very cold and the snow had a half-inch breakable crust, which made the going hard. It was very strange, too, to begin the hunt from this new angle, things looking different, not feeling quite right.

I talked loudly to Kate, my breath leaving vapor clouds in the still winter air, hoping any hunters nearby knew that deer did not wear bells or talk.

"Hunt birds, Kate. Hunt 'em up, girl." Kate kept breaking through the crust and was unsure just what to do about it. She kept looking back inquiringly at me.

"Hunt 'em up, hunt 'em up," I repeated, thinking what it would be like to be shot by a .30-06 rifle in the cold and snow. I thought of *The Green Hills of Africa* and Hemingway's description of the sound a high-powered bullet makes, audible at incredible distances, when it hits a big-game target. A splat. *Whack!* I thought to myself, figuring the impact would be the first noticeable thing—like someone hitting you in the back with a baseball bat. Then just the blood and the snow.

"C'mon, girl, find some birds. Good cover here. Find some birds."

The first time I read *The Green Hills* I was in my early twenties, and the book had read like an idyll: sun-baked hills, wide horizons, the adventure of exotic places. It was during a spring semester in college in Virginia, and the book mixed well with the tennis and the lacrosse games and the women that we used to date up the road at Mary Baldwin. We were asked to read the book in light of the author's professed experiment: to see if an unfictionalized account of his hunting trip could stand on its own merits as a book.

"Get up here, Katie. Find birds."

When I read the book a second time several years later, it did not read like an idyll. The second time around I had been appalled at the wanton killing and the reasoning behind it and had wondered at how it had been such a different book to me before.

"Hunt 'em up, Kate. Hunt 'em up."

The last time I picked up *The Green Hills*, I didn't make it all the way through. I did not see the wide horizons and rolling hills or the bloodlust. I could not see beyond the ego and the drinking and had wondered at what a perfect asshole thing it is to do, to hunt that way, to drink that way, to be proud of it. Greater Kudu and Great White Hunter: Houyhnhnm and Yahoo.

I was sidestepping down a steep pitch, breaking through the crust, trying to catch up to Kate, who seemed to be making game. But then she was off. False alarm. And then I had a queer thought that made all the sense in the world: I have never felt that *The Green Hills of Africa* was anything but a very good book.

"Find some birds, Katie girl, find some birds." The snow in the cover was taking on the quiet blue it does when darkness approaches in winter. I began to think about the stupidity of hunting in thick cover during deer season in such harsh conditions, when I can't even watch my dog work well.

Whack! I thought, just like getting hit with a baseball bat.

"C'mon. Here, girl." Enough. Darkness was falling quickly when we drove out and the snow on the road was frozen. The two pickup trucks were gone.

There are covers I don't like to hunt except with certain people. Hunting the Creek or Warehouse or Jungle is best with Jamie or another of our group that covered so much ground together four years ago, when October seemed like it would last forever and when the long lunches near the disused farmer's bridge were good, trout rising in the river near the bridge, and Kate exhausted, lying in the sun, hoping for the energy for a couple of more hours on the ridges.

The Woodcock Hotel too, which never disappoints, only hunts well for me when I'm alone or with one of two or three other people. This is a good spot that is very hard to get to if you don't know exactly what you're looking for, but it could easily get blasted out of productivity if we weren't so careful.

Once, coming out of the Woodcock Hotel (which, if the truth be known, yields more than just woodcock) a Chevy Blazer with out-of-state plates stopped to ask Jamie and Carl how they did.

"See any grouse?"

"Not many."

"Hell," the out-of-staters said, "we hunted all morning and only moved one bird."

"On a good day, maybe we move one or two," lied Carl. "And it's always in the hardwoods," he further lied.

"In the hardwoods, eh?"

"Yep. Always in the hardwoods this time of year."

"We can do better than that back in Connecticut."

"You probably can," said Jamie.

These covers—Creek, Woodcock Hotel, Warehouse, Jungle, and others—have a history that includes other people as much as or more than me. They don't seem to belong to any one of us especially. We hunt them and protect them and respect them mutually. But anyone who hunts the Endless Cover comes there with me.

Gordon came to hunt the cover with me on a perfect October day. The foliage was in full color and the woodcock flights had only just started. Gordon is one of my best friends, but he is not a hunter. He came to see what it was all about.

It was a very slow day. We made the first round of the alder thicket without so much as a false point from Kate. It was about seventy degrees that day, and working hard, hunting up onto the ridges, we were sweating freely when we stopped to make a new battle plan.

"I had no idea it would be this much work," said Gordon. "This is great."

Finally Kate started to make game in a small patch of the cover. The woodcock went up quickly without a point from Kate, and as I swung with the bird I saw I had no shot. Gordon asked me why I didn't shoot. I told him I didn't have a good shot.

But I had marked the spot where the bird put down, and soon we had Kate working the bird and I was explaining to Gordon how you could watch the dog's tail to see how earnestly it was making game, and finally Kate bumped the bird up, and I remember clearly the sunlight on the bird's wings as it dipped and veered to the right, the bright colors of the hardwoods on the ridge in the distance, the warm smell of the autumn earth. I dropped the bird with the first barrel.

"It's down! It's down!" Gordon said excitedly. Kate was on the bird quickly.

"Easy girl. Easy with that bird," I said. "That's our bird, our bird. Easy."

"I've never seen a woodcock," said Gordon as I picked the bird up, blood staining my fingers, the Endless Cover not letting me down, Kate at our feet with some pinfeathers stuck to her mouth. I held the bird for Gordon to see, and spread the wing and tail feathers out to show him the delicate markings.

It is last October and I have just left a dinner engagement with a Boston book publisher who keeps a house in Vermont. It is late and I am about forty miles from home. It is also raining steadily. Suddenly I realize that if I can catch one of the dirt roads that lead over the height of land to the south, it will save me maybe a half-hour of driving in the downpour.

But which road? I know the country pretty well, but don't recognize any of the side roads in the darkness and the heavy rain. I make a choice anyway and start heading uphill in the mud. A couple of turns onto other roads that I do not recognize—following instinct—and I am lost. Shit.

It's appropriate, I think to myself. I have been wandering all of this fall, lost, reeling from the kind of hurt that comes from betrayal, the only escape from the miasma the miles of cover my bird dog and I put behind us each day, the miles of crashing through thorn apple and alders and chokecherry and wading through waist-high hardhack. Then it would be time, driving home, to drink three cold beers slowly, watching dusk lay itself over the countryside, sweat drying and leaving its salt residue on my clothes, the beer slowly working its scam.

It's raining harder than ever, and as I gain the height of land I think I am still lost and I am exhausted from my mind's stubborn dwelling on the emptiness inside of me, endlessly trying to explain or understand it. *Shit.* But then there is something about the shadows and the rutted road and the closed-in alders. They become less forbidding, less mocking, and soon they are friendly and I realize I know just where I am. I'm in the middle of the big cover, the Endless Cover. I have come in somehow from the road that has always been the western edge to me. And quickly my mind flashes:

A bird dog is covering a thicket like a vacuum cleaner, and having already moved several birds, she is full on. Barbed-wire fences have scraped the short-haired bitch, small patches of blood staining her white coat. Clearly nothing is going to stand in her way. Suddenly, her bell stops its staccato ringing, her tail no longer waves back and forth but grows straight and rigid, and her short, muscular legs quiver with restraint and excitement.

"Your bird," Don says quietly to me. "Steady girl," he says to the dog.

"No," I say. "Go ahead. You're right there."

And he does, speaking evenly to the dog, bringing his gun to the ready position, moving his left hand up an inch or two on the fore-hand, getting ready.

The woodcock gets up, rising ten feet before veering quickly off to the right. The dog's bell comes to life again. It is a standard crossing shot and Don drops the bird.

Then we are over the fallen bird, the three of us. Don picks it up. Though we have bagged many birds that autumn, he pauses before putting this one in his game pocket and we look at it cradled in his hand: the long pliable bill, the large dark eyes, the rich chestnut-colored feathers with delicate black barring on the tips as exquisitely drawn as scrolling on a fine Spanish gun.

"Beautiful," says Don. "Aren't they lovely birds?" Nothing feels banal or cliché about what he has said, and the afternoon fades into evening, the ridgetop to the west describing a stark line against the sky, the only sound the gurgle of the small creek that twists through the alders.

My mind angles back to the potholed road and the rain beating against the windshield, but the threat of becoming lost in country I knew so well is gone. I feel an energy in this piece of land, an energy that came up and surprised me, indicating a bond that can never be broken. And for a moment it seems stupid to think that a piece of land can fill some of the void left by the recklessness of human relationships. But it can, of course, especially if you and the piece of land go back a ways together.

PICTURES OF OURSELVES AND OTHER STRANGERS

Anthony Acerrano

We begin in blackness, trusting in the certainty of dawn. Three of us, shivering in the November dark, our backs to a wind that sweeps in off the lake. Someone clicks a flashlight and a beam appears, narrow and defined, tangible, as if you could grasp and hurl it into the lake like a spear. Inside the bar of light the grass is white with frost; farther out mist rises like smoke from black water. The light swings sideways and finds the duck boat, a swirl of green and brown, thatched with rushes. Then the beam clicks off and the blackness is heavier than before.

Against the sky my breath is visible. Stars gleam. I pick out a planet, larger, brighter than the rest, but cannot remember which one it is. A hen mallard calls from the dark lake. *Whaack*-wak-wak, *Whaack!*-wak-wak-wak. Norman's lighter flares—I catch a lightning glimpse of his nose and beard, an orange flame-gleam, slightly demonic, in his eyes—then click, blackness again and a cigarette tip that streaks a tracer as it's whisked outward, then back again for another drag.

"Sure is a cold mother," John says, startling me slightly, his voice coming from somewhere on my left. I hear him chuffing warm breath into his hands.

"Wind's right," Norman says softly. His cigarette goes *pff* and glows, then flicks end over end in an arc, spitting when it hits the lake. I hear a zipper open, and an unmistakable stream of water splashes onto the earth.

"The world's best duck call," Norman says. John and I grunt in unison. It is an old joke among duck hunters, and a true one, which is why it survives the years durably, like an aged cheese.

The cold air rouses us to full consciousness, a state that seemed unattainable earlier, in the camper, when we squinted and yawned over mugs of coffee, puffy-faced, silent except for infrequent mono-syllables and grunts:

"Wind's blowin'."

"Hmph."

"Sugar."

"Here."

John stared blankly into the inky depths of his coffee cup, as if hoping to find Truth there, while Norm gazed through his smoke at a radio which crackled out the morning ration of unpleasant news . . . wars, famines, protests, political speeches—the usual fibrillations of modern civilization. I stared at both of them and tried to formulate something clear in my mind, something that might resemble a rudi-mentary idea, but this proved impossible. I slurped coffee and stared at our reflection in the black glass of the window, three men coming slowly to life in a wind-rocked camper in the middle of Montana, lis-tening to reports of distant wars and local tragedies, preparing to shoot ducks. I studied these men in the glass and wondered who they really were, and what exactly it was that they were doing, and why. This was a large effort for so early in the morning, and I soon gave up on it, but the picture stayed with me, frozen, impressionistic, like a painting; titled only: A Scene from Life. There were far better titles, of course, and more precise ones—and somewhere, a singularly per-fect one, but I could not, at the time, think of what it should be. A perfect title requires true understanding, something I didn't have just then, maybe would never have. I blamed this inadequacy on the early hour, on a mind not yet entirely shaken free of sleep. And later, when we went outside and crowded into the duck boat, when Norm started the outboard and moved us slowly away from shore, the motor dron-ing hypnotically, mantra-like, I began humming along with it deep in my throat, unconsciously seeking harmony, and I thought again of the three men in the window—smoking, sipping, staring; dressed in chest waders and camouflage, wearing shell vests and duck-call neck-laces. They seemed like characters in a foreign movie, or figures in a sepia-tone photograph from some old and yellowed book, mysterious entities, frozen for an instant in a tiny portion of the context of their lives. It was up to me to fill in the rest, to write their stories, to weave the background, the history, the pain and joy that brought them to this isolated moment. And: to read the surface of their eyes, to guess what occupies their minds. For in the painting, in the photograph—in the reflection in the window—they are empty husks, strange forms without humanity, and the urge is strong to fill those forms with spirit and life, with something one can understand.

All of which is to say that I looked at my friends, and myself, and saw strangers, husks, dressed for a morning's duck shoot, and this realization slapped me awake more briskly than could any wind. The sensation itself was not unfamiliar, being a perceptive warp that occurs without desire or intention, that comes at the oddest times—while making love, attending a funeral, eating dinner in a restaurant, standing at the edge of a wild, lonely cliff. Suddenly the world is a specular place, a trick of mirrors. Creatures move in reflection, saying and doing common things that now appear strange and curious, even bizarre, freezing for a moment into the stillness of a painting, into poses that resonate with a kind of ungraspable meaning. Undoubtedly there is a name for this state of abstracted perception, as there is a name for everything these days, and possibly this is a common enough phenomenon; I don't know or care much. I do know that my friends and I hunted for several days, and strange things happened and the mirrors appeared frequently, staying only long enough to etch scenes in my mind, little paintings for which I have not yet found titles. And I'm thinking: perhaps if they are arranged in correct but incomplete chronology, if they are connected like dots in a puzzle, maybe some kind of shape will emerge, some elusive hint of meaning will push through. A theme, perhaps. Something of interest to those who hunt and maybe even to those who don't.

So I hummed the mantra of Evinrude and felt the cold wind numb my nose, draw water from my eyes, as Norm steered us slowly over the shallow lake and the stars seemed more cartoonish than real. John's Lab, Gillis, full of years and vulnerable to the cold, nestled his head in my lap and warmed my legs with his body. He likes me, for over the years I've shot many birds over him; and I like him too, for he has eagerly brought most of them back to my hand.

Pistol, Norm's young Boykin spaniel, far too excited to notice the cold, leaned out over the bow like a Red Baron figurehead sans helmet, his long ears pinned back by the wind. John sat next to me, hunched, hooded, gloved, cheating the wind of an opening. We had all done this many times before, the three of us on this lake, but it seemed to me that this morning carried a tension, an unease of some subtle kind that we all, under direct questioning, would have denied with incredulity, even anger. So it was not a subject to be mentioned openly, as many things must not be when men, even close friends, gather in groups. A kind of code seems to be at stake, adolescent undoubtedly, but something a man learns at a very early age and never, throughout his years, fully comprehends.

Now the boat turns landward, toward the blind which we cannot yet see, and now we are a painting again, a collage of shadows, three men and two dogs in the early-morning dark, steering for a point of rushes. Now we are husks again, for these men are only duck hunters in a picture. The picture cannot convey the slight tension, cannot, for that matter, indicate the depth of friendship, or how this friendship evolved, and how these three men, even as friends, know each other in the full human exchange of minor annoyances, petty jealousies, and subtle competitions (and in bursts of camaraderie, moments of love and joy, of deep pleasure in mutual companionship). The picture shows only duck hunters approaching the blind, and so it cheats reality, tells far less than what is true. I say that there is a suppressed tension between these men, but I cannot fully tell why without changing the picture into a novel, or a confessional, wherein it can be elucidated: "See, this man has done such-and-such and the other has been a kind of whatsit to him, and then the third man came along and made the first feel a bit calibrial about him, and the one is secretly blemfious of the other and sometimes, when they get drunk together, it all comes out, naked and glaring like a shadeless lamp." And then, only after these historical lines have been connected, can these husks be filled with spirit and their limbs plumped out with real flesh; and only then can the picture carry its true load of meaning: these three real human beings crowded into a duckboat with their dogs, steering for the blind on a point of rushes; not figures in a scene, but people living and acting in the full context and complexity of their lives.

But this is not a novel, nor is there space for a proper confessional, so:

The bow nudges shore and Pistol leaps out, freezing for a moment when Norm yells at him, "You *son*ofabitch!" But both the dog and the season are young, and it is a pardonable sin after all, and I see the flash of Norm's grin. "Oh hell," he says, "I don't blame him." Gillis leaps out next and the two dogs prance around, crackling rushes, sniffing, stopping to void bladders and bowels in an orgy of physicality. I step onto the mucky shore and am handed cased shotguns, boxes of shells, and assorted oddments of paraphernalia.

The decoys are already out, set the evening before, so all there is to do is get settled in the blind and watch the sky change shades and colors, listening to the gabble of ducks, the sound of wings, the occasional yammer of a coyote or the lowing of some dawn-chilled, forlorn cow.

It is not long before the first duck comes in and the first shot is taken, the shotgun sounding outrageously loud and rude in the morning. It is Norm who shoots. He sits in the duckboat, alone, slightly in front of the blind. John and I, hunched behind a curtain of reeds, watch his gun come up, see the oncoming bird hit the wall of shot and go flinging across the sky like thrown garbage, splashing into the lake. Pistol is after it in a second, and Gillis, at our feet, whines and fidgets. John grabs his collar. "You *stay,*" he says, and the threat in his voice makes Gillis lay back his ears guiltily.

More birds come in, mallards, while Pistol is still in the water. John and I shoot. He misses and I hit my bird a little far back; it lands in the water kicking. Gillis marks the bird and splashes after it, chases it down and brings it, still thrashing, back to hand. Droplets of blood trickle from the bird's beak; its eyes, glossy black beads, stare at me, but I cannot read meaning in them—not terror, fear, panic, hate— nothing but glassy inscrutable black, in the center of which shines a pinpoint speculum of light that will soon be extinguished. Clamping down my distaste for this suffering I have caused, I grasp the bird by the neck and wring it firmly. The legs still kick, the beak works open and closed in quick spasms, the light still shows in the eyes. Frowning, I wring the neck again, feeling the warm down in my hand, feeling the meaty neckbone twist in my fingers. Wings flap hysterically, blood spatters on my coat sleeve. Clinically, I know the neck is broken, the bird is dead. I lay it next to Norm's duck, which lies rumpled, heaped in the brown matting of fallen rushes. My bird twitches. I look away at the sky for more incomers. A flock sweeps in. Norm shoots and hits, I do the same. John misses, cursing. I look back at my bird lying in the grass. Its beak moves fractionally. I mutter to myself, *"Shit."*

Norm takes in both birds, which the dogs have retrieved. One is still alive. He wrings the neck quickly and throws both birds onto the pile. The one moves its head and flutters its wings feebly. My first bird is still now. I reach over and give the second one a quick coup de grace. I look at the pile of sodden, crumpled corpses and think of Ortega: "The cadaver is flesh which has lost its intimacy, flesh whose interior has escaped . . . a piece of pure matter in which there is no longer anyone hidden."

A line of widgeon appears in the distance. Norm gives them his *peep-peep* call and they bank suddenly, heading our way. When they're over the dekes we all rise and shoot. Birds fall; the others whistle away. John curses in exasperation. Normally he is a good shot but this morning he has not hit anything. Norm, in front of us, can see none of this; he only hears our guns boom and sees birds fall. He's standing outside the blind now, sending Pistol after a fallen bird. John leads Gillis to the water and points him toward another downed duck, which floats like crumpled newspaper forty yards out. Gillis cannot see the bird, and is not trained to hand signals, so he splashes out tentatively and looks around, then comes back to shore. John points again and yells, "Fetch it here!" Gillis splashes out, stops again. John swears, yells louder.

Pistol brings the first widgeon back. John is still yelling at Gillis, trying to get him on a line. Norm points for Pistol, sends him after the duck Gillis cannot see. Trained to signals, Pistol beelines out. Gillis, anxious to please, splashes back and forth in the shallows, searching desperately for something to retrieve. Pistol marks the bird and grabs it, turns back toward the blind. "Goddamnit, Gillis," John says. Norm says nothing, watching Pistol with pleased eyes. Gillis still glances around anxiously. John grabs his collar and yanks him back from the water. I look away, feeling sorry for the dog, feeling bad for John.

Just then a lone widgeon comes winging in from the right, stupidly, suicidally, somehow blind to the three men standing upright before him. Norm is busy with Pistol; John, gunless, is holding Gillis. I alone stand there with shotgun in hand. The bird keeps coming. I bring the gun to shoulder, tracking the bird. Norm says distinctly, "Don't miss." Eyes are watching. I shoot the easy shot, across and incoming and miss. Jack another shell in, shoot and miss. The bird flares; I pump the last round in and swing. Shoot. Miss. Fall to one knee and shake my head. "Shit," I hiss.

I look over. Norm smirks. John, who has not hit a bird all morning, smirks a bit too happily. I pretend to ignore it, but it is a picture that etches in my mind. I make a feeble joke and we all head back to our places.

When the next flock comes in John and I shoot, and we both drop birds. Norm sends Pistol and yells, "Must be John doing the shooting." John laughs and I look at him but say nothing.

Later I hit a fast-moving shoveler too far back, and it sets its wings and goes into a long wobbly glide, hitting the water far away, immediately swimming for the shoreside reeds.

"Crip!" I yell out, but Norm shakes his head. "We'll never get that one," he says, and is right.

I think about the bird, wounded, unable to fly, hiding in a tangle of reeds, panting, and I feel contempt for myself, wonder what it is I'm doing here on this brilliant fall day. A line from R. D. Laing comes involuntarily to mind: "We are all murderers and prostitutes." And Nietzsche: "There is no feast without cruelty." I think about natural cycles, about suffering, about ways the bird will die (a fox, a coyote, blood loss, hypothermia . . .); think about ways it would have died naturally (a fox, a coyote, disease . . .), think that there is no end to this kind of thinking, to these pictures out of context.

By noon the shooting has stopped, the sky is endlessly blue, the sun is warm. We pull up the decoys and head back to the camper. In the boat I look around at the sky and water and trees and mountains, at my friends. By the camper we joke and laugh and pluck three birds for supper. Whatever tension there was is gone now. At sundown we mix martinis and sit on the tailgate, watching a blush of orange spread over the lake, watching distant knots of widgeon and teal and shovelers and mallards beat their way outward, to a cornfield perhaps, or a row of wheat, of barley—wherever it is they head with such singular purpose. And then the geese come, a long low-flying V, wavering in silhouette against the orange sky. They honk mournfully, filling the valley with their sweet noise, while we watch in silence, tending to our own inward peace.

Eli's ranch is a vast sprawl of bluff and prairie, twenty square miles of eastern Montana rangeland. The sun is not quite up yet as we drive a pickup through a maze of gates, up to the high stubble fields that hold hundreds, perhaps thousands, of sharptail grouse. We drive slowly, the three of us cramped into the cab, guns racked behind us. Now and then the truck spooks a hidden flock of grouse, which lifts in a raft from the stubble and glides far into distant fields, where the birds flutter down like giant, winged flakes.

Norm, who is driving, suddenly hits the brakes. "There!" A small crescent head appears forty yards to the right, peaking above the clipped straw. John and I jump out, calling from the bed of the truck Gillis and a golden retriever named Jim. Norm roars away in a swirl of dust. We load our shotguns while the dogs, as usual, sniff and pee.

The orange pickup circles wide to the left, then cuts through a far field and circles again, stopping. We wait a few minutes more, giving Norm a chance to get into position at the end of the field. Then we call the dogs and begin our march.

The stubble is frosty in the dawn cold, crunching underfoot. From up here we can see for miles, can pick out the serpentine lines of Interstate 90, can see the wheat-colored bluffs from which Custer made his arrogant, suicidal, and final attempt at genocide.

Twenty yards into the field a flock of sharptails lifts up, far ahead and long out of range. After the main flock leaves, stragglers pick up here and there, an endless number of them. The dogs perk their ears and mark the flights. Jim bolts after them but, surprisingly, stops when I call him back.

We walk. Birds flush everywhere, wildly, everywhere but in range. I hear the distant pop of Norm's gun.

The sun cracks over a low bluff. Bands of orange light make hatchwork on the fields.

When we reach the end of the field Norm is leaning against the pickup.

"Anything?"

"Nah."

"They're spookier than shit."

"Tell me about it."

We try other fields, but none of us flushes a bird in range.

"Fuck 'em," Norm says. "Let's find some roosters."

We drive down over thin dirt roads, through gates, into large fields edged with native grasses, broken by islands of cottonwoods, October gold, fluttering in the morning sun.

The dogs find scent immediately, crisscrossing, tails whirring. We run after them. Gillis puts up a rooster, which Norm kills. At the shot a flurry of hens lifts up, chucking, dropping pinfeathers and banking against the blue sky. Jim runs ahead; I pant after him. He circles wide and works back, flushes a rooster toward me. I shoot and miss.

"That Jim has bird sense," I say to Norm, who nods agreement. "He's been around."

I see this picture in slow motion, in Technicolor, a brief fragment of timelessness:

Jim running at the edge of brown grass and golden woodlands, running russet, autumn-colored in the low sun, tail high, loping past a tiny creek that cuts silver through the trees. Ahead a freak cottonwood arcs over the trail, rimmed with yellow leaves, and I bend under it just as Jim lurches forward, pushing a rooster into the air. The bird is frozen against the blue sky, chuck-chucking, wings blurred, caught in a band of light, of color. And I, bent under the cottonwood trunk, gun barrel pointing at the dirt, I can do nothing more than watch the bird and the picture vanish as if by magic.

*   *   *

After lunch, Eli comes into the ranch kitchen, wearing overalls and a John Deere cap. There is a cow stuck in the mud, out on the far reaches of the ranch, stuck for two days now, and Eli would like to extricate it with our help.

"Why didn't you pull her out earlier?" I ask as we drive away in the pickup.

"Aw, she's a croaker anyway," Eli says. "No great loss either way."

A croaker, I learn, is an animal that in all probability, for various physical reasons, won't make it through the year without substantial, expensive care.

We drive far back into the hills, back to where the grass is thin, where sage pops up now and then, back to a lonely pond near a barren rimrock. A small herd mills near the water. One beast, brown and white and alone, lies deep in mud at the pond's edge, her head barely above water. She stares at us as we pull up, in what appears to be a mixture of curiosity and fear—and, possibly, hope.

The sun is bright and warm, the wind blows and claps off the rimrock, over the sparse grass. The place is heavy with the stink of cattle, of urine and manure. We walk through the muck, behind the mired cow. Her ears twitch back to listen, and I notice a great, bulbous growth swelling beneath her anus. A croaker.

Eli fastens a harness under her neck, fitting it around her shoulders, which are barely above the mud line. "You old bitch," he says. We all grab the harness and pull, and the cow's eyes roll in alarm and she bucks and pushes against the mud. We strain and heave but she is sunk too deep and cannot be budged. My hand, spattered with mud, reeks of cow shit. I wipe it against the dry hair on her back as Eli says, "Old bitch. We'll have to use the truck."

He hooks the drag tackle and I listen to the wind. She's been sunk here for two days and nights, cold nights. I imagine what this would be like, and whether, for a cow, it would be an ordeal of fear or confusion or dull acceptance, or successive stages of all three.

The ropes are set and Eli signals. Norm guns the truck and pulls away. The harness lifts the cow's back and sinks her head beneath the water. Eli calls for Norm to stop. The harness is too far back. I watch the cow's neck, the head submerged, and look frantically back at the truck. Bubbles boil the surface. I'm about to speak, to plunge in and grab her neck, when Norm jumps out, yelling, "She's drowning, Eli! She's drowning!"

"Ain't much of a loss," Eli mumbles, and waves Norm ahead. He leaps in the truck and roars away. The cow is jerked from the mud and skidded onto dry land, where she seems suddenly huge, scuffing over the dirt like a great lifeless plank. Her legs stick out straight and her ribs heave as she chuffs out a breath. Water spouts from her nostrils.

"Old bitch," Eli says.

She lies on her side, eyes open and dim; her body a slather of mud, looking not like a cow but like a cruel experiment that failed. Barely breathing, she lies there in the sun. I listen to the wind beating, sweeping over us, and I look at the cow, feeling a great weariness, her weariness, and the wind sounds eternal, soothing, filled with a spectral wisdom and peace. In the body of the cow I feel the sun and hear the wind that strokes me like a soft hand. I am not frightened anymore, only very, very weary, and all I want is rest.

"Can she make it, Eli?" someone asks.

He shakes his head, pulls off his cap. "Doubt it. She was a croaker anyway. Only kept her so she could raise her calf. Ain't much of a loss."

"Let's shoot her, Eli," I say, hearing urgency in my voice.

"Naw," he says. "Better not. Should talk to Dad about it first. He'll drive up tomorrow and decide what he wants to do."

"Jesus, Eli, and let her stay like this for another day?"

He smiles. "Doubt she'll last the night. Cold'll get her, or the coyotes will come down."

I look up and see John and Norm standing nearby, squinting stoically. Behind them the rimrock, dry and wind-beaten, glows in the sun.

Driving back, Eli smiles at me. "Old bitch wasn't much of a loss. Only good for baloney. Probably worth fifteen bucks at most."

I nod, say nothing, think of the difference between animals and four-legged beef machines.

We drive through the brown hills, under a blue sky that reaches on forever.

In the morning John and Norm and I will hunt the river bottom for whitetails. One good shot means meat for the winter.

TOKENS FROM A DREAM

Charles Gaines

Friday, October 26, 1979. Got a late start and didn't get into the woods until two o'clock. We had decided to go up to Danbury and D.B.'s old covers instead of back to Courser Hill. A partly cloudy, snow-showery day, temperature in the low forties. There were birds, a few, everywhere we went. In the big alders Dick got one and we downed another that Buddy couldn't find. In the strip across the road I got two and Dick missed one on a back-to-back doubles shot. Buddy very good in here, though tired. I got one more across from the bridge and when we left that area we had four woodcock and a grouse that Dick stalked up onto the sand hills and nailed. We had said earlier that a perfect end to the week would be five woodcock to carry us up to thirty, and two grouse for dinner tonight. We went next to a new strip of alders up at the top of the hill and Dick shot the fifth woodcock. Then we went to the big alder patch in the field by the culvert looking for the second grouse. I missed a pointed woodcock on the left edge and flushed a big cock grouse that seemed to fly to the upper right-hand corner of the cover. We started working the front edge back in that direction. Dick flushed a woodcock, which he got on his toughest shot all week. As he was walking over to pick up the bird he flushed the grouse again and killed it, and Buddy made a beautiful retrieve. We hugged each other and quit right then—on our thirty-first woodcock of the five-day shoot and second grouse of the day. It wasn't yet five o'clock and there was light, but that was enough—it was the end of the week and it was perfect.

Dick Wentz and I still talk about that day and the ones described in the four preceding pages of my shooting journal for 1979. It was his first trip back to New Hampshire since he had left the state for a better job in Chicago three years before. It was the first time we had seen each other since then and we wanted to wring as much out of those days as we could, so we concentrated on it and did just that. For five days we hunted with other people and by ourselves, in old covers and new ones. Most days we hunted from early in the morning until dark, in snow showers on the last day, and in freakish eighty-degree heat on the first two. For lunch we'd have grinders and beer in the Jeep, parked by a cover, and throw Buddy the scraps through the screen in the back. Buddy was only six that fall, but the arthritis he had developed from the rat poison was already so bad that he would be limping by noon and hunting on nothing but his unhurtable love of it by four o'clock—so bad that more than once that season, watching his painful progress through the woods, I'd be forced to imagine not having him to hunt with anymore.

My journal entries say that Buddy found birds for Dick and me in almost every cover we went into during those five days—from the first, the big alder and pine cover in Henniker where Buddy had pointed his very first bird for me four seasons before, to that last shadowy strip of woods in Danbury where he brought the second grouse to Dick's hand and stood there grinning and lame, and eager to go find another bird before dark. And because we had plenty of birds and plenty of time and an agreement to cut that time out of sequence, to let nothing coming into it or going out of it intrude, we were free to hunt with something close to the pure abandon we had hunted with in graduate school, and rarely since then. We felt the weather, the passing of daylight, and the layers of remembered times in those old covers—recalling Tommy Tucker's comment on the trees in Hopkinton, Don Burke's "Can you make it to the clearing?" in Danbury, Jason Meyer's valiant puffing through the Henniker alders, running out of shells with Richie White on Courser Hill—in the same way you'd swim down through thermal levels in a farm pond, registering and pleasuring in each with nothing more than our senses. At night, after we washed the blood off our hands and squared the dog, we'd build a fire and drink red whiskey and eat late, then go to bed and not dream.

In rituals, the Kung Bushmen of southern Africa became the giraffe and wildebeest they prey on. For those people, hunting is an art, a transforming religion and a way of life. It is none of those things for

Dick Wentz or me, but for those five days it was for both of us a fine savagery, shared with a dog. Now, reading over the five-year-old notes that record that time, I realize that I do not need them to re-member everything I want to remember about those days, and countless other shoots as well, both good and bad, over the seven-year period I've kept the journal. For a number of years I wondered why I continued to hunt birds—why I continued to let myself inflict suf-fering and take life with a shotgun. For a number of years I worried that private question like a bone; now I don't much anymore, but when I do I know I can find at least a partial answer to it in the pages of that seven-year journal; I have stayed with bird shooting long enough to learn to concentrate on it sometimes, and therefore to pos-sess much of the time I've spent doing it. Really possess it, not in the mind, but in the senses, where it stays. I can call up any number of those days and feel them whole. Most of my days, perhaps like many of yours, are lost in a general blur of movement. But those days with Buddy and Dick, and a few others like them—I didn't covey-shoot those days. I picked each one out and dropped it clean.

When he was a boy, my father came very close to shooting his own father in the back with a shotgun while quail hunting in north Florida. The incident haunted him for years, and he did not handle a gun again until he was a middle-aged man. When he finally did take up bird shooting again, he did so with ceremony and a grave atten-tion to detail. One of the details to which he attended most carefully was me.

I was twelve years old when he and a group of other men leased a twenty-thousand-acre quail plantation in south Alabama called Midway. The place came with a columned pre–Civil War house, a cabin on a bass lake, a dozen or so good English pointers and setters, two red hunting wagons and four pairs of mules to pull them, horses to ride after the wagons, a number of black men to drive the wagons, to guide, and to train and handle the dogs, and God only knows how many quail. Midway was a paradise, and I wanted in on it. I had been shooting skeet for a year or so, often with higher scores than my fa-ther, but he had not yet let me hunt quail or dove with him. Though he badly wanted me to learn to bird-hunt, he did not yet trust me to carry and shoot a shotgun in the field. If he was a little more cautious on this issue than most fathers are, he was also right to be. I was a vain, irresponsible, scatterbrained kid who believed there was nothing I wasn't born knowing how to do—the type of kid who really *does* incline toward bloody accidents involving innocent people. My father had to deal with that fact, just as he had to deal with the memory of his stray shot in the north Florida quail cover. He also had to deal with my nonstop pleading to be allowed to hunt at Midway. And so he came up with a solution. At the time, I thought that solution cruel beyond imagining. Now I think of it as the single most brilliant piece of parenting I've ever seen.

My father bought me a Crossman CO_2-powered pellet pistol and told me that as soon as I killed a flying quail with it I could trade it in for a shotgun.

"A *pellet pistol?*" I bellowed at him. "You can't do this to me!"

I might as well have told him to wait until my agent heard about this.

"If you want to hunt at Midway, it will be with the pellet pistol. Until you kill a quail with it."

Nobody, I pointed out, could hit a flying quail with a pellet pistol: I'd still be trying when I was forty.

My father told me he knew of a man who could shoot dimes out of the air with a pistol, and a dime was a hell of a lot smaller than a quail. It would teach me good gun habits, he said, safely; it would teach me not to hurry my shooting; and it would teach me not to covey-shoot.

"Not to what?"

"You'll see," he said. "And don't curl that damned lip at me."

That first season was an agony of embarrassment. There would be my father and his friends, some of them on horseback, some riding in the wagon; three fine dogs on the ground, whipping like blown scarves over the cotton stubble, and three more in the kennel at the back of the wagon whining for their shift; out front on a spavined horse would be Fate, the head guide and dog-handler, an old, thin black man who knew most of what there was to know about mules, dogs, and quail; and thirty yards behind the wagon, trying at least to sit his goddamned horse well, there would be me, truculent and ashamed.

Somewhere out front a dog would go on point and Fate would raise his right arm. Whoever was driving the wagon would yell "Whoa, mule!" and two men would step out or get off their horses and walk toward the point, cradling good shotguns. When one of the men was my father, he would probably remember to turn on his way to the point and wave for me to come along and, hating my own eagerness, I'd jump off the horse, pull the Crossman from a sorry little holster, cock it and point it carefully at the ground, and run after him like a Pekinese. There would be a bird dog, quivering like an arrow in a tree. My father would motion me into an angle on the point from which I could not possibly shoot anyone, then he and the other men would flush the birds. There were big coveys then at Midway, and the quail would burst out from everywhere, sounding like a herd of horses snorting, and so filling your senses that for the moment there was nothing in your world but rocketing quail. There is still no natural occurrence I know of as exciting and as difficult to watch as a covey rise: fifty birds can all seem to blur into one and then be gone, variously and magically, before you can blink. If you covey-shoot at the blur, even with a shotgun, you can go for weeks or even months without killing a quail. With a pellet pistol, I am here to tell you, you could covey-shoot for decades without killing one.

It took me all of that first season and part of the next to make my eyes pick out a single bird from a covey rise and stay with it, concentrate on it, blank out everything else around it. It took me most of the first season to learn to hold the one measly shot I had until that single quail had leveled out. And it took me two full quail seasons before I finally dropped a bird. I'm still not sure I killed it. A big pointer named Jim with a head like a splitting wedge brought the bird to my father, who had shot in the same direction I had. My father turned the quail over in his hand.

"This the bird you shot at, Skip?" he asked me.

"Yessir. Either that one or one that looked just like it."

"He's got a pretty big hole in his back. Must have been your pellet." He grinned and tossed me the bird.

Someone could have opened the bird with a knife and found the pellet if it was there. But no one felt inclined to do that, least of all me.

The next week my father gave me his 16-gauge Winchester

Model 21 double, which I shot for the last weekend of that season. That gun is still the only one I shoot at anything smaller than a duck. It is now worth five times what my father paid for it, and much, much more than that to me—but not so much as the lesson that got it for me.

Tuesday, March 30, 1983. Clear, cool, snow on the ground. 6:30 p.m. A big wind that blew all day has died. Cold for this late—a still, chill, blue evening with a full moon rising and snow reflecting the late light. A new lamb in the barn and another on the way. The pond, which was almost clear, has refrozen over Buddy's frogs.

I've filled two notebooks and part of this one with notes on shoots with him, and he has always been the biggest part of my pleasure in those shoots. Last fall his arthritis almost shut him down. Then his pancreas got suddenly worse and he couldn't digest his food. He lost weight, got better for a while with medicine, then this month lost a lot of weight again. Now he has diabetes, and the vet says he doesn't have much of a life left. In a half-hour Patricia and I are going over to Dr. Jocelyn's to see him for the last time and to be with him for the injection. It's not a bad night to go to sleep for good. This Sunday is Easter.

In college I didn't hunt at all. In Ireland, where my wife and I moved right after college, I hunted only once or twice in two years, even though I had gone to the trouble and risk of smuggling the Model 21 into the country at the bottom of a crateful of books.

During a year and a half in Georgia my appetite for bird shooting started to return, and by the time I got to graduate school in Iowa I was starved for it and made a pig of myself, hunting almost every day of the two seasons I was there for quail, pheasant, ducks and geese, even illegal doves. I hunted almost always with Dick Wentz, and neither of us had a dog. Occasionally we'd go out with someone who did, like Vance Bourjaily and his springer, Bix. But eighty percent of the time it would be just the two of us, trotting down corn rows toward each other to flush pheasants, and making our own water retrieves on ducks, by swimming for them if we had to.

It wasn't that I had forgotten what a dog adds to bird hunting;

it was just that I didn't need it then. Or later in Wisconsin, where Patricia and I moved after Iowa and where I continued to hunt like a man stuffing food into his mouth with both hands.

For the three years before Iowa, I had been on a self-imposed diet of W. B. Yeats's verse plays and Walter Savage Landor's poetry, of trying to write wispy, melancholy poems and plays myself, talking an off-the-rack brand of expatriate, academic radicalism, and analyzing nineteenth-century European novels down to their comma patterns. One night in County Galway I talked in my *sleep* to Thomas Mann. There was not much animal protein in that diet, and my response to what seemed to be more of the same fare in graduate school was to run for the nearest pork-tenderloin sandwich. Plenty of days I would hunt for twelve hours straight. When there was nothing to shoot, I'd go looking for carp with a bow and arrow. Too often, when I went to classes at all, I would go late, dressed in bloody field clothes, and sit in the back in a happy, overfed stupor, thinking about jumping wood ducks on the Iowa River. For *four years* after I first arrived in Iowa City, all I wanted to do was catch fish, kill birds, and smack a few draft-card burners in the mouth. You could forget about the watercress sandwiches, Jack—and that included bird dogs. Back then, I wanted to be my *own* goddamned bird dog.

Vance Bourjaily has written that in hunting there is "not sport so much as self-renewal, an acknowledgment that one is of natural origins and belongs first to a world built by forces, not by hands; and the hunting which gives shape and purpose to the sojourn, becomes a rite of simplification, in relief of our overconnected domestic and working lives."

By the time my family and I left Wisconsin for New Hampshire, I was desperately simplified, in bad need of connections. That was fourteen years ago. Now, often, I am in bad need of simplification, and am sometimes desperately overconnected. Now I would not hunt at all without a dog.

A Brittany spaniel named Bangaway Buddy was the first bird dog I owned. I was thirty-three years old and he was two when I bought him. For the first five seasons in New Hampshire, I learned what I could about New England shooting over other people's dogs. Though I hunted often during those first five seasons, I was no longer starved for it. Neither was I in any hurry to get my own dog until, first, Dick Wentz left the state and then Don Burke. Without Dick, who had been my constant shooting companion for most of the past nine years, and without Don Burke, who with his English pointer, Echo, had accounted for most of what I had learned about grouse and woodcock, I found myself at the beginning of my sixth bird season in New Hampshire feeling suddenly and self-consciously sated on hunting—as if, still eating, I had looked up to find that everyone else had left the table.

I thought I would try not shooting that fall. I thought about everything I would get done with the extra time I'd have. I thought about how genuinely relieved I would be not to have to wring another wide-eyed woodcock's neck or lose another crippled pheasant.

Then I went out and bought my first bird dog.

Buying Buddy was for me an effort to find a new way to continue doing something I loved to do but had done too much of—a kind of morning-after pledge to drink only white wine from now on. Also, I hoped I'd find through him some way to address the discomfort I had begun to feel with killing birds for sport. I had run out on being able to hunt as unfeelingly as an animal hunts, and I believe most of us do run out on that sooner or later. We are men and are doomed, or blessed, finally, to hunt as men, with our hearts as well as our heads. I am an educated man living in the late twentieth century, I told myself: it is only natural that there be some ambivalence in my hunting, as there was in my father's. I decided to give myself a chance to continue to hunt, soberly—with a dog, with my heart, and with my ambivalence instead of against it. I would take it into the field with Buddy and me and share a lunch with it. And if, after a while, we couldn't get along, maybe I could teach this Bangaway Buddy how to herd sheep.

He was an orange-and-white Brittany, not a pretty one, who grinned, picked fights with larger dogs, ran deer when he could, and refused to be housebroken. There was nothing even vaguely elegant about him: he was a pug with staying power. During the second year I had him he got into a cache of rat poison in an apple orchard near our house, along with six other neighborhood dogs. All the other dogs died. I helped a vet give Buddy five full-body transfusions, all we could give him. The vet believed he would die. He lived, but with permanently painful joints and a deteriorating pancreas.

I was more interested in hunting with Buddy than in training him and he was never what they call a "finished" dog, one who quarters to a whistle, sits before delivering a retrieved bird, and is steady to wing and shot. I admire shooters with the expertise and patience to train all those things into their dogs, but I wanted more to learn from Buddy than to teach him and so I pretty much let him hunt the way he wanted to.

And aside from occasionally ranging out too far, his way was always fine for me. He was out there to find birds, point to them, find them again when and if I shot them, and bring them to me. And he did all those things with so much relish that he had to learn to grin to show it.

All good bird dogs love to hunt, but Buddy loved it to distraction. I have a half-acre trout pond on my property that is full of frogs. When he could not hunt birds, Buddy hunted the frogs—walking around and around the pond until he found one, pointing it sometimes for minutes, and finally pouncing on it. Not just for an hour or two, but *all day* every day he would do this, from the first appearance of the frogs in May until the opening day of bird season in September.

A bird dog wears its heart on its sleeve. Its intensity in the field is all we can really know of its love to hunt; and since it is bred to hunt, a bird dog that hunts with diffidence is as horrifying as one that hunts with love is stirring. Buddy once held a point in a tangle of alders for a full thirty minutes, waiting for me to find him. When trailing a running grouse, the intensity and joy of bringing all his senses to bear at once would seem to spill over him and gleam on him like a coat of paint. On a number of occasions as he was about to go on point, I actually heard Buddy catch and hold his breath, and saw him roll a thrilled eye at me as his head locked up. And near the end of our time together I could sometimes feel his concentration mingling with and strengthening my own: feel my own nostrils dilate in his casts for scent, my own breath catch when he went on point, and my own senses focus and strain toward the bird through his. Given an acuity and determination from the dog that I could not give it, this shared concentration became an end in itself. It led me to a new and lasting reason to carry a gun after game, and it gave me permanent custody of the time Buddy and I spent together. What I remember from Iowa is the hunting. What I remember after my first season with Buddy are the hunts.

Musing on a sundial, Hilaire Belloc observed that "loss and possession, death and life are one/ There falls no shadow where there shines no sun." Hunt for long enough and you will know that those sentimental words are true. Lose a dog you have worked with and loved and you will know it too. That evening in March Patricia and I drove over to the vet's and spent ten minutes with Buddy in the car, feeding him cold steak. Then I carried him back inside and held his head on the stainless-steel table while the vet gave him the injection. He died in less time than it takes to blink your eyes twice, and he took much of the best of me with him; much of what I have of gentleness, patience, and endurance had gone into him. But he left me with as much as he took. Death is on our breath every day as we live, and in our sleep. In the chlorophyll-dead trees of New Hampshire in November there is the sure life of acids and minerals, and beavers thrive beneath the dead ice of winter here. I have another dog now, a yellow-eyed, houndish eighteen-month-old Brittany named Tucker. I shot my first bird over him last October in the same cover where Dick Wentz and I began our five-day shoot five years ago, the same cover where I shot my first bird over Buddy. Last fall I found out that Tucker will run deer when he can, and this spring and summer that he will hunt frogs around the pond, all day every day.

> "If a bird falls, it is like being able to bring back a token from a dream."
> *Vance Bourjaily*

I have three children, from fifteen to twenty years old. None of them has ever killed an animal or a bird, and none intends to. All of them would have taken up shooting birds if I had made an issue of it, and I would have liked their company. But there are too many issues being made over hunting now for me to want to add to them, and hunting, if it is to mean anything, has to be entered and engaged in as privately as a dream. My children may have sensed in the past few years some finickiness in my hunting, a ceremonial, detail-attentive carefulness that reads to them as enervation, and been put off hunting by that as I nearly was by misreading the same qualities in my father's return to hunting. If so, I am sorry I have not been easier to read correctly.

It might also be that the urge to hunt has simply been bred out of my children, as it has out of most Americans now. If that is so, I regret their loss in one way, while in another I am happy with it. There is life in that death too, and there are other ways to learn to concentrate and not to covey-shoot.

THE FOURTH DAY

Lionel Atwill

After two scotches and a lunch of yellow potato salad, a flaccid pickle, ham and cheese hidden in a hard roll, and an indecipherable sweet wrapped so securely in foil that one might imagine its glutinous filling containing nuclear waste, I found what might make life complete: a Desk Director System 600, only $995.00. Technology, I thought, is the god of contemporary man.

I found the Director in a *Sharper Image* catalogue hidden in the seat pocket behind the barf bag. "A quantum leap in desktop efficiency," according to the copy, the Director was eight square feet of greasy black leather wed to a phone, a "vacuum fluorescent" display panel, and more buttons than I have fingers. It did everything: compute, place calls, store numbers, flash the date and time.

And there was so much more! The Wizard of Wine, a digital sommelier in burgundy plastic that winked its LCDs appreciatively at a '49 Mouton-Rothschild. An electronic ocean (with rain and waterfall features) to soothe the harried with the gentle rhythm of crashing water. A pith helmet sporting a solar-powered fan.

Had the plane not landed at Denver, and had I not had to sprint for my connection to Steamboat Springs, I would have ordered them all. Life could be so pleasant, lubricated by technology, organized by quantum leaps of desktop efficiency.

But for now, they would have to wait. More intrinsic things took precedence: elk.

My friends Bob and Bart and I were bound for the mountains. For the black timber. For a week we had contemplated for a year. For a chance to call in and bow-hunt rutting bulls.

We had arranged with an outfitter to hunt his leased ten thousand acres and to stay at his tent camp and eat his wife's food. But we had insisted that the hunting would be according to our plans. At our pace. We wanted to do this one ourselves: find the elk, call in a bull, drop him with an arrow, and get him out.

We took an open jeep to camp over a webwork of dirt roads that twisted through farms and around mountains. We traveled silently, sucking in dust with each breath, until the road narrowed to parallel ruts and the guide said, "This is it." The trip had taken an hour, and when we pulled up next to the tent, another ten minutes passed while we cleared our lungs and wiped off our glasses, drained our bladders, and unloaded our gear.

And then we could take it all in: the mountain rising above us, a rupture in the plains, dark with spruce, dark and foreboding; the small grove of aspen behind the tent with three horses and a mule standing in its shade; the cook tent, its doorway framing the guide's wife, wiry and smiling, a pot of hot coffee in her outstretched hand; and a game rack inordinately high to my eye, until it hit me that elk are four times the size of deer. "Great, beautiful," we muttered, because that was all we could think to say, and we disappeared into our tent to shuck our traveling clothes and put on hunting gear.

The elk, we were told by the guide, lay in the black timber, shaded from the heat of the day. We would have to climb, starting early so we could approach them upwind, from the top of the mountain down. And we did.

We got up at three, something none of us would do for any reason but to hunt. We drank lots of coffee and held silent conversations of nods and looks. Then the time came to put aside the dreams and the talk and really do it, do what we had thought about for the year, so we climbed the mountain.

We were enthusiastic but awkward that first day, our bodies out of synch with the rough country—panting, slipping, sliding, falling, making too much noise, seeing too little sign, sweating in the heat of midday. We would stop and call, "Ough-weeeeeee-ugh, yugh, yugh, yugh," but without great conviction, not knowing if we sounded like elk or merely like fools. Our momentum came from memories of meetings and phone calls and plans and practice back home, not from any inner drive, not from a hunter's soul. Not yet, at least. But we did it all the same.

That evening we held to the ritual—drinking straight from a bottle, smoking evil black cigars, and telling exaggerated tales of the day. Our good humor came less from satisfaction with our hunt than from a need to hold to the script we had written. Soon, though, the reality of the day surpassed the fantasy of our drama. Tired, dehydrated, frustrated to a degree, we went to bed.

On the second day we drank twice as much coffee. Bart limped noticeably, bruised from a fall. The bravado was gone; we had had one chance and had not found our game. Now we knew we would have to sweat and suffer, to battle not only the cunning of the animal but the heat, the blowdown, the brush, the rocks, the branches that slap faces and trip feet, and our own growing reluctance to push, to keep to our plan. (Where did it come from? we began to wonder. Whoever thought we could hunt this creature? Whoever thought we would want to?)

We were late getting started that second day. Gray morning light was chasing shadows from the trees when we left the cook tent. The elk, we knew, would now be making their daily pilgrimage from lowland feed to the black timber. We had missed those subtle pre-dawn minutes when the forest guard changes, when the night feeders turn to twittering birds. We cherished those last minutes by the camp stove, coffee in hand, more than the primordial lure of the mountain. Yet we felt guilt in missing the first hour of hunting light.

By accident, perhaps by intention, we met up in the woods toward noon and frittered away several hours over talk and food and tobacco. We had seen sign, all of us, but no elk as yet. Might as well enjoy ourselves, we thought, and we stretched out for an hour's nap before separating again to work slowly down the mountain to camp.

But things changed that evening. Bart had seen a bull. Not across a high park or on a far ridge, but up close, where the musty smell of the beast drifted to him, where he could watch muscles ripple beneath coarse hide, where he could hear branches crack under hooves and limbs brush against polished antlers. Very close, but not close enough for a shot. Yet the presence of that beast steeled Bart, renewed his vigor. He drank hard from his bottle of rum and smiled and laughed. His purpose had returned. He was anxious for the morning. His enthusiasm fueled Bob and me, but at the same time we were jealous of his small triumph.

On the third day we knew where the elk lay. We reached the woods well before dawn, split up, as was our custom, and climbed. As the sun came up, our calls cried from three ridges. Nothing answered. We pushed the mountain hard now, and our bodies co-operated. The stumbling was over. Eyes and ears were attuned to the woods, but some element was still missing: a sense of the animal. We knew, intellectually, where he fed, where he slept, where he rolled in piss-dampened mud, but intellect fell shy of telling us *when*.

But we were close. A cow and calf moved past Bob in the late afternoon, out of sight but near enough for him to hear the young elk's weak blats. Bob had tracked them, following prints and drop-pings through the black timber. They never knew he was there.

Bart returned to the place where he had seen a bull and in the distance spotted a spike moving up a trail. He called, but his squeals and grunts intimidated the young animal. It answered once, a shy assertion, then trotted off.

I saw no elk but I came on fresh tracks and glistening dung, which I picked up without hesitation to feel its warmth and to know, then, that I was close to the animal, close in distance, closer in mind.

That night we didn't talk much. We discussed what we would do in the morning, but it was perfunctory conversation; we knew now where each of us chose to hunt. We ate our food with purpose and drank some whiskey before going to our tent. We had washed our clothes that afternoon, and now in the flickering yellow light of a lantern, we collected them from a makeshift line and stored them outside in plastic bags with small twigs of spruce. We touched up our arrows, laid out clean socks, and went to bed.

The clock didn't have a chance to ring in the morning. We woke, dressed quickly, and got to the cook tent before the coffee boiled. Bart put on camouflage while he ate his eggs, and Bob, usually chatty in the morning, merely mumbled through a mouthful of toast and pota-toes as he pored over a topographical map.

I felt wide awake long before I should have, full of energy, light-footed and sharp-eyed. It was a feeling I've known in athletics, a confidence that comes after much practice, a sense of being able to do almost anything well and without thought. We all had it; even the guide, who had spent most of his days sprawled in a hammock at camp, was wired.

By jeep we drove halfway up the mountain, then checked our gear, slung quivers and daypacks, pissed, waved, and started to climb. The sun had yet to show itself, but the first birds of morning were tuning, and a rustle in the bushes told us deer were returning from their nightlong feed.

I reached the summit in darkness and, damp from the sweat of my climb, shucked my shirt and pulled on a sweater I carried in my pack, then sat on a rock to watch the sunrise. The cold, damp morning air, which normally I escaped in folds of wool, today felt invigorating. I could taste the oxygen in it, and the scents it brought me—damp earth, spruce, a skunk in the distance—were true and sweet. The birds were louder now and the black sky began to fade to light. And in the distance an elk called.

I find great pleasure in moving well through the woods. There is poetry in a patient stalk—one step, a breath, a hard look to cut through the gloom and the trees, to pick out a creature before it picks out you. This day I stalked well. I worked along the barren ridge of the mountain, just beneath the crest so as not to be caught in silhouette on top. As I came on an outcrop that would force me from my path, I stopped and heard on the far side the rhythm of something walking. I drew an arrow, nocked it, and dropped slowly to a crouch.

Above the rock appeared a mule deer, first antlers, then head, eyes, neck, body, and legs. He moved casually like a kid coming home from school, a foot-dragging, offhand gait. He was a big deer, the best I had seen. I watched as he moved toward me, then drew. I laid the arrow on his chest. It was an easy shot, fifteen yards, quartering toward me. But I let off. The lure of the elk was too strong now, and should I shoot this deer, I would spend the day and part of the night dragging him down the mountain. There was time in the evening for mule deer, down on the flats where a jeep could do the work. He dropped down the mountain on the far side. He never knew I was there; I felt good about that.

Below the ridge lay the black timber, dense spruce clogged with blowdowns where the elk liked to bed. I headed there to call. In the woods I found piles of droppings and trails freshly scarred from elk's hooves. They had been here yesterday, I now knew; they would be here today, I thought. I found a big blowdown and put my back to it, nocked an arrow, and called. No answer, so I waited ten minutes and called again. Still no elk. The bull I had heard at first light had moved to a draw to the east, I thought, but another should come here, so I called again and again, five or six times over the hour.

No elk answered, none appeared. I decided to move down the hill toward the lower ridge where Bob had seen the cow and calf. Staying in the shadows, I walked at the pace of an old man through the trees. I took four hours to get down the mountain. Twice I jumped deer from the cover of a streambed; the second stood and watched me from thirty feet, and I knew that I was moving well, so well that the deer did not know exactly what I was. I could have shot the second, like the big buck on top, but I didn't. Elk on the mind.

But not on the mountain. In midafternoon I broke into the sagebrush. Bob stood by some rutted jeep tracks leading back to camp; he too had seen no elk. But neither of us was disappointed. We both felt keyed to the woods, to the animals, to what was now a mission. We decided to go back to camp and rest for a few hours, then return to two water holes by which we both had passed. Deer tracks skewered the ground around the water, and we reasoned that the deer would move there toward evening to drink. An elk might not go down this day, but surely something else would.

We should have been able to sleep, but we couldn't, couldn't even stand to stay in camp more than an hour. The mountain was our siren now, and the louder she called, the harder we drove ourselves. Bob and I hiked back to the water holes by way of another ridge. We hunted along the way. Bob did the calling; I scouted for fresh sign. We picked up a well-used deer trail leading to the water holes, and by the time we got to them, we were pretty sure we would get a buck tonight.

Bob dropped off at the first hole. I walked three hundred yards to the second and found some good cover in a clump of stubby evergreens. I cut shooting lanes, got comfortable, and settled in.

I've been bored waiting for my wife, waiting for trains and planes, waiting for halftime to end in the Super Bowl, but I've never been bored waiting for game. When the stand is good and you have camouflaged yourself well, when you know you can shoot over 270 degrees, when the wind goes down and the shadows stretch out under the honey light of evening, there is too much to do to get bored. Just listening carries such intensity that a mouse scrambling through the duff is louder than a rush-hour freeway; a deer foot falling is a kettledrum's beat. Smells and sights are amplified beyond reason, and time's passage is condensed.

So it was in my clump. An hour passed, an hour and a half. The time of half-light came when animals move and visibility fades. I rocked forward on my haunches like the predator I was and tensed. Then, high on the mountain, came the trilling call of an elk.

Great confrontations are charted in advance, I believe, and this one had been written over the year, perhaps over the centuries. But it was not to be mine. I had forgotten to bring my call; Bob had his. He answered the bull, the animal replied, and I knew that I would be but a spectator to this hunt. Because I was so close, however, close in distance, and close in a bond that had formed with Bob over twelve months of preparation and over four days on the mountain, close to an animal that now possessed me, there was no jealousy. As the bull bellowed again, then tore up a small tree not a hundred yards from me, jealousy would have been too refined an emotion to consider, for my every instinct was focused on the elk. I was a predator, part of the pack.

The elk came in. I heard him attack another tree, then call again. Bob replied softly; he was the challenging bull, unsure of his rival, perhaps intimidated. The elk charged through the brush. A hush enveloped the mountain.

I waited twenty minutes in my clump of trees. No rational thought compelled me to stay there, no ponderous analysis: "If A equals B, then I should do C." My guts told me to sit tight; my guts told me to watch for that bull, to keep my arrow ready. And then they told me to move. Stealthily, I crawled out of the spruce. I skirted Bob's position and dropped into the grass near his water hole.

Then from the tree line a hundred yards away I heard the elk's death rattle—a mournful bellow, the sound of life escaping, played to the throb of my own beating heart. And silence.

We met beside the water hole, waited in silence for half an hour, then tracked him down. Bob's arrow had taken him above the heart, piercing lungs and liver, draining him of blood in less than a quarter-hour. God, he was big: five points to a side, the tines still coated with fresh mud and strips of the trees he had thrashed. We could barely turn him over to make the first cut, and after gutting him, we had trouble dragging him three feet to slant his body so the blood would drain. By the light of a flashlight, we dressed him out. My hands trembled; I felt a reverence for this beast. His quartering was a sacred rite. Later, back at camp, at night when the meat was hung and the hide salted, the head caped and the ivory pulled and polished, we fried up great ropes of tenderloins, rare and tender, and reverently ate them: our communion of the fourth day.

We hunted on for two days more, but our appetites for the kill were blunted. We worked, but not with the drive that came from the pits of our stomachs on that fourth day. Some primordial notion told us that the meat was in, that eight hundred pounds of elk is enough for three men. I ambushed a cow on a trail and drew on her at ten yards, but didn't fire. Bart had shot at a spike bull and passed too. We were not being sentimental; we just didn't feel the need. The rite had been celebrated. We had transcended the need to prove ourselves, to put antlers on the wall. Our motivation to hunt and kill that mighty beast had come from a more atavistic source, which had possessed us on that fourth day.

Then it was over. We fortified ourselves with whiskey to face the world and to drive off the remorse that came when we left the black timber for the blacktop of town. And how quickly the transition was made. In hours we were in an airport, in the cramped seats of a plane, and then, with my mind still on a mountain, I was flipping through a catalogue—a bible preaching blissful existence through technology. I wondered if someday, a million generations from now, men would be possessed by an atavistic yearning for digital convenience, for flashing lights and electronic waves. Somehow, I thought, it would never measure up. Some things we can live without.

MY CHUKARS

Charles F. Waterman

It had been several years since I had heard chukar talk—soft cackles high in the rimrock and sage—but it was unmistakable, saved in a treasured part of my memory. I began to plan.

I had never seen that ridge before, but it was familiar—ragged sage clumps among patches of slide rock and rimrock walls that had crumbled away in sections. It was like ridges of other years in other places, wasteland to those who are not called to arid mountains and sleek gray birds. The love of dry western hills is an acquired taste.

Without the dog the hunt would have lost something. He was a Brittany this time and he had never seen a chukar. There had been pointers and setters on other slopes, all of them addicted to chukars. The Brittany heard the birds and pricked his ears slightly, but the sound was more mystery than attraction. He fiddled near the truck and waited for me to establish a route.

The pointing dog is a refinement, unlike any other canine. Only the hunting dog has so strong a tie with man the hunter, a partnership through the thousands of years. When the chukar calls are silenced by the hunter's nearness and their exact location is unknown, the dog is no mere possession or servant but a full-fledged partner and collaborator. For that matter, he is in charge for the time being.

And this once I needed no companion other than the dog. It was better to climb the ridge without conversation, and I had the feeling that here I was farther from concrete and sirens than I am when on really high mountains where it is called wilderness.

I began my ascent, not directly toward where I thought the birds were, but at an angle to give us altitude. Chukars may be chased up or across but they are *hunted* down from above, and chukar hunting in rough country is truly that. It is hunting of a fascinating kind. I am reluctant to call it *shooting* or *gunning*, for it is not that simple a game. It involves a maneuvering that reminds me of chess tactics. Before any shotgun can be pointed, the trick, and it can be a difficult trick, is to put the birds in the air and to do so while they are in range. And some of the fascination is in the newness of the combination of a bird from Asia or the Mediterranean with dry, crumbling mountains of America, mountains that are not stylish for climbers in shorts and orange backpacks.

There is no American chukar tradition, and I am a veteran at a game I do not care to promote. It is lonely in chukar land—a contented loneliness of a place the world passes by, not because it is so difficult to reach, but because for most it lacks the fascination of high, timbered mountains and because it is called wasteland. I recalled another hunt when I looked across hazy canyons, standing by a rancher with a costly English shotgun over his arm.

"I can see a long way here," he said. "Big trees close in on me."

But on this later day I was alone with the dog, climbing slowly for half an hour to reach the ridge's crest, which is always a little farther back than it appears from halfway up. The rimrock was in three strips, a layered little mountain, and the ridge was broken by a ravine coming in with a creek that would tumble down into the big canyon in wet weather. There had been no rain for some time, but there was green and a little gold in the notch where the creek came in, and although chukars can live without creeks, they are glad to have them. My birds (already they were *mine*) were not far from the creek and I estimated that they were in a shattered outcropping above it.

None of this hillside chess had impressed the new dog as yet. He worked closer than usual, though, closer than he had worked for quail or Hungarian partridge, somehow knowing that this was a different game and he was a student of something he did not understand. We had started with the sun just over the ridge, but now it was getting warm for October and the dog lolled his tongue a little as he eyed me. He felt my anticipation and shared it—or did I imagine that?

At the top the ridge softened into a flat where there was more earth for the sage to use and there was considerable grass and rabbitbrush. There was sign the ridgetop had been used as a feeding ground by the chukars, there was sign of coyotes (how many birds do they catch?), and a jackrabbit took off in a teasing lope as if not all of his legs were synchronized. This time the dog simply glanced toward the rabbit, somehow knowing that great things were afoot and his weakness for rabbit chases would be out of place.

As I began to move along the ridge toward where I thought I had heard the birds, I heard a new call, this time closer to me—a happy complication, for there were more birds than I had expected. The dog stopped, pricked his ears at it, and stared at me. Was this strange sound a key to our mission?

"It looks like more birds than we thought," I mentioned to him, "but we'll just stay up here and try to work down on them."

I was about to go into the situation more deeply but stopped, a little embarrassed, aware that half a mile of slide rock and dwarfed sage had already made me a sort of happy part-time hermit who talked to a dog rather than to himself. Or was it the same thing? It was the feeling I had come back for, a feeling somehow returning quickly in chukar country. It always had, since the day I saw my first chukar sentinel in full dress on a sharp outcropping.

I tried to keep the dog close as I walked slowly along the ridge-top, only a few feet from a precipitous drop-off of some twenty feet. The breeze came in little puffs, and although I was moving against it, for the most part it was unreliable, as wind tends to be in broken country, and I had no idea of what scent the dog might catch on such dry air. I'd reached the top through a slide where the upper rim had been breached by centuries of desert weather. Desert? Well, the strict definition probably fits that particular range.

The dog began to work scent with the mysterious instinct that separates game birds, even unfamiliar game birds, from other creatures. He paused but did not point, head up and stub tail flagging, and he slowly turned his head toward the little precipice. They must be down there, I thought, but I had heard no calling for some time. What I did hear was a tiny scuffling sound somewhere over the cliff, chukar feet as they hurried to a new position, and then it was quiet again except for another puff of breeze, and this time the dog stiffened a little, his tail barely moving. Almost a point.

I stepped to the edge ready to shoot, and a dozen birds went out below me—farther down than I had expected—in squealing, cackling flight. I heard the wings plainly and I heard their alarm calls, but although I am a connoisseur of chukar cackles before they take to the air, I am a little vague about sounds they make when flushed and I am excited. I had no reasonable shot, for they had dived hard and then swept up and out some fifty yards below me, their wings driving, and then set as they began to sweep to the right, a wad of hurtling specks with the valley floor as a backdrop, going down and around a lump of mountain, appearing once more much farther down and barely visible to glide somewhere into the slope far past the little canyon *my* creek came through and where *my* chukars must be.

Though I had not yet approached *my* birds, this was why I had come—to see mountain chukars sweep into a canyon against a backdrop of sage, stone, and yellowed cheatgrass, wild birds descended from Asians and adapting to a country I learned to love, partly because of them. Here, somehow, I felt the chukars and I were beginning a game that someday would have its own traditions like those of ruffed grouse in old apple orchards and bobwhite quail in palmetto fringes by abandoned Dixie cabins. With the chukars I felt less as if I were borrowing something from earlier hunters. I had first come to the gray and tan mountains only shortly after the chukars themselves.

The dog was now hunting chukars, certain he knew the scent but still not knowing where birds might be. He worked the rimrock but made frequent short forays a little above on the more level ridge crest, and he panted with excitement as much as from the growing heat.

We reached the bluff over the little canyon where the creek, now only a seep, came through our slope and I sat down a little back from the brink to listen. I held the dog with me with whispered orders and I fingered a chukar call but did not use it. I looked at the shotgun, one that somehow goes with my chukar hunting, although there is no such thing as a chukar shotgun.

It is not a new gun and I never knew the original owner, which may be better. It is light and fast and side-by-side and the scroll engraving is modest, and although it was made in England with a proud name, it is not one of the most costly ones. It may be that its earlier owner had shot driven partridge coming over a numbered butt, partridge so nearly the same as my western chukars that only an ornithologist could list the differences. I like to think that, but I really don't want to know the gun's history or even exactly when it was made. It has honest scars and the blueing is worn from the tang on the straight grip. It is such a possession that makes me hunt, in this case more compelling than a new gun or a new anything. It is part of my chukar hunting and I can recall how each of the newer scratches and gouges was made. The old marks have smoothed almost into the wood's patina.

I heard the chukars again with a little disappointment. They were not directly below me but on the other side of the creek and its little canyon, so the dog and I trudged upstream and then crossed and climbed above where they seemed to be. On that side of the creek there were only small outcroppings of rock. Which one? I was careful to get high enough and I suddenly had some help from the direction I had come. From back there a chukar began calling insistently and I actually made him out, a speck atop a boulder but in a location we had missed. He got an answer from our side and then I was almost sure I knew what clump of rock my birds were in. I came down on it from above, and the dog moved cautiously with me. He pointed from a long distance and then broke to move up.

I finally reached the upper rocks and looked down. At their base was thick grass, a jumble of stone fragments, and a bit of sage, and I was sure I saw a trace of movement there. Probably a bird a little surprised to see me and trying to improve its hiding. The dog pointed down, big-eyed and trembling.

Until then chukar sounds had directed our hunt. Now it was silence that meant we were near the birds. A call from across the little canyon got no answer. I moved my feet and our birds flushed noisily, but there were only two of them, taking different routes.

Quite often shots like that are the good ones. The little gun seemed to move by itself and I saw a bird crumple as it went straight away. I looked for the other and it had curved its flight, going down, a route few gunners are trained for, but I was in too much of a hurry to make a careful mistake, and I shot it too and it fell into the little seep at the bottom of the canyon. When the dog had found them he was a chukar hunter, a veteran who would listen for the thready cackles and who would be hard to hold in a canyon when the sounds came from above.

Two birds were enough in the silent land. Only a few days before, when the season opened, trucks had bristled with shotguns along the valley trails, and water-hole snipers had compared scores. There were the youthful hunters aboard the pickup truck with the roll bar and enormous tires who sympathized with me, not noticing the bulge in my stained vest.

"Chukars," they said, "wouldn't be up on these mountains. There's nothing for them to eat up here. If you want chukars you get them around the grain fields or along the creeks."

The opening-day raiders do not understand the other game. You do get chukars in and around grain fields sometimes, for even chukars will accept wheat or barley if it is not too far from the cliffs and talus. But then, despite the patient disavowal made to me by tolerant ruffed grouse experts, ruffs have been pointed and shot in the stubble—with their crops full of wheat.

In Oregon, the stubble fields were on the benches formed by enormous erosions, vast gashes with precarious slopes and jutting rock cliffs, dwarfing the threads of rivers that had carved them through the ages. The chukars lived on the slopes and fed on the bench fields. They walked up in the evenings, and dogs and gunners who awaited them there generally saw them flush at long range, drive briefly, and then swoop dizzily down to unseen havens in the canyon walls, tilting up as they landed to reflect a bit of light from their set wings.

But take the dog along the steep face beneath the field's edge, and when he goes birdy and quarters up toward the stubble, you know the covey has gone that way. Follow them and the dog is likely to hold them. Then, although incoming chukars are unusual targets, you should have your chances as they pass you to go for the edge. Another game of chess.

Chukars always call, the instant experts say. "Noisy birds with taunting cackles."

But they do not always call, and miles of tawny hills can be a puzzle. The chukar has a great deal of room and some of its favorite resting places appear to a studious observer the same as a thousand other such places where a chukar is never found, so it is certainly hunting rather than mere shooting.

In Washington, the golden eagle had ridden on thermals over the river canyon since before I started to climb, his height hard to judge, for so great a wingspread is always broader than I can imagine. Suddenly there was some change in the bird's attitude, no earthward plunge, just a tighter spiral losing height, and it came downward almost to the canyon's rim. There it hovered as if about to plunge on some unseen prey. Whatever it had sighted moved, however, and the big bird took a few short, quick wing strokes, only to hover for another moment, then turn away in frustration.

I was already plodding up and across while the eagle ascended again to take up a new station at great height. If I had read him correctly, the eagle had sighted moving chukars from his high station, had come down to test for a weak or crippled bird, had caused the covey to move away, and had lost it somewhere in the rocks. With the dog's help I should be able to find the birds, but even when I feel like an expert I often find nothing, and a puzzled dog eyes me questioningly when I order him to "hunt close" repeatedly and fruitlessly.

This time, though, it went so well I longed for an audience, preferably someone who had killed thirty red-legged partridges in half an hour as beaters drove them down a Spanish mountain. Perhaps I was a little jealous, for I have never been to Spain.

I climbed to the canyon's rim, discussing my plan with a stubborn dog who had caught a whiff of chukar on the way up and took a dim view of the encircling movement; but a dog's point from below would probably make the birds run up to the rim, then fly down at an angle, giving no shots at all. We were above the birds and they *must* be in the scattered boulders below me. They were.

The dog pointed uncertainly, and before I got down to him the birds stormed out. Remember, they will fly out and then turn down, almost a straightaway. I got one of them, and my second barrel, pointed too carefully, missed as the bird disappeared below the muzzle, but although I remember the stooping eagle better than the falling gray bird, without the gun I would not have been there, and it is the gun that made me the hunter, a part of the scene.

Some chukar seekers have known the drab desert mountains since long before the chukars came from Asia, and the birds are new attractions in a beloved land—an excuse for pilgrimages to solitude, a way to become a temporary part of a landscape changing only with seasons and centuries.

In our creekside camp at dusk there wasn't the faintest murmur of traffic. We heard a coyote's choppy song, and with the last bit of light a single horse (wild?) slouched on the skyline.

"When you get used to this country, you have to come back," my old friend had said. "Drove a bunch of cows through here when I was a kid."

A NATURAL NOTION

David Seybold

Leon Waddell drove into the yard and unloaded the deer from the back of the pickup. His wife did not go out to meet him, but he didn't expect her to. If it had been November or December she would have rushed out the door and made a fuss over him, acting like a mother whose son emerges from the big game banged up but also the hero. She would have told him, among other things, that he was getting too old (he was fifty-three and in better shape than a man half his years) to be chasing deer through the woods. Then she would walk around the back of the pickup and inspect the deer and announce it was the best and most handsome one yet. She would smile and say they would have the heart that night and part of the liver in the morning. And while she carried on he would stand quiet and shy and full of pleasure. He would look at something else (he could never look directly at her when she was making a fuss over him) and think how she had said the same things every deer season (every deer season he killed a deer, that is) for as long as he could remember. Then he would say that he guessed he had got lucky again and that any fool could have shot that deer. They would say these things to each other while standing next to the pickup and deer. It would be cold and their breath would show white and thin as it drifted upward in pale mists and disappeared among the branches of leafless maples. Then he would look at her and see that she was hugging herself to keep warm. He would tell her it was too cold to be outside with nothing more than a sweater on. But he knew she would stay out there with him and not give an inch to the cold. He would say that it was unlikely the deer would skin and butcher itself and that if they were going to have a meal off the animal he had better get to work. And then she would turn for the house and he would carry the deer into the barn.

But it was May and not November or December. And it was six months after the New Hampshire deer season had closed. And it seemed so . . . so unnatural to see him bring a deer home when it was warm and not cold, when the only snow on the ground was deep in the woods, when trees were in new leaf, when there were more robins than evening grosbeaks. No, she would not go out to meet him. She would stay inside and pretend not to have seen any of it.

It came to her that perhaps he had broken the law. Such a far-fetched possibility had never before occurred to her. Her husband was a man who believed in laws. Oh, he may not have always believed in the men who wrote and enforced laws, but he did believe in them. Yes, he did. And she recalled how he had explained the importance of laws to Stuart's boy. He had told the boy that laws were to people what motor oil was to an engine. He had said that laws lubricate society. They make things run a lot smoother. Without laws we'd seize up tighter than a frog's rear end, just like an engine that has run too long without oil. What you have to keep in mind, he had told the boy with a wink, is that some laws are good and some are bad. And that there's always someone changing them. Even when they don't need to.

She saw him limp and knew that the deer had not come easily, that he had had to work hard to get it. Then she saw how small the deer was and she sighed. Her husband never shot small deer. He wouldn't even shoot a doe unless it was the last day of the season and every buck in the county had eluded him. The poor thing, she thought, so small and frail. I hope it didn't suffer. And then she put the kettle on.

He had seen her watching him from the kitchen window. She'll stay put, he thought, and worry and wonder until I let on. That was the way of her whenever something out of the ordinary happened. Something would not be the way it was supposed to be and she would put herself behind the crowd. Oh, she'll be in a tizzy, all right. She'll have that kettle boiling up a storm in no time at all. Well, I can't say as I blame her much. No sir, I can't . . . me with a deer out of season and all. I expect she'll have to wait to hear about it, though.

If I don't get the hide off this little fellow right now the meat will spoil and then there'll be no sense to any of it.

He hoisted the deer by its hind legs from a beam. Most deer he had hung from the beam were heavy and required muscle, and they were long and cleared the barn floor by only a foot or so. But this one was so light that he never even strained to hoist it, and it was so small that a child could have stood under it.

He had thought that skinning the deer would be fast work. But the deer's lightness worked against the process and it wouldn't hang still while he fisted the hide down toward the head. Most deer had hung heavy and solid from the beam, like a boxer's body bag, but this one swayed with every downward pull, like a carpet on a line that's being swatted with a broom.

When he finished the skinning he wondered if he should let the deer hang for a few days, to let the meat age. He could cover it with cheesecloth or black pepper to keep the flies off and it would probably work fine. But he decided against it and broke out the butchering knives and the saw. Better to be done with it now, he thought. And he wondered if maybe he wasn't a little afraid of being caught with an illegal deer in his barn. After all, he had broken the law. He wondered what they would do to him. Would he be fined or jailed or both? Maybe they would take his hunting and fishing license away. Well, he didn't give a damn what *they* did. The lot of 'em have their heads so far up their rear ends they have to pull down their zippers to brush their teeth, he said to himself, and then worked the boning knife against the sharpening steel. He knew damn well why he wasn't going to let the deer hang, and it had nothing to do with any laws or the breaking of them.

It was pleasant work, he had to admit. The barn was cool and the air and sunlight coming in through the wide barn door carried the scent of the warming earth. Swallows swooped in and out, gathering material for their nests, which they were building under the barn's eaves and among the rafters overhead.

He stopped working then and lit his pipe. He was not in so much of a hurry anymore. And he knew it was because he was working in the barn, which always had a way of calming him. It was the place he went to whenever he couldn't fish or hunt and he wanted to be alone.

I think I'll take a walk tonight, he said to himself. And he thought about the walk he had taken the night before. He had told Nancy he needed some tobacco and that a walk to the store would do him some good. "Well, I should think it would," she had said. "You've been sitting in a truck all winter long. You need some exercise. Yes you do." Which was true. He was the town's Road Agent and his winters were spent working erratic hours driving a snowplow or sander. He wanted to see the stars again, to see the winter constellations passing into the western sky and the approach of spring's constellations from the east. His father and grandfather had taught him about the stars when he was young, and he remembered how he had announced to them that when he grew up he was going to be an astronomer. But that was long ago, back when he was still in school and working for the town only during summer vacations. Well, he could still watch the stars, and he could still take pleasure in his ability to tell of changes in the seasons by observing them as well as a farmer could who knows the land and its subtle ways.

He looked through the small window over the butchering bench and out to the pasture and pine forest that surrounded it. Signs of spring were there, too. Patches of green rye were showing around the edges of pasture granite and fence posts. He had walked through the pasture two days before, when it was raining, and the ground was turning soft. He had walked through the pasture and into the pine forest and listened as the rain fell through the limbs of spruce and hemlock and made the whole forest hiss. The brook that ran from under the pines and out into the southwest corner of the pasture was running full and he thought that maybe this year he would dam it up and make a small pond. Clayton Rowe, who put his cows in the pasture every spring and summer, had offered to help any number of times. The brook would dry up in July or August and Clayton would have to lug water from the barn to the pasture. A pond would help Clayton and the cows and keep the well water that much higher. Well, maybe I'll see my way clear to do it this year, he said to himself. And then he remembered he had to tell Clayton that a section of the barbed-wire fence had been taken down by the limbs of a hemlock that fell during an ice storm last January.

He finished butchering and wrapped up what little meat the deer had yielded and put it in the chest freezer, which was kept in a stall. He cleaned the knives and saw and stored them and made sure the lid on the trash can was tightly on. He had put the deer's head and other unwanted parts in a plastic bag and then put the bag in a trash can, to be taken to the dump on Sunday. Raccoons and skunks lived under the barn and they would try their hardest to get the lid off and make a meal of the remains.

Done and done, he said to himself. And he felt pretty good. The anger and hurt that only a few hours before had been sharp and deep had dulled. He felt tired and strangely satisfied, as if he had made right some terrible wrong.

Now, though, he had to deal with Nancy. And won't she be in a tizzy, though, he thought. Yes she will. And he walked from the barn to the house knowing he would not tell her the truth about the deer.

He had learned a long time ago that when it came to animals and Nancy it was better to lie than to let on that an animal—any animal—had suffered. And it was the damnedest thing for him to understand. She was so strong in the face of adversity and so understanding of suffering and she could see herself (and a lot of other people too) through any amount of hardship, as long as the adversity and suffering and hardship involved people and not animals. ("Why, folks have family and friends to help them through their troubles, but animals ... why, the poor little creatures are all alone." And he would say, "Except for you," and she would get mad and walk away.) Oh, she thought hunting was all right, even worthwhile, though she never referred to it as a "sport." Hunting, in her mind, was no different than farming or gardening. It was practical, a natural thing for country folk to do. That her husband enjoyed hunting did not mean he inflicted pain or suffering on the animals he hunted. In fact, she was certain he didn't. (But how, he always wondered, could she think every animal he killed had died instantly, without pain or suffering?) Why, his hunting only made him a better provider. "Why else did the Almighty put deer and partridge and ducks and the like here?" she would say. But dogs and cats and the young of any animal were innocent (dogs running deer and cats killing birds did so only because their owners neglected them and they were bored) and she couldn't bear to hear or see their suffering. When Ransom Sargent's collie got hit by a car and died she took it as a death in the family. It was truly the damnedest thing for him to understand. And at times her carrying on would make him uncomfortable, for it was impossible not to be reminded of bad shots, shots that only wounded, and of animals that got away and died and . . . and suffered. And these were also times when he went to the barn.

He walked into the house and heard her in the front room. She was, by the sound of it, rearranging the china in the corner cupboard. Busywork, he thought. He had heard the sound many times before and knew that she had rearranged and dusted the pieces so many times that by now they were probably back in their original places.

"Any calls?" he said.

"No. Stuart stopped by to borrow your bait trap. He'll be back later on . . . said he was going bass fishing over to Otter Pond."

He washed his hands in the kitchen sink and heard her walk into the room. On the counter was a pie plate filled with chunks of young rhubarb. They were pink and covered with sugar and bread crumbs. He closed his eyes and imagined the smell of the finished pie. They had not had a fresh pie since Thanksgiving. And he realized he had not eaten since breakfast. He grabbed an apple from the fruit basket and took a bite.

"First pie of the season is about the best," he said between bites of the apple.

He turned to look at her and saw her face set in dour seriousness. She wouldn't look at him, not directly anyway, and he caught only a glimpse of her hazel eyes. Handsome she is when she's pleased, blessed she is when she's peeved, he thought.

He ought to tell me, she thought. He knows I know. Yes he does. He'll wait, though, until he's good and ready. Yes he will. And she cut thin slices of butter and placed them on top of the pie.

"Guess this weather will bring things out in proper fashion," he said. "That rain and this sun will put things in a growing mood. Yes they will."

He was watching her slice the butter and waiting for her to say something. Well, I guess she isn't going to say anything agreeable, he thought. I might just as well try to get her to say something disagreeable.

"I see the Sargents put their tomato plants out. We might just as well do the same. Weather like this will tend to them better outside than we can inside."

She covered the pie with a damp cloth and said, "Sargents always put their plants out too early ... have as long as we've known them. We'll have a frost or two yet, we always do. There'll be a full moon next Saturday night and a killing frost with it. Always is. Yes there is. We'd be right to wait until the first to put them out."

She was right, of course. Not until the first of June did they plant anything but early peas in their garden. But she did speak up, he thought. Yes she did.

She went to put the pie in the icebox and he opened the door for her.

"Got a deer today," he said.

She backed up from the icebox and went to the sink.

"Oh," she said in an even voice. "How'd you come to get a deer this time of year?" My, but you do take your time, Leon Waddell, she thought. Yes you do.

"Road kill," he said matter-of-factly. "Found him up on the East Washington Road. Little thing, no more than fifty pounds soaking wet."

He looked at her and saw she had been looking at him. Her eyes were soft and doelike, motherly, as he had expected. But her expression was still stern and serious and he was surprised. It seemed to suggest he wasn't telling her the whole truth, that there was something more. There was, of course, but he wasn't going to tell her. There's something else on her mind, he thought. Yes there is.

"Was it dead when you found it?" she said. "Was the doe around? My, but how the poor little thing must have suffered." She put the kettle on and went to the cupboard for her tea.

"Dead as dead can be when I arrived," he lied. "I imagine it didn't know what hit it ... car must have been speeding right along."

"Sometimes the doe will stay right with her young. Did you see her? Oh, the poor thing," she said, refusing to give up thinking the worst had happened. And he could tell she was truly worried and upset by the way she worked her hands in the folds of the apron.

"Didn't see her," he lied again. "Why, I'd bet she had twins and when she saw and heard the one get smacked like that that she took off with the other."

The kettle sang and she poured her tea. He made a cup of instant coffee and walked into the front room. He thought it was over and

that she'd worry herself for a time but that by supper she'd be somewhat calm. He sat down by the window and drank his coffee. She
followed him into the room and took her chair by the front window.

"What did the warden say?" she said. "Did he say you could
have it?"

"I didn't tell the warden or anyone else," he said. There was a
new warden in their area and he had not been at all impressed with
him. He was young and lazy and he considered him a "roadside warden," which meant he never left his cruiser for more than a few minutes at a time.

"Then you broke the law," she said sternly. "If you don't report
that deer to the warden, won't they arrest you?"

"I don't give a damn what *they* do. As for that warden, all he'd
do is write it up in his book and take the deer to the dump. That's
what he does. He takes road kills to the dump and leaves them for the
rats and anything else that happens along."

So that's what it is, he thought. I've broken the law and she's
afraid I'm going to jail.

"Ain't anyone going to jail," he said. "Let them try and I'll tell
them what's right and what's wrong. Yes I will. Why, all he'd have
to do is dress out the deer and take it to a state home or to someone he
knows who's in need of some fresh meat. Lord knows, there's a lot of
folks who'd welcome some venison. Kiernan used to do it all the time.
Yes he did. He knew it was the proper thing to do. Yes he did. But
this new one . . . why, he's too damn lazy. Hell, he even admitted to
Jim Lamson that road kills are a waste of his time. His gut should be
empty sometime. Yes it should be. Why, if Kiernan were alive today
he'd have him across a stone wall counting chipmunk droppings
faster than you can blink your eyes. Yes he would!"

By God, but what I wouldn't give to have Kiernan back in uni-
form, he thought. Here it is 1981 and there are fewer deer in the
woods than ever before, and the game wardens these days are all
educated and lazy and throwing away any animal that might mean
they'll have to get their hands dirty. Yes sir, it's something, all right.
Makes you wonder if all that education they get takes away all notion
of what's right and what's wrong. Yes it does.

She let him have his say and when he was done they were silent.
He sat and stared out the window and she fidgeted with the folds of

her apron. Her husband was not given to such emotional outbursts. He was a quiet man who preferred listening and thinking to speaking.

"Kiernan isn't here anymore," she said in a voice that was only slightly above a whisper. "He's dead and so are a great many of his kind. Even so, right or wrong, the law's the law . . . the same now as it ever was. You can't just go off and take what isn't yours. No you can't."

She had never seen him this way. He was different and she didn't understand him. (Had she really talked to him that way, as if he were Stuart's boy?) She looked at him and saw his face was tense and that his eyes were set in a seriousness she had seen only once before—when he had found the Clarke boy drowned in the Blackwater River and told Kiernan that he knew the parents and that he'd tell them. There's something knotted up inside him, she thought. Yes there is.

"Well, I'm not going to call a man to come and get a deer that he's going to throw on a heap of trash. No I'm not!"

He had not expected this to happen. He had not expected her to argue with him, to talk to him as if he were ten years old. Why, he wondered, can't she see that me keeping that deer is my right . . . or anyone else's who has a notion of what's right and what's wrong?

She had had enough of listening and talking and not understanding. She felt empty and hurt and confused. And very tired. In thirty-one years of marriage they had never acted this way to each other. She wished they were in bed and that they were looking up into the darkness and talking to each other in voices that somehow always made sense.

"Well," she said in a tired voice, "at least the poor thing didn't suffer. That's one right thing."

At that he stood up and said he had to call the garage and tell Clark to lock up and that he'd see him in the morning. Then he told her he was going out to the barn and rebuild some of the tomato cages.

He was not a big man, not quite six feet and only about one hundred and seventy pounds. He had a way about him, though, that when he walked he appeared much larger than he really was. But as she watched him walk across the yard to the barn, she thought he looked small, even smaller than he actually was. She saw him limp and wondered what had happened to make his leg act up like that. He's tired, she thought. He's tired and upset. He needs a rest. So do I. Yes we do.

He went to where he kept the tomato cages and sorted out the ones that needed repair. He put them next to the workbench and then went through a pile of scrap hardwood until he found some old maple stakes that would make good legs for the cages.

While he worked he thought about what he had said to Nancy. He had been wrong to talk to her that way. It was not like him. And it was not like her to talk to him like she had. But he was the cause, the reason why she had. Maybe it was the deer, the truth about the deer which he would not tell, maybe it was her arguing about the law, maybe it was a combination of both. He really didn't know. Well, at least she'll never know the truth about the deer, he thought. That's one good thing. And then he pictured the deer as he had found it.

At first, he wasn't sure what it was. It could be a dog, though he doubted a dog would be so far from houses unless it was running with a pack. Or it could be a coyote feeding on a small road kill, which would be understandable.

He approached the animal very slowly, letting the pickup idle along the shoulder of the road. When he got to within a hundred feet he saw it was a deer, a very small one. He stopped the pickup and wondered what a deer was doing on the side of the road flopping around like a fish out of water.

"Now isn't that the damnedest thing," he said. "Yes it is." He saw that the deer was trying to run into the woods on legs that were only half there.

He didn't know what to do, which surprised him. All he could do was stare at the deer in disbelief and feel sick to his stomach.

"Road kill without the kill," he whispered. And he wondered: who in hell would hit a deer and not stop? It didn't make sense. It really didn't. So he sat there and stared at the deer's pathetic attempt to escape into the woods.

He got out of the pickup and walked up to the deer. He looked in its eyes and saw they were glassy and frightened and he turned away. The deer stared at him and tried even harder to escape, but its effort was futile and sad and it moved like a turtle on its back. He saw that the deer's legs were broken at the shoulders and that below the lower joints they were shattered. Its chest had been crushed and he wondered why the deer was still alive.

He looked for tire marks and saw that the deer had been run over and dragged for about twenty feet. There was a smooth swath in the dirt road where the deer had been dragged. It was as if the car had been towing a heavy sack.

He wondered what he should do. He didn't have a rifle with him and couldn't put the deer out of its misery. If he went home for his rifle, the deer would probably have died by the time he got back. He could take the deer home in the back of the pickup, but the ride back over the rutted and potholed road would only make the deer suffer more.

Without thinking he got down on his knees and stroked the deer's side, which was streaked with mud and with both dried and fresh blood. When the deer inhaled, it wheezed and shuddered under his hand, and when it exhaled, a trickle of blood and mucus ran out of its mouth and nostrils and stretched to the dirt. He put his hand under the deer's head and raised it to ease the deer's breathing. Then he sat down and worked the deer's upper body onto his lap. A sharp bone, possibly a rib, dug into his knee and he could feel the old chain-saw wound start to ache. He tried to move without disturbing the deer but couldn't. It'll stiffen, he thought.

He sat there with the deer across his lap and it no longer tried to escape. He held its head up with one hand and stroked its side with the other. He heard a crashing sound and looked up and saw the flash of a white tail disappear through the thick pine.

"This is the best I can do," he said to the deer. "I don't know what else to do. Someone hit you and they didn't stop. Maybe they didn't care or maybe they were just scared and kept going. Out of sight, out of mind . . . that sort of thing. They should have stopped, though."

No one used the East Washington Road during winter or early spring. There were only a few houses along it and they were summer camps and not winterized. The owners came up only from the middle of June to early October. Foliage seekers, joy-riders (kids and lovers), and hunters used the road, but only until either the hunting seasons closed or snow made the road impassable. He drove the road every spring to inspect culverts and check for washouts. Owners of the camps always called him every spring to see if the road was open and if their camps were still standing. No one in recent days, however, had called about his camp or the road.

When half an hour passed without anyone driving by, he knew whoever had hit the deer would not be back. Probably not even from around here, he thought. Flatlanders or newcomers.

He stroked the deer and listened to its erratic breathing. He knew it wouldn't live much longer, and that he'd better figure out what he was going to do with it.

"Well, now, little fellow, I don't figure the Good Lord created you to be killed by people driving cars who don't give a damn what happens to you. But that is the case here."

He shifted his position ever so slightly and realized his bad leg was numb. He thought about the newcomers and how in general they didn't understand country life. Oh, they were nice folks, for the most part. But it bothered him to see them buying land and then posting it to keep hunters, and everyone else, away. If they were working the land, raising crops or cattle, anything but just letting it sit there, he might understand. Most, however, weren't doing a damn thing but paying taxes and saying it was theirs. They're changing the way we live, he thought.

As quietly as a trout slips from sunlight into shade the deer died. There were no last great paroxysms, no last gasps for life. He simply felt the deer go limp, and he knew it was dead. And he sat there and hated the newcomers and their Volvos and Jeep Wagoneers. He hated the new warden and the people who taught the warden his trade.

It came to him that he hated these people and things just like he hated crows that destroy crops and the eggs of nesting birds. There was no way to stop them, either. Not really. You would try something, but they would figure a way to beat it. They would get together in large numbers and take whatever they wanted until they completely destroyed the very thing they wanted. Then they'd move on and do it all over again somewhere else.

"Know what killed you?" he said to the deer. "The times. The times are changing and you and your kind don't figure into what they're changing to. Somehow I always figured I'd see my way through. Now I don't know anymore. I could be wrong. I just don't know."

He decided against calling the warden. And it came to him that although the deer wasn't legally his, it also wasn't anyone else's. He could leave it right there and the coyotes and fisher cats and whatever could have a good meal off it. But then again, so could he and Nancy.

He picked up the deer ("Why, it's no heavier than a large dog," he said) and put it in the back of the pickup and headed for home. He drove down Main Street, past the Texaco station and Town Hall. He saw Jay Gurnsey going into the bank and waved to him. He knows, he thought. He's been up against changing times longer than me. Then he pulled over and motioned to Jay to come over. He watched to see his friend's expression when he got close enough to see the deer.

"Well now, look at what you have. Looks like a little skipper . . . a pretty beat-up one, at that. How'd you come by him?"

He told his friend the story and watched as his face went from anger to sadness to understanding. Yes he does, he thought.

"Well, he'll eat as well now as one in fall. Say, did you see the doe? I wonder if she had twins? Maybe she did. Maybe we should think about hunting up there next fall." And he smiled.

"Well, I think we'd be right to try. Yes I do." Then he drove down the hill to his home, figuring he'd spend some time in the barn.

LITTLE LOVER OF THE BOGS, LITTLE QUEEN OF THE WOODS

Guy de la Valdene

T he woodcock appeared on a gilded plate, intact except for his feathers, alongside a sprig of watercress and a shock of straw-colored french fries. He sat with his head tucked under his wing on top of a square of toasted white bread over which was spooned a liverish puree. The French waiter ceremoniously swept away my empty soup bowl and neatly replaced it with *"une bécasse pour Monsieur."* I was ten years old.

It looked okay, a little like squab, except that for some ungodly reason someone had forgotten to dispatch its head. Not knowing what to do, I looked to my father for guidance. He had selected a species of perch, prisoner of the deep waters of Lac d'Annecy, and had already deboned it. He laughed and advised, "Pretend you're Robespierre and cut it off. Then if you feel ambitious, pinch its bill and bite off the top of its head. The brain is what you want." It was an ambition I did not share, but the bird was delicious. I finished it with my fingers, much to the disapproval of the waiter. Visible through the nuisance of a few bones was a hunting scene baked into the plate, depicting a Gordon setter on point and a farm girl reclining on a haystack with her thumb in her mouth. After a while I discovered the woodcock, nestled beneath her petticoats in the swale of a thigh. Facing me at the bottom of the plate, the inscription read, *"Quelle bécasse!"* In France addled young girls are sometimes called *bécasses*.

My father congratulated me. "Didn't think you'd eat the toast and trail."

"Trail?"

"Insides. You know—the intestines."

"You mean the caca?"

He laughed. He loved to laugh, and he loved good food, but he didn't like to hunt. He'd done that in airplanes for three years in one war and again twenty-five years later as a member of the Free French. He wouldn't shoot things that didn't shoot back. He's dead now, and I've never been to war, so I bird-hunt.

Some argue that a hunter's concern for a species is motivated by self-interest, and I agree; others simply point in the general direction of our forefathers and mention bison. The latter group argues for the abolition of all hunting, and their morality in the matter is ticklish to dispute. Our civilization proclaims through the relentless voice of religion that man's death is but a stepping-stone to better things, but for reasons of soul, animals are not included.

I hunt the ridges, woods, and marshes, and will do so as long as I can, because that's where I'd rather be. I kill game and regret the finality of it, but given the choice of eating pork chops or wild fowl, my regrets shift to the cellophane wrappers. My interest in the preservation of wildlife is real and selfish, my interest in the preservation of mankind less so, since we are a stupid lot, doomed by overbreeding and our own arrogance.

Aldo Leopold, observer and hunter, poet of nature and doyen of this century's ecological movement, asked, "And when the dawn-wind stirs through the cottonwoods, and the gray light steals down from the hills over the old river sliding softly past its wide brown sandbars—what if there be no more goose music?"

Decades later I ask, "Will the woodcock ghost-dance at dusk when the scantlings have turned to steel? Will he sing when his amphitheaters are cemented to the ground? Will there be anyone who cares?"

Once upon a time, the story is told, a covey of gray partridge roamed the Moroccan plains of Zair. Among them, a small, pitiful individual feebly vegetated while her powerful brothers and sisters ridiculed her, keeping the best grain and insects for themselves. To survive, the little partridge was reduced to seeking out minute morsels of food in the fissures of rocks and hard-to-get-at places. Unfortunately, her short beak did not always allow her to reach her food, and she grew weaker.

The Virgin Mary, witnessing her misery from Paradise, was saddened and called her to Heaven. The partridge curled up in her hand and listened as the Virgin said, "Little bird, I am going to transform you, so that you may know the joys of life. Thrown out by your kind, you will now live alone in the serenity of the forests, where along with silence you will also find an abundance of food. You will be the elegant hostess of the underbrush and will generate the admiration of those who love nature. Your capricious flight and your intelligent defenses will allow you to escape your pursuers. I will protect you."

The Virgin laid three fingers on the little bird's head, leaving three brown transversal imprints now called "the Virgin's fingers." The bird's beak lengthened, her plumage took on a golden hue, and she flew back to earth as guardian of the forests.

So was born the woodcock, also called Our Lady of the Woods.

The American species is *Philohela minor*, which can be translated as "little lover of the bogs." The scientists have reclassified it several times, most recently naming it *Scolopax minor* to return it to the genus of the European woodcock, but to me it is *Philohela*. The European woodcock is larger than our American bird, but very much like it. The French have always regarded the woodcock as special and worthy of adulation. Unlike our bird, it is referred to as the Lady of Velvet Eyes, Queen of the Woods, Enigmatic Gypsy, the Divine One, and Sorceress. Others think of *les bécasses* as cuckolds.

Physically, woodcock appear gentlemanly, even portly. I observed one years ago, strutting across a sandy two-track, chest thrust outward, tail fanned, bobbing up and down like a bullfrog, and I expected him to pitch over and plunge his bill into the ground. The behavior was a sign of nervousness, I'm told, but it was certainly disguised with élan.

In hand, the bird is a delight. From the crown of his head to the tip of his tail, his orbicular shape quite simply fits as if he'd been born to be palmed. Gauguin might well have painted him, cupped as an offering in the hands of a girl.

The woodcock's plumage deserves special attention. Overall, it is not unlike the color of a freshly killed brown trout or the skin of certain reptiles. Subtle beauty exudes from this relic of another age whose survival depends on camouflage. Both male and female have identical coloration, and, except when young or during the molt, it remains for all intents and purposes constant throughout the seasons.

The feathers, woven like bractlets on an artichoke heart, are at times suffused and at other times notched, barred, edged, and tipped in kaleidoscopic patterns, incredibly specific and purposeful.

Everyone's perceptions of colors differ and vary with respect to light and taste. Some find woodcock dull when compared to other species. Personally, I find that bruised peaches, reflections of gravel creeks, and the whip of red foxes evoke his memory. But then so does Pan.

An old gamekeeper who was not above doing a little poaching when the larder was empty told me, "Above the partridge belongs the snipe, and above the snipe the woodcock, and above the woodcock there is nothing." Woodcock should be roasted or made into salmis. So declare the great chefs of past and present. The exquisite flavor of the bird imposes simplicity.

It is part of the biological progression that every form of life is hunted. *Homo sapiens*, no longer threatened with extinction, nevertheless perseveres in the tradition by killing his peers, his motives ideological and self-centered. The rest of the natural world, including those who hunt their own, hunt for food. So much for soul.

Regardless, fall belongs to the hunter. Fall in Michigan has the overwhelming effect on me that the Louvre Museum in Paris had on Russell Chatham. A distinguished painter, Russ was overcome by the presence and number of masterpieces in one place. He told me later that it had scared him and made him aware of his shortcomings by reminding him of the passing of time. In much the same way the raging explosion of fall completely disorients my perspective of time and space. More often than not, I feel closer to Mars than I do to my car. The earth is my museum, and its abundance confuses me. A piece of ground no larger than a canvas could take months, even years, to understand.

So I wander, always bemused at nature's impeccable order of things, and I get lost, because I follow my dog and never pay attention to where I'm going.

The texture of woodcock hunting cannot be grasped without a dog. Through the nose of a good one, the innards of the sport—the chase and the kill—are classically dramatized. The flow of action follows an inevitable course, premeditated and acted upon in collaboration. The setting is romantic, the action bold, the denouement stylish and heroic.

My love of the sport demands companionship other than human. I have always owned a dog and would feel naked and ashamed killing birds without one. The nagging aura of indulgence that more and more shrouds my hunting prompts the need for a scapegoat. As an active partner in the paradox, my dog fills the requirements.

She's not a pointer but an old yellow Labrador bitch who has outlived three cars and who in ten seasons has traveled a hundred and fifty thousand miles to and from cover. She is not particularly good-looking, and other than when hunting she is awkward. Elevators and slippery floors worry her, and she walks on or in them stiffly, with her tail tucked between her legs. She is easily confused. She stares lugubriously and for too long into full-length mirrors, snores when stroked, sleeps unless hunting, and enjoys turning over garbage cans. Her coat is velvety soft. She is inordinately deep-chested and used to be very strong. She now is very wise.

We have done everything together for a long time. We have slept under the same covers on cold nights and rested on huge boulders that shaded feeder creeks three thousand feet above ranch hands who could not hear our howls of joy. We have killed well, and we have killed badly, but we have mostly been honest. Her coat has lost its sheen, and the years have pulled her skin tight to her frame, but she still looks at me from within dark sockets, and her eyes are aware of things I don't understand. Whatever they recognize, however, will someday become plain to me, and I too will be caught looking achingly at an old friend I love.

These memories remind me of collages. The picture is my life, and within it the fragmented facets come and go, prismatically shaped and pasted one on top of another like unrelated abstractions. A deer grazing in a specific apple orchard is remembered in the bouquet of Calvados brandy. I feel a woodcock whenever I handle a quail, and taste him in snipe. I see autumn under the surface of beaver ponds and hear grouse drumming in local tire establishments. Dental braces remind me of birds and the passing of time.

A long time ago, before my friend Jim Harrison and I really knew how to pick and choose our cover, we spent an afternoon on a bluff overlooking the Manistee River. It was one of those clear, quiet, invigorating days that fall is all about. A few moments after we entered the woods we killed a woodcock and two grouse. Always concerned about the potential "skunk," we were pleased it was off our backs and without ado began to discuss the evening's recipe. An hour later four more woodcock graced our game pouches. We went on, pushing through the woods and working the edges of dirt roads, shooting well and picking birds every few minutes. We stopped at eighteen, nine woodcock and nine grouse. Jim and I always stop one bird short of the limit. Why? I have no idea except that it's a penalty of sorts, perhaps the penalty of reason.

When we reached his driveway, we were greeted by his wife, Linda, and eleven-year-old daughter, Jamie. They walked to the car, rolling their eyes at each other and timidly inquiring about the hunt. In those days our daily bags were invariably slim, and that question usually did not elicit glee. We were purposely somber when we opened the trunk, but for once the entire boot was filled with feathers, abandoned pell-mell on top of the guns. Linda exclaimed, "Oh, my!" and giggled through her hands, while little Jamie simply stared in openmouthed disbelief. She was wearing braces, and young girls wearing braces have ever since reminded me of that special day eleven years ago.

Nick Reems and I hunt well together. We walk at the same pace, seem to know where the other one is without having to shout, and naturally take our positions on either side of the dogs. We work to cover and instinctively leave ourselves room for wild flushes.

One afternoon we hunted a small woodlot shaped like a horseshoe. We worked the edges, thirty yards apart. Soon enough the bells fell silent, and turning to the sound of a shot, I heard Nick's warning. The woodcock spun up to the crest of the trees and flew high over my head. A high, incoming bird vertical to the shooter used to be thought of as "the king's shot," possibly because it is not very demanding and certainly because it is pretty. The woodcock fell correctly, the skeet load killing him at the apex of his flight. He tumbled with his head to one side and looked like a small pillow, an inanimate object arching through the air, free of life. He landed in the clearing behind me.

We found Nick's bird but were still looking for mine when Nick's dog, Cochise, went back on point twenty yards to our left on the edge of the woods. My friend was doubting my bearings. "Must be your bird," he declared. I knew better because I recognize death, but I honored the dog and circled through the underbrush, leaving

Nick in the clearing. Over the years I have stared at a million leaves looking for woodcock and have been rewarded with a million enigmas, but this time the bird's image jumped out of the puzzle a scant yard in front of Cochise's nose. He was tuckered on the ground facing away and watching me out of his famous eyes. There ensued a time warp of sorts, during which the only suggestion of motion was the dog's shivering flanks. A minute passed, and never taking my eyes off the bird, I called to Nick, who implied it might be my cripple. It wasn't. I never moved, but the oppression finally sprang the woodcock into flight.

After the pleasure he'd bestowed, I didn't shoot, but, not having been there, Nick dropped him as he curled low around the bend of the woods. We found my bird a few minutes later, lying in the open where I thought he should be. Air-washed, the fallen bird had eluded the dogs; they hadn't smelled him even though they had done everything but walk on him.

I often think about that bird on the ground and am glad the occurrence is rare. It would be morally and psychologically impossible for me to kill woodcock after seeing them bundled up like elves in the leaves. I punish myself enough by canting cripples toward the sun and looking into their pupils before crushing their heads with my thumb. I don't know what I am looking for, but what I see is a dark reflection of my face. Killing is already too serious and precarious an affair for me to be that calculating an executioner. Birds in flight are targets, but on the ground they incarnate a form of latent freedom for which we have all longed.

Roads and rivers, stars and instinct, impel migrating woodcock, both males and females, to their destination. But in the fall it is the males who linger. With little else but necessity urging them on, they defy nature's caprices, noodling from cover to cover, and pay for their mistakes by dying. It is in most cases the bird without memory, the yearling, who is most vulnerable.

The woodcock flew slowly and deliberately, his wings cupping the northerly flow of air like bowed paddles. Ten days before, he had been in Canada, living on the edge of a road inside a long, thin strip

of alders. Sometimes as many as twenty other birds lived in the com-
mune, while other times he was alone, but there was always food, and
when he left he was heavy and strong.

 He felt good, but that evening he had left footprints in the snow
and for the first time something worried him on. It was the same in-
comprehensible fear he had felt when the sound of a bell material-
ized into the face and then the eyes of a dog. He had dealt with
enemies before, but never one that merely scrutinized him. The re-
peated sound of a distant whistle finally broke the spell, and he flew
away. A week later he was far to the south.

 He was not alone in the sky. He could hear and sense, even when
he flew by himself, other migrations above him. The wind had gath-
ered his entire class and was moving it under cover of darkness to a
destination he remembered—or instinctively knew—as being boun-
tiful and warm. Already the leaf fall was less pronounced and the
ground softer.

When things are not right, or when tedium ponderously wraps
its hands around my neck, I think first of fixing a bite to eat and then
of going hunting. It used to be fishing, but for the moment I want my
gun and my dog. It makes no difference where, because anywhere
I'm allowed to carry a gun is far enough from civilization for me to
imagine myself surrounded by tigers.

 Children, with their vision, are closer than adults to nature and
in a sense know how to guard it against any reality other than its
own. Later in life, beauty, which in nature is uncomplicated, has the
power to express itself in contrasting ways and is perceived by our
complicated minds as feelings dictated by knowledge and time. It is
possible to be saddened by natural beauty, as was the case for me
after my father died.

 A month after I laid him to rest in France, I joined Jim for our
annual October outing. My father had suffered, and since he had
been a proud man, subjected to months of hospital-related igno-
minies, my loss was tempered during the weeks immediately suc-
ceeding his death by a feeling of relief. It wasn't until Jim and I drove
across the cornfield adjacent to the woods overlooking our bend in
the river that the improbable beauty of the moment triggered my
loneliness.

The trees, some older than my father, beckoned his memory, and for the first time since the horrid shrill of the early-morning phone call I cried, knowing that nothing would ever be quite right again. My old friend, with whom I have shared almost everything two men can share, was silent for a moment and then asked, "Are you crying because it's so beautiful?" I replied that I was crying for my father. Jim looked at the mosaic of leaves bordering the dirt road and at the quaking aspens brushing against the window of the car and gently declared, "This is the right place to do that sort of thing."

A HUNT WITH THE INNUIT

Angus Cameron

Pegged out on the tundra was a polar bear hide, and I remember being astonished at its size. Almost any skin looks as if it had come off an animal much bigger than the carcass, but the bear skin was so big that it seemed, well, unlikely that a bear's body could have been so huge as to wear it. The young boy Ajak, sixteen maybe, stood by, black eyes shining, waiting for praise, and I was happy to accommodate. Mightily impressed, I must have let a lot of my feeling get into my response. "Jesus," I said, "Jesus, but that bear was big!"

We were a few yards from Kisik's tent, where I had gone with the young hunter to see the skin of his first bear. Kisik, who had temporarily adopted the parentless boy, was as proud of the achievement as Ajak was. He sauntered over to us and asked, "You want to hear about that bear? Ajak not speak English, but I help."

Kisik said something in Innuit to the young hunter, who nodded eagerly and began to speak in steady cadences, a flow that I knew was narrative. He was telling me the story. Soon Kisik interrupted him: "He saying, 'I coming back from Beechey Point with dog team when Nanuq come in sight. He stand up, then dogs see him. Oh, they go crazy, jumping and falling over each other and while I try unhitch they all tangled in traces . . .' "

The boy, excited by his recollection, stopped for breath while Kisik continued his translation, catching up with the story. " 'Nanuq, he run away. I say to myself, 'Oh, dogs soon catch up to you all right.' "

The simple facts were that the great beast soon turned at bay ("Nanuq more mad at dogs than scared," Ajak told us), and while the dogs snapped, yapped, and danced in and out to escape the swipes of the bear's paw, Ajak took his rifle from its sealskin scabbard and walked up close to the frenzied scene. Kisik's translation of the climax was terse: "Ajak say, 'Next time that bear stand up on hind legs, I shoot him. He dead right away.'"

I was, of course, full of questions. "Where did you shoot him?"

Ajak sensed my meaning before Kisik could repeat the question in Innuit, and he answered with a gesture, jabbing rapidly and repeatedly at his own throat with a forefinger. He was grinning proudly.

"How far away was he?"

Ajak turned quickly to Kisik, eager to understand and answer the question. After a short exchange the boy waved his hand back and forth from his own chest toward me, measuring that distance by his gesture. I got his meaning at once, for I was standing no more than five feet from him: point-blank. But the real climax of the story came when I thought to ask what rifle he had used. When Kisik had passed on my question, Ajak bounded away to his tent and reappeared with his rifle. It was a Model 23-D .22 Hornet—excellent for woodchucks.

When young Ajak had basked in my astonishment and admiration and had returned to his tent, Kisik said, "Boy's first bear big thing, you know." He pondered for a moment and then added, "Every bear big thing, though. A hunter remember them all just like the first."

This all happened in 1949, a year that could be said to mark a watershed in Eskimo life. At that time The People (Innuit) of Alaska's Arctic coast were still living the hunting life; caribou, seals, whales, walrus, and fish still constituted their diet. True, they had occasional access by dog team or whaleboat to flour and beans at Barrow or through the trader's warehouse at Beechey Point, but basically they hunted and fished to eat. That very year a drastic change began. The Navy, establishing an Arctic Research Base in Barrow, needed workers for the civilian contractors who were building the base. By 1952, the year of my second trip to Alaska, all but two or three families between Barrow and Demarcation Point (the Canadian border) were living in Barrow and working for the Navy's contractors. Airmail had come to Barrow too, and The People were now in touch with the mail-order houses—Sears, Roebuck and Montgomery

Ward. No longer were they dependent on the icebreaker *North Star* to bring to Barrow once a year the things they had ordered the year before.

Kisik deplored this development. When I camped with him in 1952 he said, "I not know what happen to those people in Barrow. Dogs all die first winter some disease. Boys quit hunting and fishing. Girls not sew, all have the poor eye for sewing clothes, spend all time in tent there watching old movies. No, I not know what happen to them when Navy leaves . . ."

This is not the place to discuss how our civilization has shattered the ancient culture of the Eskimos, and I mention Kisik's comments only because they were prompted by his reflections on the hunting life. He and I had been talking about hunting as it had been practiced before the hegira to Barrow. In three short years it had gone from the Arctic coast. Its practitioners, save Kisik and his family and one other group, were now all working for the civilian contractors of the Navy. But the tradition of hunting was still strong in Kisik and his family and was, of course, still practiced by his sons, Apiak and Oolak.

I was eager to hunt with Apiak, and expected to soon, for we were going to fly in to the headwaters of the Sagavanirktok in the Brooks Range to hunt grizzlies and sheep, and Apiak would go with us. I had expressed a desire to hunt with Kisik too, but he said, rather forlornly, "I not hunt now, too old, but I once big hunter. Did Bud tell you I was a market hunter for gold mine? Oh, I have great fun hunting and hearing stories of old men. Many old, old men not have rifles when young, hunt with bow and arrows and lances. Oh yes, I almost forgot. I have something for you when you hunt that bear . . ."

He sauntered over to his tent, disappeared through its flap, then reappeared holding out something in his hand. It was a narrow eight-inch blade. When I took it I saw that it was bone, diamond-shaped in cross section right down to its still-sharp point.

Kisik said, "You keep this when you go hunt grizzly in mountains so if you shoot and wound that bear and he come for you, you have something to fight him with." This time his big affectionate grin was accompanied by chuckles, and when I responded properly to this sally, he explained about the lance point, for that was what it was. "In long-ago days, old people say, hunters use lance to kill Nanuq. They let dogs go just like Ajak when they see bear. They wait till dogs make Nanuq back up to ice ridge, then when he stand up on his back legs, old hunter drive lance with point like this upwards—here, just below here." He touched his own breastbone. "Reach heart easy that way. Nanuq not last long after that, soon dead."

Then in a reverie he added, "Old, old man with People say he see his grandfather kill Nanuq this way. I not see it but old hunters tell story many times. Old hunters *like* to do dat." Kisik's eyes shone with admiration for the old hunters; he told the story with a hunter's pride, and I realized the key words were "Old hunters *like* to do dat." The People used Nanuq's meat and hide and his fat (not his liver, said Kisik) and they needed the hunt, but they also enjoyed the hunt, and Kisik enjoyed telling of it almost as much, one supposed, as the old hunters enjoyed the encounter.

I hunted three times with Kisik's sons that summer and fall, and concluded that I could not imagine hunting partners more enthusiastic than the Eskimos. Big game or small, it made no difference, the enthusiasm was always there. One afternoon Oolak had come over for a visit. We were living at that time in a cold frame-of-a-building that Kisik had started to construct from leftover lumber at an abandoned Coast and Geodetic Survey camp on Tigvariak Island. It had no winterizing and the windows were plastic sheets. As my old friend in Ontario, Roy Smith, might have said, "You could throw a little yaller dog through the cracks in it." Suddenly Oolak pointed at the window and said, "Akapirik"—ptarmigan. Like a boy released from the thrall of piano practice—he had been helping Sheila, my wife, mend nets—he bolted for the door. He returned with his brother's 12-gauge pump shotgun. I loaded my 12-gauge L. C. Smith and joined Oolak, who was obviously going to fire at the birds sitting. Hastily kneeling and trying to shoot parallel to the ground so he could hit more than one bird, he pumped two shots at the sitting birds—and missed! He fired a third time, and I thought I saw two birds topple over. The remaining birds froze, out of sight. Only then, in his excitement, did he think of me. "You shoot?"

I motioned him around to my left, for I didn't like his excitement behind me and to my right with a loaded gun. Then I walked in and flushed the birds. It was late enough in the year so that the family coveys were already flocking up; there must have been fifteen birds in the covey. In the first rise, half a dozen birds got up and flew into the sharp west wind, squawking raucously. If I had set out to impress Oolak I couldn't have arranged things better. I swung on two birds flying in tandem, and both dropped at the shot; with the second barrel I bowled over a far-flying single.

Oolak literally jumped into the air in his enthusiasm, for these birds were the first, his father told me later, he had ever seen killed on the wing. He kept saying in a rising crescendo of excitement, "Good-good-good-good!" He pronounced it "goot-goot." It was clear that he felt handicapped by his small English. Later I learned that when he told Apiak about the shoot, he said, "I try that next time, more better fun."

Our next time, however, was a hunt not for birds but for caribou. This hunt was a serious one, as the two families were out of meat and had been making do on fish alone for several days. It all started when, glassing upriver with the big spotting scope that we had mounted on an empty fifty-five-gallon gas drum, Oolak spotted a band of caribou crossing the river. Grabbing our rifles and making for the boat, we were soon at the point in the river where the caribou had crossed. Once ashore Oolak went ahead, bent over in a stalking crouch, his black water boots making squashing sounds in the wet canals that surrounded the tundra's bunchgrass clumps.

Suddenly he turned to me, grinning. "Shoot now," he said, using up about half of his available English. In his enthusiasm, he was simply unable to wait, and wait he should have, for the caribou were already over three hundred yards away. But they were not spooked and might have been stalked to closer range after they went over the horizon. The leading bulls were on the skyline and adding distance at every step as they slanted up the side of the long, rolling dune.

But Oolak took his own advice; he raised his Hornet offhand, took quick aim through the little Savage's open sights, and fired. Then he fired again. Then, turning to me, he repeated, "You shoot." He said it with a big smile and in a tone that seemed to say, "Hey, aren't you going to get into all this fun?"

Now that the bulls were spooked I quickly sat down on the edge of a pinguk and held the cross hairs of the four-power scope at the shoulder line of the nearest bull, now more than four hundred yards away. The .300 Weatherby roared but I had done something wrong. Probably I had swung too far ahead of him. In any case, I missed, and in a second the vague line of the horizon was empty.

"Tuktu-puk," said Oolak. "Many tuktu-puk." Yes, there were a lot of big bulls in that bunch. I knew that "tuktu" meant caribou and "puk" meant big.

Oolak did not seem the least bit disappointed. Grinning broadly in his most ingratiating Eskimo manner and examining his new rifle with mock criticism, he said, "Not strong." Then, thinking better than to criticize his brand-new rifle even in jest, he added, "Maybe Oolak got the poor eye."

Oolak's whole performance was typical, and I've thought about it often. The Innuit needed the hunt for the meat and the hides; for them the hunt was not a mere diversion. But if it was business, it was joyful business. A young hunter like Oolak could watch someone shoot birds on the wing and decide to try it that way himself because it would be "more better fun," though it would increase the likelihood of a miss. And he could miss a caribou and grin about it and mock himself. His zest was infectious.

It was also utterly ingenuous, for when it came to ballistics he was wholly innocent. He had never even fired his new rifle until this hunt with me. The day before, when the famous Alaskan guide and outfitter Bud Helmericks had picked up Oolak's Hornet in Barrow (and a .30-06 for his big brother Apiak), I had tried to explain things to him and Apiak. Though their father, Kisik, normally translated all that needed to be translated, his English was not up to the unfamiliar concepts of trajectory and sight adjustment. I could only hope that the new rifles had been roughly zeroed at one hundred yards at the factory, and I hoped, too, that Oolak would confine his shooting to head shots; I had visions of lots of wounded caribou as a result of Oolak's hunting with the Hornet. Of course, I knew that Eskimos killed caribou with the puny .22 Long Rifle load; I also knew that Paneak, nominal leader of a band of inland Eskimos in the mountains south of us, used nothing but a Hornet, and for sheep and even grizzlies, as well as caribou.

But though these friends of mine were innocent of ballistics, they were most knowledgeable about the game, and passionate about the hunt. Every night in the old folks' tent, where we ate, Kisik regaled us with tales of his own hunting and the exploits of others. And Apiak, already a famous hunter himself, would offer a few comments, which his father translated for us.

In 1952 Apiak was twenty-six, the oldest of Kisik and Oineak's children and one of three survivors of thirteen, Oolak and Lydia being the other two. His English was much better than it had been three years before when I had first met him. He dressed with style and on occasion wore an elegant fur parka with a wolf ruff on the hood. It was shorter than the traditional men's parka, designed more like a jacket from outside. I could not help but feel that in a way it was symbolic, for Apiak seemed to me to be a young man torn between a desire to continue in the traditional Innuit culture, on the one hand, and a yearning, on the other, to embrace the new city life of Barrow. I mentioned this to Kisik once and he replied sadly, "Yes, Apiak, he feel halfway between old ways and new ways."

But he was firmly attached to the old ways when it came to hunting. When Bud flew in and announced as soon as he walked a pontoon to shore that there were five caribou bulls not ten miles away, Apiak couldn't get to his new rifle fast enough. I noticed that he also brought along an old ax and a rusty U.S. Army entrenching tool. As we collected the movie camera, the .300 Weatherby, and ammunition, Bud explained that the whole Colville Delta was denuded of caribou save for those five big bulls to the east. Knowing that the camp was out of meat, he had prospected for game. Only five bulls in the delta—that was a sudden and drastic change. Now that the mosquito plague had been ended by the chill imminence of winter, the caribou no longer needed the use of the delta's mud flats for protective coating.

The hunt was to accomplish several things—provide footage for a promotional film Bud was making, give Apiak a chance to "blood" his new .30-06, supply meat for the camp (some for immediate use and some to be brought in later by dog team), and also give Bud and me some notion about the penetration of some of our handloads for the Weatherby. We had loaded a batch of cartridges with a 250-grain Barnes bullet, a bullet heavier than those with the heaviest loads produced commercially, and we planned to use these cartridges later on a grizzly hunt.

As we taxied out into the river for our takeoff, Bud said, "I hope it doesn't suddenly decide to get colder. It's hovering just above thirty-two now and if it drops much we might have an instant freeze of the controls from takeoff splash when we come back." Always something, I thought, to watch out for when you're flying in the bush. As we made our run, I looked over my shoulder at Apiak, who was sitting behind me. He was grinning in pure delight.

A few minutes later Bud dipped a wing and the caribou appeared below, like flies on a screen. We located all but five, but noticed that two of them lay between the little lake where we intended to put down and the other three bulls. As we approached the lake I said, "Jesus, that looks awfully small to get out of."

"Yes," Bud said, "but I checked it out before I came into camp. We can get out—if the controls don't freeze."

He landed and taxied the pontoon tips hard against the low shoreline. When the plane had been staked out, we began what turned out to be an easy stalk. The tundra appears flat from above but, being entirely made up of loess—windblown materials—it has gentle ripples in its surface, low dunes of ancient deposit. A half mile or so ahead of us toward the caribou (happily upwind) was a dune just high enough to screen us as we walked erect. We had to crouch and finally crawl for no more than the last fifty yards or so.

Bud set up to get movie footage of the action, then urged me to try for the closest bull. We agreed that the animal was about three hundred to three hundred and fifty yards off. We also agreed that we didn't know where the Weatherby would hit at that range with the 250-grain Barnes load. We had sighted in the rifle to print the load three inches high at a hundred yards and, comparing it with commercial loads using bullets 30 grains lighter, we estimated that our point of impact would be ten inches low at three hundred yards and perhaps thirty-five inches low at four hundred yards. Fortunately, we had with us some very hot 150-grain loads, and I knew very well where they printed at various ranges. Both Bud and I were aware that Apiak's .30-06 might have been zeroed to be on target at one hundred yards. If so, it was out of it at these ranges.

The less said about the shooting—by all three of us—the better. At last both bulls were down, but neither was dead. Indeed, both still had their heads up, and I got a lesson in Eskimo methods. As we approached the first bull, I supposed Apiak would deliver the coup de grace with his rifle. But no, Apiak said, "Not waste bullet," and proceeded to walk straight up to the animal. Reaching carefully for the far antler tip, he pulled it over until he could put his foot on the down antler. Then, drawing his knife, he dispatched the hapless caribou as a bull is dispatched after the toreador's sword thrust. He did the same with the second bull. Now Apiak's hunting excitement passed, as he prepared to skin and cache the two carcasses. I couldn't believe that anyone could skin and cut up two big animals as quickly as he did. Using knife, hands, and feet, he skinned out both bulls. Then with his knife and ax he cut them up into wholly unrecognizable pieces. When he had the meat in two piles—the bulls fell two hundred yards apart—Bud said, "Now you'll see how Eskimos store meat when the weather is warm."

Using the ax and short-handled shovel, Apiak stripped off and rolled up wide pieces of sod right down to the permafrost—about sixteen inches down in that area at that time of year. He laid the meat right on the frozen surface, then covered it with sod, grass side down against the flesh. Then he stripped off a smaller area, placed the head on the frost, and pushed the sod in around it. The antlers could be seen from quite a distance to guide him back to the meat when the first good snowfall would permit him to use his dogs and sledge.

My day's lessons were not yet over; Apiak had a final revelation for me. After putting the meat of the second bull down on the permafrost, he did precisely the opposite of what hunters from outside would do. Instead of taking great care not to puncture the paunch while butchering, he slit the paunch open and poured its contents all over the meat. Later when I asked Kisik about this, he chuckled and explained: "Oineak and me, we like it dat way, it taste pickled goot, but young folk, they not like pickled caribou, so Apiak do one bull for us and one for him and Oolak and Lydia." The younger generation is the same everywhere—that is, different from the older generation in tastes and practices.

That night we had caribou stew from the big chunk of meat Apiak had carried back to the plane. We sat cross-legged around the pot, which Oineak set down on her best square of oilcloth, which Bud had brought for her from Barrow. Beside the meat pot she set a crockery bowl of seal oil. I knew the routine: pick out a piece of meat with the fingers, dip it in seal oil, bite one edge of the meat, then, holding it with your teeth, cut it off close to your lips with your knife. (Kisik had earlier watched our little daughter, Cathie, look on in awe at this process and had said, "Now you know why Eskimos have short nose." The four-year-old had got the joke.)

Now Kisik said, a bit wistfully, "Coming from mountains I never get used to seal oil."

I found it had a rather intriguing flavor, a kind of fishiness combined with an overtone of ever so slightly rancid bacon. While I pondered how surprised my friends outside would be to hear of an Eskimo who didn't like seal oil, the talk about the hunt eddied back and forth from Apiak to Bud to Kisik, Oolak, and Oineak. There was much laughter.

My mind turned away to the outside, to an occasion when a good friend—somewhat self-righteously, I thought—had criticized my love of hunting. "Don't get me wrong," he had said. "I don't object to hunting by peoples like Eskimos or the natives of the Kalahari who hunt for food. That's different, it's legitimate, their killing is not for sport. They hunt with no more enthusiasm than I have when I shop for food in a supermarket. But getting some kind of *joy* out of the hunt, that's something else."

How sad, I thought. Poor Bill. Not just because he wouldn't enjoy hunting, but it sounded as if he wasn't getting much pleasure out of eating, either.

My reflections were interrupted by the laughter of my friends sitting around the big pot of caribou stew. Hilarious laughter erupted at a sally from Apiak, and I asked Kisik what he was saying.

"Oh, we have fun. Apiak tell how many times you miss dat bull."

I pointed at Apiak. "Tell how many times you—"

"Oh, he do dat," said Kisik, "he say everyone have the poor eye. I guess we lucky we have meat at all."

Nothing, not even the seal oil, would lessen his delight that evening. I wondered whether Kisik or any other great hunter could ever tell which he really liked better, the hunting or the eating. It was the old question in another form: Did he hunt to eat or eat to hunt?

COMMUNIST

Richard Ford

My mother once had a boyfriend named Glen Baxter. This was in 1961. We—my mother and I—were living in the little house my father had left her up the Sun River, near Victory, Montana, west of Great Falls. My mother was thirty-one at the time. I was sixteen. Glen Baxter was somewhere in the middle, between us, though I cannot be exact about it.

We were living then off the proceeds of my father's life insurance policies, with my mother doing some part-time waitressing work up in Great Falls and going to the bars in the evenings, which I know is where she met Glen Baxter. Sometimes he would come back with her and stay in her room at night, or she would call up from town and explain that she was staying with him in his little place on Lewis Street by the GN yards. She gave me his number every time, but I never called it. I think she probably thought that what she was doing was terrible, but simply couldn't help herself. I thought it was all right, though. Regular life it seemed, and still does. She was young, and I knew that even then.

Glen Baxter was a Communist and liked hunting, which he talked about a lot. Pheasants. Ducks. Deer. He killed all of them, he said. He had been to Vietnam as far back as then, and when he was in our house he often talked about shooting the animals over there—monkeys and beautiful parrots—using military guns just for sport. We did not know what Vietnam was then, and Glen, when he talked about that, referred to it only as "the far east." I think now he must've been in the CIA and been disillusioned by something he saw or found out about and been thrown out, but that kind of thing did not matter to us. He was a tall, dark-eyed man with thick black hair, and was usually in a good humor. He had gone halfway through college in Peoria, Illinois, he said, where he grew up. But when he was around our life he worked wheat farms as a ditcher, and stayed out of work winters and in the bars drinking with women like my mother, who had work and some money. It is not an uncommon life to lead in Montana.

What I want to explain happened in November. We had not been seeing Glen Baxter for some time. Two months had gone by. My mother knew other men, but she came home most days from work and stayed inside watching television in her bedroom and drinking beers. I asked about Glen once, and she said only that she didn't know where he was, and I assumed they had had a fight and that he was gone off on a flyer back to Illinois or Massachusetts, where he said he had relatives. I'll admit that I liked him. He had something on his mind always. He was a labor man as well as a Communist, and liked to say that the country was poisoned by the rich, and strong men would need to bring it to life again, and I liked that because my father had been a labor man, which was why we had a house to live in and money coming through. It was also true that I'd had a few boxing bouts by then—just with town boys and one with an Indian from Choteau—and there were some girlfriends I knew from that. I did not like my mother being around the house so much at night, and I wished Glen Baxter would come back, or that another man would come along and entertain her somewhere else.

At two o'clock on a Saturday, Glen drove up into our yard in a car. He had had a big brown Harley-Davidson that he rode most of the year, in his black-and-red irrigators and a baseball cap turned backwards. But this time he had a car, a blue Nash Ambassador. My mother and I went out on the porch when he stopped inside the olive trees my father had planted as a shelter belt, and my mother had a look on her face of not much pleasure. It was starting to be cold in earnest by then. Snow was down already onto the Fairfield Bench, though on this day a chinook was blowing, and it could as easily have been spring, though the sky above the Divide was turning over in silver and blue clouds of winter.

"We haven't seen you in a long time, I guess," my mother said coldly.

"My little retarded sister died," Glen said, standing at the door of his old car. He was wearing his orange VFW jacket and canvas shoes we called wino shoes, something I had never seen him wear before. He seemed to be in a good humor. "We buried her in Florida near the home."

"That's a good place," my mother said in a voice that meant she was a wronged party in something.

"I want to take this boy hunting today, Aileen," Glen said. "There're snow geese down now. But we have to go right away, or they'll be gone to Idaho by tomorrow."

"He doesn't care to go," my mother said.

"Yes, I do," I said, and looked at her.

My mother frowned at me. "Why do you?"

"Why does he need a reason?" Glen Baxter said, and grinned.

"I want him to have one, that's why." She looked at me oddly. "I think Glen's drunk, Les."

"No, I'm not drinking," Glen said, which was hardly ever true. He looked at both of us, and my mother bit down on the side of her lower lip and stared at me in a way to make you think she thought something was being put over on her and she didn't like you for it. She was very pretty, though when she was mad her features were sharpened and less pretty by a long way. "All right, then I don't care," she said to no one in particular. "Hunt, kill, maim. Your father did that too." She turned to go back inside.

"Why don't you come with us, Aileen?" Glen was smiling still, pleased.

"To do what?" my mother said. She stopped and pulled a package of cigarettes out of her dress pocket and put one in her mouth.

"It's worth seeing."

"See dead animals?" my mother said.

"These geese are from Siberia, Aileen," Glen said. "They're not like a lot of geese. Maybe I'll buy us dinner later. What do you say?"

"Buy what with?" my mother said. To tell the truth, I didn't know why she was so mad at him. I would've thought she'd be glad to see him. But she just suddenly seemed to hate everything about him.

"I've got some money," Glen said. "Let me spend it on a pretty girl tonight."

"Find one of those and you're lucky," my mother said, turning away toward the front door.

"I already found one," Glen Baxter said. But the door slammed behind her, and he looked at me then with a look I think now was helplessness, though I could not see a way to change anything.

My mother sat in the back seat of Glen's Nash and looked out the window while we drove. My double gun was in the seat between us beside Glen's Belgian pump, which he kept loaded with five shells, in case, he said, he saw something beside the road he wanted to shoot. I had hunted rabbits before, and had ground-sluiced pheasants and other birds, but I had never been on an actual hunt before, one where you drove out to some special place and did it formally. And I was excited. I had a feeling that something important was about to happen to me and that this would be a day I would always remember.

My mother did not say anything for a long time, and neither did I. We drove up through Great Falls and out the other side toward Fort Benton, which was on the benchland where wheat was grown.

"Geese mate for life," my mother said, just out of the blue, as we were driving. "I hope you know that. They're special birds."

"I know that," Glen said in the front seat. "I have every respect for them."

"So where were you for three months?" she said. "I'm only curious."

"I was in the Big Hole for a while," Glen said, "and after that I went over to Douglas, Wyoming."

"What were you planning to do there?" my mother asked.

"I wanted to find a job, but it didn't work out."

"I'm going to college," she said suddenly, and this was something I had never heard about before. I turned to look at her, but she was staring out her window and wouldn't see me.

"I knew French once," Glen said. "*Rose*'s pink. *Rouge*'s red." He glanced at me and smiled. "I think that's a wise idea, Aileen. When are you going to start?"

"I don't want Les to think he was raised by crazy people all his life," my mother said.

"Les ought to go himself," Glen said.

"After I go, he will."

"What do you say about that, Les?" Glen said, grinning.

"He says it's just fine," my mother said.

"It's just fine," I said.

Where Glen Baxter took us was out onto the high flat prairie that was disked for wheat and had high, high mountains out to the east, with lower heartbreak hills in between. It was, I remember, a day for blues in the sky, and down in the distance we could see the small town of Floweree, and the state highway running past it toward Fort Benton and the high line. We drove out on top of the prairie on a muddy dirt road fenced on both sides, until we had gone about three miles, which is where Glen stopped.

"All right," he said, looking up in the rearview mirror at my mother. "You wouldn't think there was anything here, would you?"

"*We're* here," my mother said. "You brought us here."

"You'll be glad, though," Glen said, and seemed confident to me. I had looked around myself but could not see anything. No water or trees, nothing that seemed like a good place to hunt anything. Just wasted land. "There's a big lake out there, Les," Glen said. "You can't see it now from here because it's low. But the geese are there. You'll see."

"It's like the moon out here, I recognize that," my mother said, "only it's worse." She was staring out at the flat, disked wheatland as if she could actually see something in particular, and wanted to know more about it. "How'd you find this place?"

"I came once on the wheat push," Glen said.

"And I'm sure the owner told you just to come back and hunt anytime you like and bring anybody you wanted. Come one, come all. Is that it?"

"People shouldn't own land anyway," Glen said. "Anybody should be able to use it."

"Les, Glen's going to poach here," my mother said. "I just want you to know that, because that's a crime and the law will get you for it. If you're a man now, you're going to have to face the consequences."

"That's not true," Glen Baxter said, and looked gloomily out over the steering wheel down the muddy road toward the mountains. Though for myself I believed it was true, and didn't care. I didn't care about anything at that moment except seeing geese fly over me and shooting them down.

"Well, I'm certainly not going out there," my mother said. "I like towns better, and I already have enough trouble."

"That's okay," Glen said. "When the geese lift up you'll get to see them. That's all I wanted. Les and me'll go shoot them, won't we, Les?"

"Yes," I said, and I put my hand on my shotgun, which had been my father's and was heavy as rocks.

"Then we should go on," Glen said, "or we'll waste our light."

We got out of the car with our guns. Glen took off his canvas shoes and put on his pair of black irrigators out of the trunk. Then we crossed the barbed wire fence and walked out into the high, tilled field toward nothing. I looked back at my mother when we were still not so far away, but I could only see the small, dark top of her head, low in the back seat of the Nash, staring out and thinking what I could not then begin to say.

On the walk toward the lake, Glen began talking to me. I had never been alone with him, and knew little about him except what my mother said—that he drank too much, or other times that he was the nicest man she had ever known in the world and that someday a woman would marry him, though she didn't think it would be her. Glen told me as we walked that he wished he had finished college, but that it was too late now, that his mind was too old. He said he had liked "the far east" very much, and that people there knew how to treat each other, and that he would go back someday but couldn't go now. He said also that he would like to live in Russia for a while and mentioned the names of people who had gone there, names I didn't know. He said it would be hard at first, because it was so different, but that pretty soon anyone would learn to like it and wouldn't want to live anywhere else, and that Russians treated Americans who came to live there like kings. There were Communists everywhere now, he said. You didn't know them, but they were there. Montana had a large number, and he was in touch with all of them. He said that Communists were always in danger and that he had to protect himself all the time. And when he said that he pulled back his VFW jacket and showed me the butt of a pistol he had stuck under his shirt against his bare skin. "There are people who want to kill me right now," he said, "and I would kill a man myself if I thought I had to." And we kept walking. Though in a while he said, "I don't think I know much about you, Les. But I'd like to. What do you like to do?"

"I like to box," I said. "My father did it. It's a good thing to know."

"I suppose you have to protect yourself too," Glen said.

"I know how to," I said.

"Do you like to watch TV?" Glen said, and smiled.

"Not much."

"I love to," Glen said. "I could watch it instead of eating if I had one."

I looked out straight ahead over the green tops of sage that grew at the edge of the disked field, hoping to see the lake Glen said was there. There was an airishness and a sweet smell that I thought might be the place we were going, but I couldn't see it. "How will we hunt these geese?" I said.

"It won't be hard," Glen said. "Most hunting isn't even hunting. It's only shooting. And that's what this will be. In Illinois you would dig holes in the ground to hide in and set out your decoys. Then the geese come to you, over and over again. But we don't have time for that here." He glanced at me. "You have to be sure the first time here."

"How do you know they're here now?" I asked. And I looked toward the Highwood Mountains twenty miles away, half in snow and half dark blue at the bottom. I could see the little town of Floweree then, looking shabby and dimly lighted in the distance. A red bar sign shone. A car moved slowly away from the scattered buildings.

"They always come November first," Glen said.

"Are we going to poach them?"

"Does it make any difference to you?" Glen asked.

"No, it doesn't."

"Well then, we aren't," he said.

We walked then for a while without talking. I looked back once to see the Nash far and small in the flat distance. I couldn't see my mother, and I thought that she must've turned on the radio and gone to sleep, which she always did, letting it play all night in her bedroom. Behind the car the sun was nearing the rounded mountains southwest of us, and I knew that when the sun was gone it would be cold. I wished my mother had decided to come along with us, and I thought for a moment of how little I really knew her at all.

Glen walked with me another quarter-mile, crossed another barbed wire fence where sage was growing, then went a hundred yards through wheatgrass and spurge until the ground went up and formed a kind of long hillock bunker built by a farmer against the wind. And I realized the lake was just beyond us. I could hear the sound of a car horn blowing and a dog barking all the way down in the town, then the wind seemed to move and all I could hear then and after then were geese. So many geese, from the sound of them, though I still could not see even one. I stood and listened to the high-pitched shouting sound, a sound I had never heard so close, a sound with size to it—though it was not loud. A sound that meant great numbers and that made your chest rise and your shoulders tighten with expectancy. It was a sound to make you feel separate from it and everything else, as if you were of no importance in the grand scheme of things.

"Do you hear them singing?" Glen asked. He held his hand up to make me stand still. And we both listened. "How many do you think, Les, just hearing?"

"A hundred," I said. "More than a hundred."

"Five thousand," Glen said. "More than you can believe when you see them. Go see."

I put down my gun and on my hands and knees crawled up the earthwork through the wheatgrass and thistle, until I could see down to the lake and see the geese. And they were there, like a white bandage laid on the water, wide and long and continuous, a white expanse of snow geese, seventy yards from me, on the bank, but stretching far onto the lake, which was large itself—a half-mile across, with thick tules on the far side and wild plums farther and the blue mountain behind them.

"Do you see the big raft?" Glen said from below me, in a whisper.

"I see it," I said, still looking. It was such a thing to see, a view I had never seen and have not since.

"Are any on the land?" he said.

"Some are in the wheatgrass," I said, "but most are swimming."

"Good," Glen said. "They'll have to fly. But we can't wait for that now."

And I crawled backwards down the heel of land to where Glen was, and my gun. We were losing our light, and the air was purplish and cooling. I looked toward the car but couldn't see it, and I was no longer sure where it was below the lighted sky.

"Where do they fly to?" I said in a whisper, since I did not want anything to be ruined because of what I did or said. It was important to Glen to shoot the geese, and it was important to me.

"To the wheat," he said. "Or else they leave for good. I wish your mother had come, Les. Now she'll be sorry."

I could hear the geese quarreling and shouting on the lake surface. And I wondered if they knew we were here now. "She might be," I said with my heart pounding, but I didn't think she would be much.

It was a simple plan he had. I would stay behind the bunker, and he would crawl on his belly with his gun through the wheatgrass as near to the geese as he could. Then he would simply stand up and shoot all the ones he could close up, both in the air and on the ground. And when all the others flew up, with luck some would turn toward me as they came into the wind, and then I could shoot them and turn them back to him, and he would shoot them again. He could kill ten, he said, if he was lucky, and I might kill four. It didn't seem hard.

"Don't show them your face," Glen said. "Wait till you think you can touch them, then stand up and shoot. To hesitate is lost in this."

"All right," I said. "I'll try it."

"Shoot one in the head, and then shoot another one," Glen said. "It won't be hard." He patted me on the arm and smiled. Then he took off his VFW jacket and put it on the ground, climbed up the side of the bunker, cradling his shotgun in his arms, and slid on his belly into the dry stalks of yellow grass out of my sight.

Then for the first time in that entire day I was alone. And I didn't mind it. I sat squat down in the grass, loaded my double gun, and took my other two shells out of my pocket to hold. I pushed the safety off and on to see that it was right. The wind rose a little then, scuffed the grass, and made me shiver. It was not the warm chinook now, but a wind out of the north, the one geese flew away from if they could.

Then I thought about my mother, in the car alone, and how much longer I would stay with her, and what it might mean to her for me to leave. And I wondered when Glen Baxter would die and if someone would kill him, or whether my mother would marry him and how I would feel about it. And though I didn't know why, it occurred to me then that Glen Baxter and I would not be friends when all was said and done, since I didn't care if he ever married my mother or didn't.

Then I thought about boxing and what my father had taught me about it. To tighten your fists hard. To strike out straight from the shoulder and never punch backing up. How to cut a punch by snapping your fist inwards, how to carry your chin low, and to step toward a man when he is falling so you can hit him again. And most important, to keep your eyes open when you are hitting in the face and causing damage, because you need to see what you're doing to encourage yourself, and because it is when you close your eyes that you stop hitting and get hurt badly. "Fly all over your man, Les," my father said. "When you see your chance, fly on him and hit him till he falls." That, I thought, would always be my attitude in things.

And then I heard the geese again, their voices in unison, louder and shouting, as if the wind had changed and put all new sounds in the cold air. And then a *boom*. And I knew Glen was in among them and had stood up to shoot. The noise of geese rose and grew worse, and my fingers burned where I held my gun too tight to the metal, and I put it down and opened my fist to make the burning stop so I could feel the trigger when the moment came. *Boom*, Glen shot again, and I heard him shuck a shell, and all the sounds out beyond the bunker seemed to be rising—the geese, the shots, the air itself going up. *Boom*, Glen shot another time, and I knew he was taking his careful time to make his shots good. And I held my gun and started to crawl up the bunker so as not to be surprised when the geese came over me and I could shoot.

From the top I saw Glen Baxter alone in the wheatgrass field, shooting at a white goose with black tips of wings that was on the ground not far from him, but trying to run and pull into the air. He shot it once more, and it fell over dead with its wings flapping.

Glen looked back at me and his face was distorted and strange. The air around him was full of white rising geese and he seemed to want them all. "Behind you, Les," he yelled at me, and pointed. "They're all behind you now." I looked behind me, and there were geese in the air as far as I could see, more than I knew how many, moving so slowly, their wings wide out and working calmly and filling the air with noise, though their voices were not as loud or as shrill as I had thought they would be. And they were so close! Forty feet, some of them. The air around me vibrated and I could feel the wind from their wings and it seemed to me I could kill as many as the times I could shoot—a hundred or a thousand—and I raised my gun, put the muzzle on the head of a white goose, and fired. It shuddered in the air, its wide feet sank below its belly, its wings cradled out to hold back air, and it fell straight down and landed with an awful sound, a noise a human would make, a thick, soft, *hump* noise. I looked up again and shot another goose, could hear the pellets hit its chest, but it didn't fall or even break its pattern for flying. *Boom*, Glen shot again. And then again. "Hey," I heard him shout. "Hey, hey." And there were geese flying over me, flying in line after line. I broke my gun and reloaded, and thought to myself as I did: I need confidence here, I need to be sure with this. I pointed at another goose and shot it in the head, and it fell the way the first one had, wings out, its belly down, and with the same thick noise of hitting. Then I sat down in the grass on the bunker and let geese fly over me.

By now the whole raft was in the air, all of it moving in a slow swirl above me and the lake and everywhere, finding the wind and heading out south in long wavering lines that caught the last sun and turned to silver as they gained a distance. It was a thing to see, I will tell you now. Five thousand white geese all in the air around you, making a noise like you have never heard before. And I thought to myself then: This is something I will never see again. I will never forget this. And I was right.

Glen Baxter shot twice more. One he missed, but with the other he hit a goose flying away from him, and knocked it half falling and flying into the empty lake not far from shore, where it began to swim as though it was fine and make its noise.

Glen stood in the stubbly grass, looking out at the goose, his gun lowered. "I didn't need to shoot that, did I, Les?"

"I don't know," I said, sitting on the little knoll of land, looking at the goose swimming in the water.

"I don't know why I shoot 'em. They're so beautiful." He looked at me.

"I don't know either," I said.

"Maybe there's nothing else to do with them." Glen stared at the goose again and shook his head. "Maybe this is exactly what they're put on earth for."

I did not know what to say because I did not know what he could mean by that, though what I felt was embarrassment at the great numbers of geese there were, and a dulled feeling like a hunger because the shooting had stopped and it was over for me now.

Glen began to pick up his geese, and I walked down to my two that had fallen close together and were dead. One had hit with such an impact that its stomach had split and some of its inward parts were knocked out. Though the other looked unhurt, its soft white belly turned up like a pillow, its head and jagged bill-teeth, its tiny black eyes looking as if they were alive.

"What's happened to the hunters out here?" I heard a voice speak. It was my mother, standing in her pink dress on the knoll above us, hugging her arms. She was smiling though she was cold. And I realized that I had lost all thought of her in the shooting. "Who did all this shooting? Is this your work, Les?"

"No," I said.

"Les is a hunter, though, Aileen," Glen said. "He takes his time." He was holding two white geese by their necks, one in each hand, and he was smiling. He and my mother seemed pleased.

"I see you didn't miss too many," my mother said, and smiled. I could tell she admired Glen for his geese, and that she had done some thinking in the car alone. "It *was* wonderful, Glen," she said. "I've never seen anything like that. They were like snow."

"It's worth seeing once, isn't it?" Glen said. "I should've killed more, but I got excited."

My mother looked at me then. "Where's yours, Les?"

"Here," I said, and pointed to my two geese on the ground beside me.

My mother nodded in a nice way, and I think she liked everything then and wanted the day to turn out right and for all of us to be happy. "Six, then. You've got six in all."

"One's still out there," I said, and motioned where the one goose was swimming in circles on the water.

"Okay," my mother said, and put her hand over her eyes to look. "Where is it?"

Glen Baxter looked at me then with a strange smile, a smile that said he wished I had never mentioned anything about the other goose. And I wished I hadn't either. I looked up in the sky and could see the lines of geese by the thousands shining silver in the light, and I wished we could just leave and go home.

"That one's my mistake there," Glen Baxter said, and grinned. "I shouldn't have shot that one, Aileen. I got too excited."

My mother looked out on the lake for a minute, then looked at Glen and back again. "Poor goose." She shook her head. "How will you get it, Glen?"

"I can't get that one now," Glen said.

My mother looked at him. "What do you mean?" she said.

"I'm going to leave that one," Glen said.

"Well, no. You can't leave one," my mother said. "You shot it. You have to get it. Isn't that a rule?"

"No," Glen said.

And my mother looked from Glen to me. "Wade out and get it, Glen," she said, in a sweet way, and my mother looked young then for some reason, like a young girl, in her flimsy short-sleeved waitress dress and her skinny, bare legs in the wheatgrass.

"No." Glen Baxter looked down at his gun and shook his head. And I didn't know why he wouldn't go, because it would've been easy. The lake was shallow. And you could tell that anyone could've walked out a long way before it got deep, and Glen had on his boots.

My mother looked at the white goose, which was not more than thirty yards from the shore, its head up, moving in slow circles, its wings settled and relaxed so you could see the black tips. "Wade out and get it, Glenny, won't you, please?" she said. "They're special things."

"You don't understand the world, Aileen," Glen said. "This can happen. It doesn't matter."

"But that's so cruel, Glen," she said, and a sweet smile came on her lips.

"Raise up your own arms, Leeny," Glen said. "I can't see any angel's wings, can you, Les?" He looked at me, but I looked away.

"Then you go on and get it, Les," my mother said. "You weren't raised by crazy people." I started to go, but Glen Baxter suddenly grabbed me by my shoulder and pulled me back hard, so hard his fingers made bruises in my skin that I saw later.

"Nobody's going," he said. "This is over with now."

And my mother gave Glen a cold look then. "You don't have a heart, Glen," she said. "There's nothing to love in you. You're just a son of a bitch, that's all."

And Glen Baxter nodded at my mother, as if he understood something that he had not understood before, but something that he was willing to know. "Fine," he said, "that's fine." And he took his big pistol out from against his belly, the big blue revolver I had only seen part of before and that he said protected him, and he pointed it out at the goose on the water, his arm straight away from him, and shot and missed. And then he shot and missed again. The goose made its noise once. And then he hit it dead, because there was no splash. And then he shot it three times more until the gun was empty and the goose's head was down and it was floating toward the middle of the lake where it was empty and dark blue. "Now who has a heart?" Glen said. But my mother was not there when he turned around. She had already started back to the car and was almost lost from sight in the darkness. And Glen smiled at me then and his face had a wild look on it. "Okay, Les?" he said.

"Okay," I said.

"There're limits to everything, right?"

"I guess so," I said.

"Your mother's a beautiful woman, but she's not the only beautiful woman in Montana." I did not say anything. And Glen Baxter suddenly said, "Here," and he held the pistol out at me. "Don't you want this? Don't you want to shoot me? Nobody thinks they'll die. But I'm ready for it right now." And I did not know what to do then. Though it is true that what I wanted to do was to hit him, hit him as hard in the face as I could, and see him on the ground bleeding and crying and pleading for me to stop. Only at that moment he looked scared to me, and I had never seen a grown man scared before—though I have seen one since—and I felt sorry for him, as though he was already a dead man. And I did not end up hitting him at all.

*   *   *

A light can go out in the heart. All of this went on years ago, but I still can feel now how sad and remote the world was to me. Glen Baxter, I think now, was not a bad man, only a man scared of something he'd never seen before—something soft in himself—his life going a way he didn't like. A woman with a son. Who could blame him there? I don't know what makes people do what they do, or call themselves what they call themselves, only that you have to live someone's life to be the expert.

My mother had tried to see the good side of things, tried to be hopeful in the situation she was handed, tried to look out for us both, and it hadn't worked. It was a strange time in her life then and after that, a time when she had to adjust to being an adult just when she was on the thin edge of things. Too much awareness too early in life was her problem, I think.

And what I felt was only that I had somehow been pushed out into the world, into the real life then, the one I hadn't lived yet. In a year I was gone to hardrock mining and no-paycheck jobs and not to college. And I have thought more than once about my mother saying that I had not been raised by crazy people, and I don't know what that could mean or what difference it could make, unless it means that love is a reliable commodity, and even that is not always true, as I have found out.

Late on the night that all this took place I was in bed when I heard my mother say, "Come outside, Les. Come and hear this." And I went out onto the front porch barefoot and in my underwear, where it was warm like spring, and there was a spring mist in the air. I could see the lights of the Fairfield Coach in the distance, on its way up to Great Falls.

And I could hear geese, white birds in the sky, flying. They made their high-pitched sound like angry yells, and though I couldn't see them high up, it seemed to me they were everywhere. And my mother looked up and said, "Hear them?" I could smell her hair wet from the shower. "They leave with the moon," she said. "It's still half wild out here."

And I said, "I hear them," and I felt a chill come over my bare chest and the hair stood up on my arms the way it does before a storm. And for a while we listened.

"When I first married your father, you know, we lived on a

street called Bluebird Canyon, in California. And I thought that was
the prettiest street and the prettiest name. I suppose no one brings
you up like your first love. You don't mind if I say that, do you?" She
looked at me hopefully.

"No," I said.

"We have to keep civilization alive somehow." And she pulled
her little housecoat together because there was a cold vein in the air, a
part of the cold that would be on us the next day. "I don't feel part of
things tonight, I guess."

"It's all right," I said.

"Do you know where I'd like to go?" she said.

"No," I said. And I suppose I knew she was angry then, angry
with life, but did not want to show me that.

"To the Straits of Juan de Fuca. Wouldn't that be something?
Would you like that?"

"I'd like it," I said. And my mother looked off for a minute, as if
she could see the Straits of Juan de Fuca out against the line of
mountains, see the lights of things alive and a whole new world.

"I know you liked him," she said after a moment. "You and I
both suffer fools too well."

"I didn't like him too much," I said. "I didn't really care."

"He'll fall on his face. I'm sure of that," she said. And I didn't
say anything because I didn't care about Glen Baxter anymore, and
was happy not to talk about him. "Would you tell me something if I
asked you? Would you tell me the truth?"

"Yes," I said.

And my mother did not look at me. "Just tell the truth," she
said.

"All right," I said.

"Do you think I'm still very feminine? I'm thirty-two years
old now. You don't know what that means. But do you think I
am?"

And I stood at the edge of the porch, with the olive trees before
me, looking straight up into the mist where I could not see geese but
could still hear them flying, could almost feel the air move below
their white wings. And I felt the way you feel when you are on a
trestle all alone and the train is coming, and you know you have to
decide. And I said, "Yes, I do." Because that was the truth. And I

tried to think of something else then and did not hear what my mother said after that.

And how old was I then? Sixteen. Sixteen is young, but it can also be a grown man. I am forty-one years old now, and I think about that time without regret, though my mother and I never talked in that way again, and I have not heard her voice now in a long, long time.

HAWK WHO WALKS HUNTING

John Randolph

I had heard about him long before I met him. I was running a hunting and fishing magazine in Vermont and occasionally heard mention of his name, usually during deer season. The talk had a tribal ring to it. He was a mythmaker, a totemic person in a hunting society. When, as the editor of a hunting magazine, you heard, "That guy up in Duxbury kills big buck; he's good with a light," you considered two possibilities—both of them intriguing. Either the man was an extraordinary deer hunter, a killer of mighty bucks, or he was a poacher, perhaps the most gifted night killer of whitetails around. No matter how it turned out, there had to be a story in him.

In all honesty I wanted this man to be a white Hawk Who Walks Hunting, a Homeric Indian figure. Even a Pigeon Who Walks Hunting might work. After all, in Vermont's hunting circles the highest achievement is killing large bucks—night or day!

His name is Larry Benoit, and I confess I was skeptical about all I had heard. Still, great possibilities loomed: The enigmatic figure from Duxbury might be the real item, a larger-than-life figure who stalks the woods and runs great bucks to bay, executing the elusive big-game animal in a Hemingwayesque moment of grace—or something like that. I conjured Benoit. He was *Beenois* (Beenwaa), a conglomerate reincarnation of La Longue Carabine, Chingachgook, and Jedediah Strong Smith. The possibilities were Cooperian.

Even the jacklighting angle had delicious possibilities. If Benoit turned out to be just a poacher of great bucks, that too would make a story. In Vermont even jacklighters have a certain stature.

The Benoit I wanted would slip shadowlike along high-mountain deer tracks, confronting bucks with giant racks in a deadly pas de deux, the end for the great animal arranged and executed by the hunter in a sunburst instant. He would then conduct some brief ablution, a symbolic gesture to the spirit he had taken.

That was my editor's dream. But I personally needed the shadowy, enigmatic deer-killer. Deer hunting, in my opinion, had become something defiled by hunters. Deer had become meaningless targets instead of symbols. The woods had become an opening-day shooting gallery. I needed a new hero, the real atavistic item. He should admire deer like some Taoist symbol.

The official book on Benoit was clean. He had no record of fish or game violations, and the wardens I asked said he was the real item. I decided to arrange a meeting. Benoit had much to prove, but he must prove it in the woods with me in tow. I must actually see to believe. I called him just before Vermont's 1971 deer season.

"Randolph? I know who you are. I don't agree with everything you write. Yeah, I'll be hunting Vermont next month. Yeah, you can tag along. But writers don't go far in the mountains. How far can you run? Do you smoke? Two of you writers should relay it, one take the first two days and the other the next two."

There was an arrogance in his voice, an implication: "You are probably one of those mortal hunters who sit on a hot seat decked out in Day-Glo orange. You shoot deer as targets. You cannot walk or jog or sneak fifteen miles a day in the mountains—gut-wrenching, side-slipping, rubbery-legged-in-the-end tracking. I can talk *at* you, but I cannot talk *to* you. The moments that have been mine in hunting you cannot know."

I felt small and growing smaller. But it dawned on me that Benoit might have the patronizing serenity of the truly great athletes. They *know* they have a step on the rest of us. Benoit *knew*. I'd follow him if it meant crawling through the woods. Something said that if I could make it I might count coup. It would be like taking batting practice with Babe Ruth.

"Be at my house at six a.m. on Wednesday," Benoit said.

I hit the floor running at my home in Bennington that November morning at two-thirty and by three-thirty I was speeding alongside the steaming White River, worrying that it would be a very late start for deer hunting.

A Welsh-faced leprechaun opened the door of an old one-room

schoolhouse, the Benoit home in Duxbury. His hand, not offered until I thrust mine forward, was hard in the palm. I'd been told he was a carpenter, and the hardness in the bottom of his palm proved he was no stranger to hand-held tools.

"Come on in. There's coffee."

When Benoit turned to re-enter the house his movements were catlike. He had a scatback's quickness. His short stature and heavily muscled shoulders gave him a rugged yet gnomelike appearance that complemented the leprechaun face. He moved with athletic ease, yet intensity lay coiled in him like a dozing snake.

"Sugar or cream?" he asked while holding a steaming cup at me.

"Cream."

Rank coffee aroma filled the little house. I lifted the cup and sipped and turned slowly to scan the big antlers, the sneak-mounted heads along the galleried walls.

"Are all these yours?"

"All mine except the boys' mounts. That one there's Lanny's first buck. The one over there my son Shane took last year—his first."

"Which one was your best?"

"That one," Benoit said, pointing to a wide-beamed head peering down from a sneak-mount in an alcove above the TV.

"He was the smartest. Some bucks are less smart than others—none stupid. You can catch up to them on the track in an hour and they'll make a mistake. Pow, down they go, *kersplat*. Others know every trick in the book. You hunt them for days. That one . . . thirteen days. He never did make a mistake, but one day he took me up a brook. He stepped carefully, never left a track, but his foot brushed a snow-capped rock, so I knew he was in the brook ahead of me. I followed the brook for nearly a mile without finding where that buck came out. I was sure he *had* jumped out somewhere, so I finally backtracked down the brook and walked both banks. I found where he'd made his jump—a long one—out of the brook. By late afternoon I caught up to him."

Kersplat, I thought.

When Larry Benoit told a deer-hunting story there was a sonorous, fatelike cadence and tone to the telling. The ending was inevitable . . . the execution of a creature so immeasurably capable in survival instincts—smell, hearing, and gazellelike bounding—that men have deified it.

"There are two ways to kill"—the word sounded like "possess" the way he used it—"big bucks—by luck or my way. Today we'll do it my way.

"Are you afraid of the woods?" he asked. "You can't hunt big bucks if you're afraid. *All* white men are afraid of the woods. When the light falls around three, they get scared and head for the road. If you have that fear you may kill a big buck now and then, by luck, but you'll never kill the big animals in the big woods. I track them until they make a mistake, often just before dark. I'm not afraid. My father was American Indian. My mother was Welsh. We lived up on the base of the Big Jay. My brother Bing and I spent our summers in the woods. When I was twelve we headed off into the woods and walked north into Canada. We spent two weeks by ourselves. I was never afraid of the woods after that."

"What about a compass? Do you carry one?"

"Just a small flashlight. I never think about where I am until I'm ready to leave the woods at dark. If I can't get out, I spend the night where I am. My three boys know I'm okay. They'll come find me if I stay too long."

Listening to Benoit's descriptions of deer, I realized I'd never seen whitetails with a clear hunter's eye. I had never truly seen the bucks I followed up into the long woods with anything more than a hawk's-eye intensity. There was more required of a great hunter: the Hawk Who Walks Hunting view of the great white-tailed bucks.

Benoit's eye had that unblinking intensity of the true predator, a hawk sitting on a limb, its eye supernova-bright as it sweeps the meadow below. There! A mouse moves in the grass and the hawk's eye focuses with an inexorable intensity, the eye a magnifying glass bending light rays to a point, burning energy into paper. I, too, had that burning-candle brightness. It was not enough. There were other, missing elements.

What, then?

At that point in my hunting career I felt I knew as much lore and science about whitetails as anyone. I had spent nearly a decade study-ing the biology of the animal. I had interviewed the world's experts on deer physiology, habitat needs, ethology, and natural history. And

I had hunted the animals from North Carolina to New Brunswick. I had also read everything I could find on whitetail hunting, but the books, written by professional writers who were not hunters, were invariably over-egged pudding. Only in hunting with one deer hunter had I felt close to the truth.

Joe Jurek of Colrain, Massachusetts, had the hunter's eye— *coeur d'oeil*, the French call it. Joe had the hawk's-eye intensity and he *sensed* the survival thoughts of the older bucks. How does one acquire such understanding? I wondered. Must a hunter make some Faustian deal? Must one spend himself totally to gain such sagacious, almost spiritual insight?

And, more important, was Joe Jurek's insight *the* missing element, or were there *elements*? Benoit obviously had the predator instinct, he might even have the understanding, and, unlike Joe Jurek, he apparently had superhuman endurance. Joe ambushed his great bucks, Benoit ran them to frustration, fatigue . . . to fatal mistake. That, I told myself, sipping coffee and ogling the racks in the Benoit home, I must see.

The New England high hardwood forests have a way of calling a lone hunter in and possessing him in what Robert Frost called a "demiurge" place. Among their trunky hallways, the hush, broken only by the sweep of the wind or the thunk-thunk of a woodpecker, is counterpoint to the hunter's deadly intent. A raven's croak makes him pause briefly on the track. He is alone, his eye, focused on the track, follows its threaded imprint out through the hallways and blowdowns ahead, as far as his eye can see. His eye searches for an ear, an outline—a suggestion of gray-brown where an animal stands motionless . . . watching.

The hunter's thoughts flit in a limbolike trance of terribly focused intensity. His eye and mind are separate racing dynamos. One searching, the other analyzing—planning. "He may be watching me from that little knoll ahead . . . I'll circle behind the knob and if he's watching his backtrail I may catch him standing . . . On the other hand, he may have circled right to watch me from that *other* knob . . . Maybe I should circle left . . . Yes, that's better."

It was into this hardwood world, where I had spent so much of my whitetail-hunting life, that Benoit took me in tow—to pursue whitetails his way.

I expressed my reservation about the late start to Larry. After all, I said, the trip north to our Jay Peak hunting area would take another two hours. By leaving at seven in the morning we could not possibly be in the woods searching for track before nine. The best part of the day would be lost.

"That's what all the hunters think," Benoit said. "There's no need to be in the woods early, unless you know where there's the track of a big buck. We'll take our time today up on Little Jay. If we find a good buck track, the hunt begins then. By nine the light crust will be melted and we can move without making noise. You'll have time enough to push later . . . maybe too much time if your legs give out. By the way, no smoking while you're with me. A deer can smell it a half-mile off."

Larry's eldest son, Lanny, did the driving. (That's not accurate; he did the steering of the gray Oldsmobile rocketing along the toboggan-chute roads of Lamoille County, Vermont.) And while we careened I was informed of the Benoit family preeminence in dirt-track racing in eastern Quebec and northern Vermont. Lanny's prowess behind the wheel was a source of pride in the Benoit family, which, I learned, built the engines and cars he drove, often to victory.

"Where're we going today, Pop?" Lanny asked while ice-and-dirt-drifting a nasty turn near Morrisville, Vermont. Riding the very edge of control, he let the car find its line through the turn the way a skier skis the line, just on the fine edge of control/no control, following the line down-mountain. In the rear seat I felt my feet press the floor, the muscles in my thighs tightening.

"Big Jay. Up near the notch. We'll take John up where we hunted the big buck with Charlie."

Benoit's decisions were pronouncements of law in the family. His position was absolute, the revered father-chief in a tribal family unit. He was a patriarch, the real item in an American culture beginning to question patriarchates. (The Vietnam War and women's lib were working synergistically against maleness at the time—men, it seemed, were screwing up everything.) "Making war is a madness of the testosterone," is the way one female reporter put it to me at the time. The testicality of history. It made me wonder if the male test about to take place on the Big Jay was just some Neolithic puberty rite. What the hell was I going after up there in the rime ice—just a story? I resolved then and there, shaking in the back of that old gray Oldsmobile rocketing between snowbanks, to enjoy the ride.

Lanny pulled the Olds into an old wood road at the base of the Big Jay. It would be a melting day, I decided as I peed by the car and watched the yellow hole form, wondering if that hole would be the sum of my day's accomplishment. Most days spent following bucks amount to that little, but a good hole is something to admire if you've studied them much.

In snow-sign reading, the clean imprint of a big buck's track is to the tracker as braille is to the blind. And pee holes are similar in readability. Benoit could scan the impression of a large buck's foot in the snow and tell a whole story about him—his probable weight, age, size of frame (short-coupled or long-coupled), and the state of his randiness. A randy buck, in the Benoit vocabulary, meant a buck absolutely consumed by the sexual urge. A buck overwhelmed by the drive to mate would literally tear up trees, shrubs, and ground in his seasonal fit of testosterone.

Bucks make pee holes, too, and Larry Benoit knew how to tell their pee holes from doe pee holes, which, if you think about it as a matter of natural history, are made by slightly squatting deer rather than standing-straight ones. "He squats to pee" might mean a buck so small he has not yet learned to pee like, well, a man or a full-grown buck. A "skipper" is a deer that has not yet reached puberty—a fawn. No one should *ever* shoot a skipper, in the Benoit scale of values.

The ability to read sign is one pinnacle of a man's achievements in the Benoit world. As we headed up Jay Peak, he began his instruction at the first deer tracks we encountered.

"See here," Larry said, stooping to examine three tracks. "This one is a buck, the other two does. See how the little does dink around. This one walked over here to sniff, then over there to nibble. Does can never decide what they want, just like a woman—'Oh, what's this over here? Oh, no, I forgot that over there!' Look at the buck track here. Look at the depth of the impression. He'll go about a hundred and eighty pounds. Notice how long the stride is between his front-foot and rear-foot tracks? He's got a long frame. Notice he does none of that doe-dinking . . . stop here, smell there, nibble somewhere else. He knows where he wants to go and he goes there. See how straight his tracks are?"

I had discovered a missing element: White men no longer know how to track animals, especially whitetail deer. It was as if I had never hunted deer at all. To me deer had been targets, although I had added the biological picture, supplied by wildlife experts. I had just entered the woods with Larry. Actually, I was entering it for the first time, an ingenue.

He led me up the Long Trail, halting now and then to explain something about a track here or the imprint of an antler there, where the buck had halted momentarily to gnaw fern roots and his rack had dented the snow.

"See? It's a buck all right, and his rack is fair."

Larry held his Remington .30-06 pump along the tine imprints to measure the rack's width. He laid a rifle cartridge in the buck's track. Its rounded nose nearly reached the point of the buck's right toe pad; the primer lay at the heel of the pad. "Notice how deep the track is. This buck sinks pretty deep, but it's a wet snow. He *should* sink on snow like this. A heavy buck has a big track *and* a deep track. This buck is going to bed. He'll be on the ridge above. From here on we go slow. You keep back."

"Fifty yards?"

"A hundred. You make a lot of noise when you walk."

I make a lot of noise! I'd practiced walking quietly in the woods for thirty years, from New Brunswick to North Carolina!

I fell back, sullenly watching Benoit sneak swiftly up through the hardwoods, pausing here and there, then moving on, always with a coiled-spring alertness. Something had happened to him; I could feel it. I was not behind him anymore, although I could feel he sensed my presence as a potential intrusion.

The woods had changed. The tense hush seemed suddenly drawn taut. The figure ahead moved intently, stooping briefly to examine a track in the soft, wet snow, then pressing on. His movements were insistent and deliberate, in the manner of a skilled boxer stalking an opponent. I had never felt empathy for a whitetail before, but I felt it now. Fate had dealt this buck a malignant hand. I glanced at my watch: 10 a.m. The duel was not made yet; the buck had not been jumped—was not aware of approaching danger. I had the feeling he was close by, perhaps even watching the backtrail that had led him to his bed in the woods above. I wondered if the kill would be sud-

den—a foolish buck—or a prolonged race across the mountains followed by a dusky denouement. That possibility made me worry
about my legs. I felt fresh, but I hoped that a marathon would not be
necessary. "Let him do it somewhere between here and exhaustion,"
I implored. I'd endured a forty-mile forced march of thirteen hours in
the Marine Corps, but ten years had taken their toll. And this uphill-
downhill leg-wrenching had me apprehensive. I didn't want to quit. I
knew Benoit expected it.

Something had changed again. The way Benoit stooped to examine something betrayed a relaxation. He motioned and I jogged uphill
to him—huffing.

"He's jumped. See here."

Benoit pointed to a kidney-shaped depression in the snow. Its
size would have impressed the most jaded deer hunter, and it made
me gasp.

The size of the shape did not impress Benoit at all—he'd seen
big deer beds before. It was the leap prints that the hunter pointed to.

I had never known how deer sense a man's presence on a wind-
less day. (There was not a whisper of wind that day.) Benoit explained that mountain air drifts upward in the morning and
down-mountain in the evening. We had walked uphill toward the
bedded deer. Our scent had preceded us, and with a great bounding
leap the deer was gone.

"What now?" I asked, resignedly.

"Stay back," he replied as he trotted off on the track. *Kersplat*, I
thought, wondering who would fall first—the buck or me.

Benoit jogged away through the gray, snow-filled woods and I
followed, my camera thumping on a Kuban strap at my chest. The
buck slabbed the sidehill, heading down into a long beech tree basin.
Occasionally Benoit would hesitate, sometimes stooping to examine
the track, but as long as the buck ran, he ran. We were near the valley
floor once more by the time the hunter halted and crisscrossed the
woods, peering at the ground first this way and then that. I could run
no longer but walked with long ground-devouring strides. When I
caught up, I was sweating profusely—one shirt drenched and steam
rolling off my wool shirt. Before speaking, I tore off one of my shirts
and tied it at my waist. Benoit still crisscrossed the woods looking at
deer tracks that ran in all directions. I wiped my face and watched,

now more intent on what he was doing than on my physical well-being.

His movements were purposeful—check this track, then that—and almost before I could query him, he found direction and began to walk off on one track.

"What happened?" I interjected before he could get far. He halted and returned. "Look," he said, leading me quickly through the maze of tracks. "That buck has tried to confuse us. He ran in here among the tracks of these other deer and then came out there."

I examined the fox-and-geese track patterns but could find no trace at all of the buck's path through the little deer yard. Benoit was already off and running as I completed my examination. I watched the figure moving, ever moving, away through the slate-gray beech stands. A hunter's moth flitted by me on silent, tremulous wings and I considered briefly what Benoit knew about tracking and the instincts of deer. And I think at that instant the full range of his understanding and abilities struck me. I glanced out through the woods at him: Had he inherited this instinct from his Indian father? Was it from this understanding that his irony—his scathing view of white hunters—came? I ran after him. He never looked back, but kept boring on, his savage alertness riveted on the track ahead.

It must have been an hour later that I finally saw Benoit pause and stoop briefly to examine the track. He let me catch up, and while I removed my second shirt and tied it too around my waist and mopped my brow, he read sign.

"Bucks get mad when they're in the rut and you follow them too long. See here? He stopped and tore the ground up. He doesn't like us pushing him."

The buck had pawed the ground furiously, throwing snow and mud out and away from his pawing. He had torn a sapling to shreds with his horns and then, perhaps sensing the imminent appearance of the thing that stalked him, had trotted on. His movements were also purposeful, the track straight and directed, unlike the dinking-here-and-there tracks of the does we had crossed in the little deer yard. His presence was imperial, but now, it seemed to me, he was worried. I too was worried—for the buck and for myself. I hoped that we could stop and lunch. It would give me precious minutes to sit and raise my legs, a stamina-saving trick I'd learned from an old Marine gunnery sergeant.

Ahead, Benoit gulped one of his patented brownies, a thick and massively heavy and chocolaty, doughy bar that sustains his charges through the woods. There would be no rest stops.

I let my mind wander a bit as I followed the figure jogging and walking ahead along the track. Where the hell would son Lanny be at this point? Perhaps somewhere up on Little Jay. I imagined him dogging another big racker, the poor animal nearly distraught with rage and frustration at the thing that followed incessantly and would not let go. The buck wanted to chase down does to screw, but the man back there just kept coming. Larry said Lanny was the closest thing to the perfect deer hunter he'd ever seen, perhaps even better than Grandpa Benoit, the full-blooded Indian who killed giant bucks when there were no deer in Vermont according to officials of the state's Fish and Game.

Larry felt Lanny knew more for his age about whitetails than he had as a young man. He also said Lanny's physical abilities were awesome, if employed impetuously. One day, while following a buck Larry estimated at 275 pounds dressed, Lanny had taken off on the track like a scalded dog. "Let him ramble," Larry said with his characteristic leprechaun twinkle. "By noon he'll have the buck or he'll be whipped. Then we'll take over." Benoit, fifty at the time, played his hands slowly. Son Lanny blew the big bucks out—running, sneaking, slipping and sliding along ridges, charging with a Stygian scythe. The Lanny stories had already, at age twenty-six, established him as heir to the throne.

"He's tired."

The voice startled me. Larry had let me catch up and in my reverie I had not seen him standing by a tree, waiting.

"See how his tracks splay. His legs are tired. Bucks don't get much sleep in the rut. We jumped him this morning before he could rest after rammin' around last night. He'll make a mistake now."

The light had fallen. I estimated the time at perhaps three-thirty in the afternoon. One hour of daylight remaining. I wondered if I could make it. My legs were rubbery and my thigh muscles ached agonizingly with each step. I could not think of the deer anymore. I glanced at Larry. How could a man so much older than I rivet his intent on a buck when he himself must be exhausted? We had crossed the mountain's crest four times. I estimated our trek at seven miles. Sweat burned in my eyes.

"What now, Larry?"

"You drop back a bit more. He's angry and he's tired."

There are physical barriers to break in endurance sports, and only the great athletes break them with relative impunity. I simply could not concentrate on the buck ahead anymore; my own physical needs were an all-consuming imperative. The deafening cathedral hush of the forest was gone. The quiet joy of walking with a wild animal ahead, to be glimpsed at some point, was now agony. Yet when I could take an instant to watch the hunter ahead, he seemed not only fresh but presciently aware of something. He walked poised now, and as we neared the top of a ridgeline he signaled for me to hold back, lifting and dropping his right arm without turning.

Benoit moved slowly with catlike efficiency. I had a vision of a lioness stalking—ears perked. Did the buck sense the imminence of his fate? If so, then the events before me had an existential grandeur. I happened to be at the nexus of fatelike currents, of things that had happened before on Benoit hunts but never with a witness.

I saw Larry suddenly run forward along the track and then the unearthly stillness was broken by a rifle report, and then another and another.

Despite my agony, I dashed forward to the crest of the hill. Benoit stooped, looking the woods floor over carefully.

"What happened?"

"He jumped. Not because of me. There was another buck here with a doe. He was going to drive him off. I thought he'd jumped because he smelled me. I ran ahead to get the shot as he ran away, but he jumped and ran with that beech between us. I shot, should have had him. Missed."

Benoit took me carefully through the tracks and the story they had written in the soft snow. In the gloaming light we walked it over and talked it through, the way a pitcher talks his way through the what-ifs of his pitches after a lost game.

I wondered how so much effort could produce so little. How could a man repeat such effort day after day, with the split-second chances so slim, the rewards so seemingly fruitless. Was he different from ordinary men?

"We'll get him tomorrow."

"I have to be in Bennington for business," I replied, knowing that I could not possibly last another day of such physical pounding.

Two days later Lanny killed the buck, a 180-pound eight-pointer. When Larry called to tell me, I thought of the buck whose fate had turned black. To the Taoists such an animal is a symbol of immortality, very close to the Benoit view of things, I thought. But with an important exception: The great bucks have something that Larry Benoit wants now. I learned what by examining his rifle.

Larry Benoit's rifle is an Indian talisman of power. As he describes it: "I like to personalize my rifle—give it a little more life than the folks at Remington put into it. I usually carve a deer scene on the stock, paint it with oils, then lacquer it. I also use brass studs to mark the number of bucks it's knocked down. I tie a portion of a deer's ear onto the top of the sling. It's an old Indian custom. Deer have the keenest hearing of all animals, and Indians tied a piece of deer ear to their bows for good luck."

His rifle is a sacred totem. And his tattered green-and-black shirt he also considers a source of his power. He will not part with the ancient Johnson shirt, and he stitches its rips together for yet another season.

Yes, this is Hawk Who Walks Hunting. He is the man who holds totemic power over white-tailed bucks. And perhaps no other one, except son Lanny, has it.

THE CANDY JAR

Richard Wentz

Except for my years of early childhood, I can't remember a time when the handling of fly rods and shotguns has not made for magic moments in my life. I suspect it's not odd, then, that all too often I can't help but recall a late afternoon in November 1976. We had just moved from New Hampshire to the suburbs of Chicago, and the Mayflower crew had had its share of problems unloading the truck. I don't think any of us had truly believed that morning we could successfully squeeze our belongings into the small house we had rented in Rolling Meadows, Illinois. By noontime, I had given up all thoughts on whether this carton should go here or there. A cold, hard-driving winter rain had whipped us all day long, but around four-thirty, with darkness coming on quickly, things looked mercifully to be drawing to a close.

Shortly after five o'clock I signed the load release papers, and asked if anyone cared for a drink. I'd kept a bottle of Early Times in one of the suitcases, and while I scrambled over bedroom boxes looking for it, the crew's kid member scrounged up paper cups.

He was the kid who had shown repeated interest in the fly rods and shotguns. He had carried the cartons marked "Firearms" and "Fish Rods" very carefully to a far corner of the house. He was a big, high-spirited kid. Thick in the neck and shoulders. I imagined him bench-pressing medium-sized U-Haul trailers when he wasn't unloading Mayflower trucks.

The four of us had collapsed with the whiskeys on a wet, filthy living-room carpet. For several minutes everyone was too damned tired to talk. Finally the kid lit a cigarette and jerked his thumb toward the back part of the house.

"You know all that huntin' and fishin' stuff I put in that little bedroom?" he asked. I said I had watched where he put it and appreciated his hauling it back there with extra care.

"Well, I grew up around here, and there's something you ain't got that you're gonna need."

I told him my bird dog was put up in a kennel, if that's what he was talking about. I told him the dog was a shorthair and that he had grown up in New England hunting woodcock and grouse.

"I'm not talkin' about a bird dog," he said, taking a drag on his cigarette. "What you need you can't put in a kennel, and Mayflower can't pack in a box."

"I don't exactly follow you," I said. I took a long sip of whiskey and looked at the quiet, middle-aged crew boss, who for the first time all day had taken off his hat. He started to laugh, and I could sense an empty feeling begin to spread as I listened to the wind still blowing strong through the willow tree by the front porch.

"What the kid's getting to," he said, "is that what you don't have out here is a place to hunt."

Actually, the move to Chicago was not my first go-around with the Midwest. There had been graduate school in Iowa City, then two years of Green Bay, Wisconsin, where I owned a loving but worthless golden retriever and met my wife. What I guess made the Chicago move so difficult was the rich texture of a fistful of bird seasons following Green Bay. Two years of work in Washington, D.C., led to teaming up for a second time with a man named Robert Tucker, who had been a close friend throughout my undergraduate years in Virginia. I had missed all six feet five inches of him for a long time. Big shoulders, big hands—"Yank," he always called me, and I put up with that only from him. In November, I found myself shooting quail on weekends in the familiar sawmill country of his "Southside" Charlotte Court House home. After pushing hard all day long behind pointers through thick, dark stands of spruce pine and sunlit patches of Korean lespedeza, we'd head home exhausted in the truck to plates steaming with fried country ham and chicken, red-eye gravy and biscuits, butter beans and snaps.

Then came six years in New England, and frequent hunts with

another old college friend, Charles Gaines. During this time my wife and I lived in four different rental houses: one on the edge of a small town; another surrounded by a bright stand of white birch deep on a backwoods gravel road; a beach house perched high on a hill overlooking the Atlantic; and a poorly designed chalet next to a warmwater pond where the shorthair rolled in the yard upon rotting, sunbaked bluegills through long summer afternoons.

Like happy children, Gaines and I replayed Iowa seasons together—at one point he and his family lived within a mile of us on the narrow, twisting gravel road. Each fall we hunted waterfowl, grouse, and woodcock with the same impish-grinning abandon we used to share in cornfields and Mississippi River sloughs. Always, between us, there has run a deep-rooted, blood-brother kind of kinship. Over the years, it has made for a natural rhythm and balance that floats us above even the flattest part of a bad day. Working my young shorthair across cramped, spongy covers of speckled alder and long stretches of quaking and bigtooth aspen high on windblown hilltops, we would make our way out to the nearest road come evening in the rich, shadowy autumn light. But when a job on which I'd been working for over a year suddenly folded, I knew there were no more options. Both he and I were aware that as I said goodbye to New Hampshire on a warm, muggy day in November, a period of our lives had passed which would not be duplicated again.

Seven bird seasons have gone by since that November afternoon and we have moved twice. Home is now an old white Cape on a piece of property we purchased northwest of Chicago—a place former owners called Twenty-nine Oaks (all but one of them are still intact). We have a vegetable garden, several shagbark hickories, an apple tree, a cottonwood, and enough daylilies, spirea, jasmine, honeysuckle, trumpet creepers, prairie roses, and lilies of the valley to help us sometimes forget that we left New England behind. There is a good-sized kennel set up in the grown-up half of our backyard acre, and Corey, the old shorthair, has made his manner of peace with a new yellow Lab pup.

What the kid tried to tell me seven years ago, though, rubs like sand in a tight-laced boot. Bird hunting, as I grew up doing it, does not come easily in northern Illinois.

*   *   *

"They look like pheasant tails," I said. It was early afternoon on a hot, hazy Saturday in July 1979, and I had just walked into a place called the Prairie Pub for lunch and a beer. The Pub is located on the west end of the tiny town of Garden Prairie, some seventy miles outside of Chicago in Illinois' Boone County. My eyes were still adjusting from the midday glare, and shadows cast by a revolving, fluorescent Old Style beer display behind the bar made it difficult to be certain if pheasants had in any way been involved with the feathers sticking high out of an old glass candy jar next to the cash register.

"What's that, hon?" the waitress asked. I had chosen a place to sit between the pool table and the jukebox. Given the noise from the window air conditioner, a country song, and the White Sox game on TV, it was understandable she hadn't heard what I'd said. Yes, they were pheasant tails, she explained, and for one reason or another, the Pub's owner, John Ryan, had not tossed them in the trash. She had, in fact, made a point of mentioning the feathers to him because sooner or later they were a good bet to attract bugs. There weren't, on the other hand, very many of them the past couple of seasons, she pointed out. Not like years before when the jar was routinely stuffed full of the long, black-banded chestnut tails.

By the time she returned to my table with a bottle of Old Style, I had sized up the menu hanging on the far wall. I passed up the barbecued ribs, the Prairie burger, and the Garbage Basket (a batter-fried assemblage of onion rings, zucchini, mushrooms, and cauliflower) for a pork tenderloin sandwich. I couldn't recall having ordered one since long-ago days in Iowa. The Prairie Pub's tenderloin came with fries and a choice of applesauce or coleslaw. When I asked the waitress if they had any mustard other than the yellow kind in the jar on the table, she headed into the kitchen and came back with a small ceramic container on which was scribbled "stone-ground horseradish mustard, 9/17/'77."

"John said to tell you he thinks you'll like this," she said. I hit the pork sandwich with it heavily, and after my first bite motioned as best I could for another beer. Though the mustard had momentarily knocked the breath out of me, I suspected I was going to like John

Ryan. I decided to ask the waitress if he could join me for a quick chat after things slowed down in the kitchen. "There's a question or two I want to ask him about pheasants," I told her. Meanwhile, I went about catching up with the White Sox, who at that moment had tripled against Milwaukee in the bottom of the fourth.

It was nearly two o'clock when John Ryan pulled out a chair at my table and sat down with the sigh of a man who had spent a long lunchtime on his feet. He was younger than I had imagined—a pleasant, boyish-faced forty with thinning blond hair matted damp across his forehead from the Pub's kitchen heat. The jukebox was silent; most of the noon crowd had departed, save a few customers who had settled in for an easy, air-conditioned summer afternoon.

"So you want to talk pheasants," John said. "That shouldn't take us very long." He pulled two paper napkins from the holder and idly rubbed several grease stains on the sleeve of his light blue shirt. "Our hunting business is down at least seventy-five percent. We used to have bird hunters, but camping is the thing now, and snowmobilers when we have snow. There's deer, of course, seems like more bow hunters every year, and trappers—plenty of coyote and fox. But the seasons when we used to draw for the longest pheasant tail at five o'clock on Saturday afternoon are pretty well kaput."

"How come?" I asked, tipping back an empty Old Style bottle I forgot I had drained during a strong Sox rally in the sixth. It was not as if I didn't have a handle on the answer; it was simply one of those questions you ask when you're picking up as many local details as you can.

"I'm not a hunter," John said, "except for when we used to fool with rabbits when we were kids along the railroad tracks. There's just not much interest left in the pheasant-tail contest, mainly because the population in this neck of the woods has really petered out."

He would get no argument from me on that. Had I been forced to rely on wild birds for my first two seasons in northern Illinois I might well have left my hunting gear in the back-bedroom closet, where the moving kid had carted it in the Mayflower box. But thanks to a business contact in the spring of 1977, I was offered membership in a small, inexpensive hunt club that released pen-raised pheasants out past Woodstock, no more than an hour's drive from our house.

What I didn't know when I paid my first year's dues was that even this game farm's days were numbered. When I first saw the pink plastic survey ribbons fluttering from the burr oaks during a cold, windy hunt in December 1979, I knew it was the last time around for Corey and me at the little Woodstock club. Acorn Ridge, its acreage was to be called—just one of many upper-middle-class housing developments that had begun to mushroom in the late 1970s out along the final commuter leg of Chicago & Northwestern's railroad line.

"What do you think of this?" I asked John. It was a classified ad Robert Swan had sent me from the *Crystal Lake Daily Herald.* "Attention, hunters," it read. "Garden Prairie hunting ground available. Enough for 10 or more. Duck, deer and pheasant. Also can be used in summer for fishing or picnics. Include your family. Phone after six p.m." Swan had worked with me on a federal arts project in Green Bay ten years before. I lost track of him through the 1970s, but discovering that he lived in Evanston and played viola with the Chicago Symphony was one of the high points of our move to the Midwest.

"All depends on how you look at it," said John, returning the news clipping. "Like how much the guy is asking, and how bad you want to hunt." He pointed to my empty Old Style bottle, but the heavy lunch had left me feeling stuffed.

"It would run two thousand dollars over two years," I said. "The owner sees it as what he called a recreational investment. At least that's how he put it when I drove out here last Sunday and he showed me around his place."

John shook a cigarette from a pack in his pocket and turned to watch three customers make their way through the Pub's front door. "You play it out however you're going to play it," he said, "but if I were you, I'd save my money. That's one hell of an expensive picnic spot."

I thanked him for the advice, and stood up to figure the waitress's tip as John walked around the far edge of the bar toward the grills. "Say, John," I suddenly thought to call after him. "What used to make for a Saturday-afternoon winner?" He thought about that for a moment, then grinned. "Twenty-seven inches would do it," he laughed. "But five bucks says you won't come up with a rooster tail to stick in that jar."

There was a time when the ring-necked pheasant enjoyed a high standard of living in Illinois, particularly through the early 1960s when the federal soil-bank program routinely guaranteed him the kind of quality housing that no longer exists today. Clean farming practices, designed to produce that extra bushel of corn or wheat, have obliterated fencerow cover and brushy field edges so critical to pheasants in search of a bite to eat, a bed to nest in, or a corner to hole up tight from predators. In 1962 and 1963, for instance, Illinois hunters harvested more than a million pheasants each season. This is not to say that the Prairie State ran in the fast company of Nebraska, Iowa, or South Dakota, but some counties regularly hosted two hundred pheasants per square mile in the soil-bank years. Now those counties support fewer than a bird per square mile.

Some of those statistics held poignant meaning for me in the summer of 1979, since I knew the four hundred and fifty dollars which Swan and I had put together to lease land would not translate into a lot of pheasants. Its only justification was the fact that for the first time in my life I was staring at an autumn that offered me as much hunting opportunity as an empty box of 16-gauge shotgun shells. Compounding the problem was the severity of Illinois' past two winters. Heavy storms had dealt a deathblow to northern Illinois pheasants. The birds literally froze in the bare remains of cash-crop stubble buried beneath record depths of ice and snow.

On a Saturday afternoon in early November, the farmer finally agreed to lease us 180 acres. There was a soybean field that we knew would be clean-cropped. By the time a combine vacuums a field like that, you can putt a golf ball on the field's surface and count on it rolling evenly for ten or fifteen yards. The 180 acres of corn was my main concern; just how it would be cut the farmer couldn't say, but he did think he'd hold off on plowing and disking it until spring. This was important, I had explained to Swan. Given even a little corn-shock stubble, we would at least have some decent cover to run the dogs before hitting a nice-looking slough that snaked across the middle of the corn.

Though the slough was not much more than twenty acres, it was thick with sandbar willow, hawthorn, young box elder, and cottonwood. Reed grass plumed eight feet high on the northern end, and buckwheat-colored cordgrass grew sharp-edged and tangly in the slough's moist center. Off to the east ran a sandy-bottomed stream called Coon Creek, a piece of water that the farmer claimed held nice panfish "and a northern or two." Suddenly, there seemed to be a few shotgun shells left in the box after all.

You have placed yourself on a risky edge when you call a man who sits atop an eight-ton International Harvester tractor a dirty name, but that is what I did on a morning in late November when Robert Swan and I arrived at our hunt acreage and saw the last of the corn being plowed underneath the ground. "You must have got your wires crossed somewhere, Bud," he called down to me from the cab with the big diesel engine whining high in the frosty fall air. "You'd best take it up with Bill. If he says the corn goes under, the corn goes under. Now move your ass out of this furrow, and call off your god-damned dog."

We hunted our four-hundred-and-fifty-dollar twenty-acre slough hard through the rest of the season, and on January 6, 1980, I went to the Prairie Pub and paid John Ryan his five-dollar bill. ("Five bucks says you won't come up with a rooster tail," he had said.) Heavy black field mud curled around the rungs of the Pub's barstools; there had been a three-day thaw, but weather reports promised cold Arctic air was to blow in soon. Robert and I sat down at the table by the jukebox and ordered rare Prairie cheeseburgers, stone-ground horseradish mustard, chili, and fries. We had seen one rooster all season—a bright-plumaged, long-spurred cockbird that Corey had locked onto tight by the east side of the slough. "Whoa, whoa," I had said, and the big bird had cackled up out of the cord-grass and swung wide toward Robert off to my right. His little over-and-under cracked once, twice, and we both watched the pheasant sail high across Coon Creek through the tall red oaks on the other side.

When the waitress brought our check I mentioned to her that the total looked to be a mistake, as it included only one lunch, not two. "John said to tell you your five dollars wasn't a fair bet this year," she said. "See, hon." She pointed toward the cash register. "He threw those old buggy pheasant tails out in October. And he threw the candy jar out, too."

THE GREAT SHOT

David B. Wilson

He started out in the morning. Early. Sounds glared out in the pre-dawn: spoon in the coffee mug, twang of the egg skillet, running water; and then those few minutes of silence while he stared into the coffee mug because it was blacker than the night outside the window.

He put the coffee mug down and stood and picked his pack off the other chair. He took up his old 16-gauge pump by the case handle and tucked it under his arm so that he had a hand free to lock the door. He put on his cowboy hat and went outside. The rain muffled everything, even the closing of the car door. The car started with a cough and he backed her out and put her in forward. It was a twenty-mile drive to the new place and he drove slowly, thinking that the rain would keep the birds on their roosts. He found an old sweet song on the radio and let his mind wander.

No other cars on the road. In the fringe of the headlights the desert began. The sun wasn't rising. He flicked the radio off. You never can rely on the weather, he thought, not even in Arizona.

At the dirt road, mile mark 105, he pulled off. The sun began to brighten the sky behind the clouds.

He always felt refreshed walking in the rain in Arizona. The smell of the desert during a rain was as if every parched particle was singing in harmony.

The old car rattled like she was dying over the potted road except when all the loose joints hummed crossing the cattle guards. Two miles down the dirt road he pulled the car off to the side and stepped out. The air was still and rainless, the sky a flat gray mat. Early in the morning the weather was always his mood.

He opened the trunk, put the pack on, and slid the Featherweight Ithaca out of its case. He tucked it under his arm and filled his pockets with shells. He shut the trunk softly, listening now. He wanted to hear the quail. They would be moving soon.

The wash he intended to hunt ran southeast and bent due east around a hill a mile or so away. Smaller washes led down to the wash from the surrounding hills. The land looked creased, like the skin around an old man's eyes.

Walk in the wash till you hear birds, he told himself. In the early morning the birds moved off their roosts in the mesquite trees in the washes and could be found in numbers, groggy from the cold night. They were easy shooting but he didn't like to shoot them in the morning. He liked to walk the wash to see what he could. Sometimes he'd stop to search for artifacts. Today he just walked.

From sunrise on, the birds moved higher onto the hillsides, grazing. They were like cattle the way they grazed together, and had some of the characteristics of some people the way they called to each other and seemed so gregarious. But they're not people, and later, on the hillsides where the shooting is a challenge, he might shoot some for dinner. The breasts were delicious braised in butter and garlic and ginger root and the legs were good, deep-fried in oil with a flour and curry spice coating.

Today, with the rain, the birds would hold tight and flush sporadically. He looked forward to trying the birds that flushed out behind him, the ones he couldn't see flush. He heard birds chuckle off to his right in the mesquite and he walked into the trees, dropping low under the branches. A thorn caught in his ear and he stopped, staring at the droplets of water at the base of the mesquite spines as he unhooked his ear. He crouched through the prickly brush and stood. The birds saw him and flushed, two, then three, and then the rest, showering water off their wings as they went. He took a step and one more went out. He watched them fly up the hillside, cup wings, drop and flare down on the other side of the hill.

He cut across the wash, through slow granular desert sand, and went up over the hill after the birds.

They lay on the far side of the hill in ones and twos, the way he liked to hunt them. He was sweating from the climb and he felt purified sweating out the poisons in the cold air.

Two birds went out at his feet, giving his heart a little jump, and he raised the gun and pointed the birds, heart racing out with them through the air over the hills. He walked through the desert grasses flushing the birds and pointing them with the gun, watching them as they dropped out of range.

Then he lowered the gun and walked through the rest of them, not watching as they flew. He wasn't in a hunting mood yet. Something was wrong, something seemed missing. He walked on. Now he looked into the distance.

In the distance the hills grew larger and then turned into mountains. Above a certain altitude they all had snow, starting on the tops of the closer hills and traveling off like whitecaps into the mountains.

There was frost in some of the wash bottoms in the distance where it hadn't rained. It looked as if it got colder the farther away from the road you were. It had stopped raining. Something else was wrong. Something was wrong with the land. He turned around. Behind him, far away, the twin stacks of a copper mine rose like cigarettes out of a pack. He saw how the sulfur smoke poured out of the tops of the stacks and blew north and south with the prevailing winds.

He turned away from the mine and went deeper into the country after the birds. Much of the land was barren of cacti and only sparse patches of grass grew. The birds ran out ahead of him, appearing and disappearing. Farther and farther he walked into the desert. This was not his desert.

The birds outran him, scurrying over the top of another hill. There was no cover for them to hide and hold.

It started to rain, big drops spattering on his hat, and then it stopped. He had been walking in the barren path of the sulfur smoke. He looked back again and could see that the vegetation on the leeward side of the hills was not much thicker. He could hear birds calling, "Chi-ca-go, Chi-ca-go." No—it sounded like they were asking, "Where are you? Where are you?" They were calling from the east.

As he walked toward the calling birds he thought about a hunt in the rain three weeks ago. The rain had turned to hail, then snow. From where he'd sat, under the outcropping in the arroyo, he'd seen the saguaro cacti light up, looking like dead men walking off into nothingness. And he remembered how every time the rain stopped he'd set out again, only to be driven back as the rain changed to snow or hail. And lastly he remembered how, when the sun finally won through, all the desert creatures had come out in it and he walked so close to them in a kind of truce brought on by the weather.

He stopped. He had come to the top of a ridge. Cacti grew along the slope below him down into the wash. He could hear birds chuckling in the wash. It was lucky there were still birds, and good cover for them to hold in. He turned back and looked out over the barren strip of land.

"Damn," he said under his breath.

He stared out at the snow-covered hills. Coyotes yelped back in the hills and it grew into howling, a sound like laughter the way it echoed.

He put his gun to his shoulder and fired a shot into the sky over his head. The report seemed to snap the air into a vacuum.

The coyotes stopped their howling and their echoes faded away.

And he heard the rain. At first he thought it was the lead pellets falling back down on him. Then he realized it was the rain and he laughed.

He turned away from the barren land and walked down through cholla and prickly pear to the wash. He was careful to avoid the cholla's vicious travelers that had spines like porcupine quills.

ACROSS THE LINE

Thomas McIntyre

The Cessna 206 Stationair, loaded (short of tying bundles to the roof) as much like a Mexican *autobus* as a bush plane could be, wobbled over the snowy crest of the Baird Range, and on the other side the country below opened out into an emptiness more extreme and beautiful than imaginings. Only not "empty" in the least, merely a land without people.

From my seat behind the pilot, cocooned by an unconscionable payload of dunnage only somewhat restrained by cargo nets, with my feet delicately poised upon two one-gallon cans of gasoline and my Jones cap held upside down in my lap in the event we encountered turbulence, I could look down on moose loitering in the sparse stands of timber and a grizzly, brown as Swiss chocolate, loping over the tundra. After an hour of that the plane began its descent, and I began to see caribou too, clopping along in small bands. I tried to point them out to my friend Big George, contorted in the copilot's seat like a draft horse told to wait in the car, but he could not understand my voice above the drone of the engine. At last, there was the Noatak, perhaps the last purely wild major river extant in North America; and then, at a position along the river that the pilot would describe in terms of precise navigational clarity as the "second S after the straight after Warren's cabin," there was the canvas wall tent, already raised against the elements and radiating whitely in a stand of tall shimmering willows on a high bank, with Fred and Louie in their rolled-down hippers, waving as they walked, coming to meet us on the rocky beach where the pilot set the plane down as smoothly as a serving cart stacked with china might be pushed along a street of cobblestones.

Hot damn, Alaska!

That had been the idea all along, of course: *Alaska.* Four of us (two flaming Californians and two resolutely good ol' boys, one from Mississippi and the other from Arkansas; hunters, but hunters who had never before attempted *anything* so intemperate as venturing into the barren Arctic by themselves), gone north—68° of north, a hundred miles or more beyond the Circle—in September to look for caribou *all* on our own; to be beholden to no one but ourselves for a while; unattended by the retinue of guides who normally accompany such affairs; babes in the wild (any and all "woods" left entirely too far south), perhaps, but if nothing else, righteous in our collective ignorance and ready to see what we could learn. We were up for it, we told ourselves; we were confident. Then, after we had unloaded the 206, we four stood and watched it depart, watching until it *blipped* out in the gray sky; and that being very much that, we *were* in Alaska, for better or worse.

"What in the *hell* are you doing?" Fred was asking me a few minutes later.

"Mothballs," I said, sowing white balls of pungent naphthalene around the perimeter of the small camp.

"*Moth*balls?"

"They say bears don't like the smell and keep their distance."

"*Whoa-ho-ho-ho-ho!*"

Nonetheless, I remembered the tundra grizzly (old *taqukaq* to the Eskimos) I had seen on the way in and went right on broadcasting those mothballs.

"Is this *all* the whiskey we brought?" I asked that night, hunkered beside the pale willow fire under the yellow tarp behind the tent.

"I knew he was going to ask that. I *knew* it," Fred declared to Louie. I grinned. Everything was all right. Tomorrow we hunted.

Big George would kill a caribou in no other way than with his pistol (as on another caribou hunt, a sixth of the way around the world, he had been determined to take a bull with nothing but an arrow from his compound bow, and ended up using a bullet from a

.308). In Big George's case, his pistol was a .44 Magnum that fit his hand about the way a .22 kit gun might fit yours or mine. And he *could* shoot it. But he had also brought along a .375 H&H Magnum rifle to deal with a bear if a "situation" arose, because the Arctic grizzlies, we had heard, were no laughing matter—except maybe of the most hysterical variety.

I had my .375 as well, a veteran of African and elk hunts, and, notwithstanding that, an unmitigated piece of junk. To our rifles we added pack frames with our daypacks and cold-weather clothes, and headed downriver the next morning to look for caribou.

Our camp sat beneath a very high bluff that Louie and Fred would climb to glass for caribou, while Big George and I worked along the edge of the wide flat that fanned out downriver from our camp, the flat rimmed with hills inland. The day was warm and sunny. As we walked, I could feel the pack frame lying comfortably against my back and the sweat soaking coolly into my wool shirt in a mild westerly breeze. We soon learned, though, the utter futility of trying to walk around on this tundra and still-hunt.

There was, first of all, no cover to speak of, with the possible exception of some poplar trees at the river's edge and the very marginal irregularity of the land's surface. Stalking, therefore, short of crawling across the highly aqueous ground on one's belly like a serpent, was out of the question. Even walking on the tundra was exacerbated by the hassocks of grass it was made up of. These were too close together to step between, and too unstable to step upon; it was like treading across a mattress stuffed with pumpkins, and the footballers' tire drill would have been outstanding preparation for it. And if you did see a caribou, he would likely be two miles away and moving; and after forty minutes of walking on the tundra, you might be barely lucky enough to reach the spot where you first spotted him— only he would no longer be there. We would, it appeared, have to find a place to wait where the caribou—who were made to walk, and run, on this terrain—would come to us. It was the Eskimo way, I assured Big George.

So we climbed up on a hill and dropped our packs and rifles and got out the spotting scope and almost at once sighted a herd of twenty caribou two thousand yards away at the farthest western brink of the flat, where the river cut a bend around it. There were no fewer than six bulls in the herd, standing out with their white-haired necks against their gray bodies and with their large antlers among the cows' curious dwarf growth—caribou being the only one of the world's deer whose females carry antlers—and one of the bulls carried an excellent set of antlers, rising and flaring out from his head in vast multi-tined arcs.

At the sight of the caribou we hurried to gather up our gear and go after them, but before we got even halfway down the hill, the herd reached the river and crossed the wide gravel beach, then forded the fast icy water, only their heads showing, and came out dripping on the other side where we could not reach them. Now, though, we knew where their crossing was, and worked our way along the edge of the flat to it, seeing shed antlers of past years poking out of the tundra like the bone-white stalks of last season's harvest. At the crossing point we saw where we could wait the next day, wait in the spindly poplars by the river's edge for the caribou to come to us.

The next day, while I waited in those poplars, I remembered the previous day's sun. This much beyond the Circle, its light looked weakened, withered by the distance it had to come to reach so far north. It seemed only robust enough to glance at you askance up here, and even at highest noon it delivered you of a shadow long as the tail of a black comet. But it was still the sun. Today, in an east wind, I sat in snow falling in perfect hexagonal flakes—the Eskimos, it is said, have names for some two dozen classes of snow; what name might they have for this?—feeling my feet and hands grow numb as I glassed with my binoculars.

Big George dragged fallen limbs and finally entire trees down behind a barrier dune on the beach and built himself a fire to stand next to. As I moved my binoculars across the hills encircling the flat, and the taller hills behind them, rising above each other until they reached the black Iggiruk Mountains in the distance, I catalogued from those around me and from my memory the sounds I recognized now as being of the Noatak. They were: that of a raven, clucking; of gulls; of a bird I did not know; of the wind in the poplars; of the wind in the aluminum tubes of my pack frame; of my snuffling nose as I daubed the raw tip with Chap Stick; of the river itself and of ice cracking in small pools and ponds at night (Fred and Louie bounding out with handguns into the darkness at this sound, loaded for bear; Big George and I yelling at them to go back to bed); of the sometimes passage of light aircraft high above us; of the burning of wood in the campfire or in the tin-can stove in the tent; and of the human voices inside the canvas at night. It was not much of a list, but I would, I guessed, put it next to all the sounds *you* may have heard that day.

That night, after no sightings of caribou, I thought, too, of the chores of camp that got divvied up among us, starting with building a fire with the poor willow wood in the stove in the morning and keeping it burning; cooking breakfast; carrying water; sawing wood and splitting it; washing dishes; burning all the trash that would burn and crushing all that would not so it could be carried out with us when we left, every scrap; digging latrines; cleaning and oiling guns; patching rubber boots; fixing dinner; and, after ten hours or more of hunting on top of all that, collapsing, ultimately, onto a cot and drawing the hood of a fat goose-down sleeping bag over your head.

That night, also, we ate the last of the fresh meat we had brought in with us. It was now clearly time for somebody to go kill something.

The most fundamental understanding of hunting's meaning—its essence—is arrived at by a human only at such times as this when he is made to realize, in no uncertain terms, that in order for him to enjoy the pleasure of red meat again in this lifetime, a fairly large mammalian organism must be located, run down, put to death, and taken apart *tout de suite. That* is when one truly discovers what this most ancient of *sports* is all about, when the belly seizes the helm. I have also seen this carnivorous satori more than once overtake adamantly non-hunting people who have come along on a hunt for laughs, people who until that hunt had only a vague or uneasy concept of the chain of stern events required to transport animal flesh from on-the-hoof to wrapped-in-plastic-and-under-glass, and who would never *dream* of taking any creature's life themselves—have seen such people, to their own very genuine dismay, cry out, "Somebody go kill something, all right?" And it was to this same pass that we—hunters all—had come as well.

The next morning Big George and I were back at our stand. It was early when we heard the distant shots, but we would finish out our day here before going in to see.

In the afternoon a large herd of cows and calves appeared on the ridge across the flat from our stand and stampeded down it. They proceeded around the edge of the flat, coming toward us in that sort of inexorable shuffle of theirs, then crossed the river just below us, running in a high-stepping trot when they reached the other side, their stunted-antlered heads and short tails held erect, the river sparkling on their hides. When Big George and I returned to camp, there were caribou antlers lashed to pack frames and caribou meat already on the camp stove.

Meat, we all thought with deep fondness, the way one might recall Mom on Mother's Day. *Meat.*

Fred, swaying inside the tent that night, a large white plastic cup in his hand, hooted happily, "I know of hardly *any* other folks in Tippah County, Mississippi, who have spent today packing caribou down off a mountain on the Noatak!"

In the following days we would eat caribou stewed, chicken-fried, barbecued, and caribou bourguignonne, then go through the same menu all over again. It became imperative for one to remember how generally bleak matters had once been when there had been no caribou meat in one's life.

Sitting on stand one morning, patient as a glacier, I glanced over at Big George down on the beach by his well-tended fire. Three hundred pounds and closer to seven feet than he was to six, he stood naked to the waist, holding his steaming woolen undershirt up to the smoky flames to dry the sweat soaked into it by our fast two-mile hike from camp. His chest and back showed as thick a pelage as the spring coat of a grizzly. There was a trace of snow in the air, and I was glad there was nobody else around to witness this rather disturbing spectacle of nature.

The next morning before setting out, I was squatting over the slit latrine, watching the side of the wall tent a little distance away, thinking of nothing much in particular—or of no more than: When will that bull caribou show up where I *know* he must? Fred and Louie, who had hides to flesh that day in camp, were inside, trying to figure how to make a brand-new backpacker's gas stove go. Neither had operated one of these apparatuses before; and I could hear their fiddling and interchange of concepts, and the occasional reluctant flipping of the pages of the instruction booklet. I could also hear a match being struck and a squeaky valve being opened. Then I heard a *whoosh* of something incendiary sucking all the oxygen out of the interior of the now orangely lit tent as its canvas flapped and the frame shuddered as Fred and Louie each vied for the privilege of being the first individual to break the world tent-evacuation instantaneous speed record. But the first thing to appear outside the tent was neither of them, but a great yellow ball of flame, not so big as the sun, streaking through the air to crash to earth, followed in short order by a trotting Louie, who dashed a bucket of water onto its fiery remains. Then Fred's bemused head emerged from the tent, and both he and Louie turned to look through the trees toward me where I squatted still, shaking my head in grave disappointment at them as they smiled sheepishly, the Brothers Snerd.

The snow had been heavy the night before, but early that morning it was not falling. I was halfway out to our stand—Big George lagging far behind, having hit upon the formula that the only way not to sweat, and therefore not need to strip down every day and dry his clothes by the fire, was to walk at a pace approaching a single kilometer per hour—when I saw a herd of caribou on the ridge opposite our stand. Bending double, I slunk through the low willow brush and dropped off the steep bank of the flat to the beach of black gravel and stones below. I trotted to the stand, but as I peered up over the rim of the flat, I saw, again, only cows and calves, and watched them go on to cross the river, velvet still hanging in tatters from the antlers of some of the cows, the white antlers under the velvet stained red with blood.

At nine a.m., from far beyond the big bend the river made below us, there came the sound of ten rapid shots, then a single clear, placed one. At ten a.m. the snow came.

In heavy snow at noon, I now heard on the Noatak the sound of outboard engines. I turned and saw two open boats traveling upriver with the skinned carcasses of three caribou lashed to the covered bow of one. Seeing Big George and me, five men in two boats put in to our shore. We walked down and greeted them. They were Eskimo hunters who had come from far, far downriver, looking for caribou for the winter. Three were young men wearing baseball caps with the names of Alaska corporations on the crowns. One of the two older men had a face round and full as a fall moon and wore horn-rimmed glasses that made him resemble a village mayor or high school principal. The fifth man, though, had a lined and weathered face surrounded by wolf fur trimming his parka hood. His eyes were permanently squinted and his smile calm as a sheltered inlet. As the others chatted, asking us about caribou, describing how the river was below, he stood silent, settled; and my eyes kept being drawn to him. His was the face of one of the people who with their spears and dogs, and without a backward glance, had given ancient chase to the bison and the mammoth and the caribou, *tuntu*, crossing the land bridge of Beringia into a land no men had seen before. He would know himself not as "Eskimo" but as Inupiat or Inupiak or Innaupaq—probably each some variation on that shifting theme of "the human"—and would likely feel at home anywhere he was in pursuit of game. As I looked at him, I knew who had fired that solitary shot. Then we all shook hands again; and they went on upriver (Mercury and Evinrude, it seemed, now also part of the way of the Eskimo), leaving us in the snow.

For a seventh day, Big George and I set off from camp to sit and wait for caribou. The snow was fresh on the flat that morning, and in it was the new track of a small wolf. I pointed this out to Big George. I followed the wolf track along the edge of the flat until it suddenly turned and dove off the flat and onto the beach below. A few steps more and I found the reason in the diggings and the track of a medium-sized grizzly. I pointed this out to Big George as well.

"What am I supposed to be looking at?" he asked.

I remembered that Big George had never seen a grizzly track before and was probably looking for something much smaller. I drew a large circle around it with the toe of my boot.

"Oh," Big George said quietly. "Grizzlies don't *stalk* people, do they?" he inquired with no minor concern.

I shrugged. The tracks moved off across the flat. We continued.

Later that day I saw a red fox running across the tundra, his tail tipped in white. For a moment, out there hundreds of yards from me, he paused and looked back, his eyes golden and mine, behind my binoculars, brown. Big George came up from his fire and watched the fox with me.

We were both, after so many days, getting *weird* out here on this Arctic tundra, no doubt about it. As the halfhearted sun came out, Big George began the telling of this tale—how much of it fantastic, I neither knew nor cared—about "these girls." What the hell, let's make it *three* of them! About the blue chlorinated water of a Southern California swimming pool. About the hot afternoon sun and iced cocktails. Heated baby oil may have even played some role in the story. By the time the telling got to extremes, we were both howling out of control, adding parts that appealed to us, our sides aching from the laughter as great salty tears rolled out of our eyes. As I said, we had been out here a long time.

As we came in giggling at sunset we saw the two boats of the Innaupaqs coming back downriver. On the bow of the rear boat the severed head and antlers of a very fine caribou bull rode high like the carved prow of some victorious Norsemen's ship. The hunters waved to us, and we waved back to them as they sailed by.

Watching them go, I felt within me the certain knowledge that a bull caribou would come to us. *Would* come to us.

In camp I told Fred about the track of the grizzly heading off across the flat.

"Well," Fred drawled glumly, "I know where he went."

He and Louie had found the bear's print that morning in the snow ten paces from the cold campfire under the tarp behind our tent. Why the bear had stopped, then turned and shambled off, Fred could not say. I could.

"Mothballs."

"Whoa-ho-ho."

"Now, Freddie," Louie admonished him, "we don't know that they *don't* work, do we?"

"You got any more of them?" Fred asked me, having thought about it awhile.

At midnight, Fred awakened us all to tell us that the northern lights were showing in greens and yellows in the sky. I had read that the aurora is the earth's magnetosphere, activated by atomic particles driven forth by the solar wind, projecting a luminescence onto the pole's upper atmosphere—in all, a force perhaps equivalent to the movement of a million caribou. It was also, at this advanced latitude, directly overhead and looked bigger than the mind, making us feel smaller than four grains of sand tossed out upon a beach as we stood, shivering, staring into it.

On the ninth day, the wind still out of the east, Big George and I were on our way to our stand when we saw on the opposite bank of the river a herd of over fifty caribou cows and calves running. We watched them, then went on and set up again.

All day we waited, then decided, at last, to leave here for someplace else. There would never be a caribou bull coming by. As we started in, the wind shifted to the west and I glanced up at the ridge across the flat and spotted flecks of white. I slipped out of my pack and got out the spotting scope and, turning it all the way up to thirty-six power, I saw three bulls feeding toward us, their antlers far above their heads. I told Big George we would wait here after all.

We watched the bulls for two hours as they came on. They fed toward us in a cluster. I told Big George which one I wanted. We kept waiting, kneeling in the low willow brush. Then as they began to get near, Big George slipped down to my right, to the upriver side, as we waited with our backs to the Noatak, and as the caribou moved forward, two halted out at two hundred yards and began to graze, while the largest one, the one I had wanted, continued on till he was sixty yards in front of Big George, who no longer was giving any thought to using his pistol but had his .375 ready. Big George was mouthing silently to me, "Should I shoot?" and I nodded, and when he fired, I held on the second-biggest one, still out there two hundred yards away on the tundra, and when he snapped up his head, I fired my .375 and missed, and heard Big George fire again, then I fired again at the caribou running off now, with the third caribou in tow, and heard Big George fire once more, and I fired and hit the caribou—hit his right antler and shot it clean off—and out of the corner of my eye I saw Big George's caribou still running, then saw it collapse at the instant I heard Big George's last shot, and I got up, reloading as I ran, splashing across the tundra flat, sitting down to fire again at the caribou, then seeing it was impossible now as the two ran in a wide arc and made the river and swam the Noatak to its far side, one minus an antler but in every other respect the very picture of health, I just watched them go.

I slogged back to where Big George stood admiring his dead caribou, oblivious to everything else around him. A bull *had*, after all, come to us, but not to me. We got our packs, and while Big George field-dressed and back-skinned the bull, I worked on the cape for him. The sun was out and warm, and now was one of the parts of the hunt I could still enjoy: the part of the taking apart. Even if I had not shot well—trying to remind myself of the basic fact that if you hunt long enough and often enough, you will miss—I could do this well. I could indulge in the antiquity of the knife and hide, the knacker's art, which was perforce the second-oldest craft after the spearman's. After we had the caribou apportioned, we loaded him onto our pack frames, over a hundred pounds of him apiece, and carried him back to camp, where we came in calling, "Halloo, the camp!" and Louie and Fred ran out to meet us, carrying a large white plastic cup for each of us.

The next day, I added to my camp chores the careful turning of the ears on the cape of Big George's caribou, until they were blue fleshless puffs. Then when the lips were split, I laid out the hide in the shade and, kneeling, poured salt onto the inner side, the "blue hide," rubbing it into all the extreme fringes of the cape, the white salt stinging into the many small cuts on my hands, and I leaving my hands in it to remind me of something about the pursuit of game, something of the sharpness of it. I also wanted to be able to remember the feel of doing one job right.

Louie and Fred and Big George had decided to extend the hunt and push downriver to look for moose now, but I had previous commitments in the Lower 48. They wanted me to come with them, but I could not. When the bush pilot returned on the agreed-to day to collect our camp, I, without a caribou to my name, went with him on the first leg, the 206 filled now with wild meat and hides and antlers, back to Kotzebue, a thousands-of-years-old Eskimo trading settlement on the tip of the Baldwin Peninsula on Kotzebue Sound off the Chukchi Sea, named these days for a German admiral who was once in the navy of a tsar.

Kotzebue was an odd combination of the American frontier, modern times, and the most foreign town I had ever encountered. The heirs of those who had followed *tuntu* and the mammoth now shrieked over the muddy streets on three-wheelers and dirt bikes, wearing dark glasses, their long raven hair flying out from underneath baseball caps. At night, many drank in the loud, low-ceilinged, incredibly smoky Ponderosa, the "Pondu" of local renown, until the fistfights broke out. That night in the Pondu, I excused myself as I slipped through the crowd to reach the bar, and then had someone kick my ass. I wheeled and saw the most beautiful Eskimo girl I had ever seen, a drink in each fist, those fists held up like a boxer's gloves, her eyes fierce as she glared at me. "You're excused!" she barked.

I awoke next morning in the hotel, washed, shaved, and alone with a headache, and wanted above all else for the bush pilot to fly me back out to the moose camp, to the wild once again. I wanted to go *right now*, but told myself I could not. I could not just go off and spend an entire season trailing game for no better reason than just to chase it and be at home with it. That was not done by someone who had the sort of serious commitments to fulfill that I had.

I was still telling myself all that that afternoon at the airport where the commercial jets and military transports landed and took off. I waited uneasily in the small airline-terminal building that trembled from the roar of engines; then, remembering brightly that I had half a pint of bourbon left in my daypack from the day before, I did the only sensible thing under the circumstances and slipped into the unoccupied men's room and finished the whiskey, dropping the empty into the trash. I stared at myself in the mirror and wondered, then, what it was I had learned by crossing the line out onto the tundra. That I could survive? That I was maybe not as ignorant of the wild as I had thought? That even in letting the game escape, I had still captured it somewhere within me? That I could not, finally, tell you why I was leaving? No, I could not answer any of those questions or I might not board my scheduled flight.

Back in the waiting room a man was sitting with two large cardboard boxes at his feet, smiling this almost Zen smile. I myself was feeling right friendly now; resigned, I thought.

How was he doing?

Pretty good, he told me.

Been hunting?

In a way. He was a paleontologist.

Oh, got your digging equipment in those boxes?

No, he told me, grinning wide-eyed now. That happened to be a baby mammoth.

It also happened to be, for me, the last straw.

WHEN NO ONE IS LOOKING

Gene Hill

It was nearly a two-hour walk to the woodcock cover that I favored, not a major expedition when you're fourteen, but still, two hours is two hours. I'd been looking forward all week to this Saturday; according to the old-timers, everything was perfect: a full moon, a northeast wind, and mild nights. If the birds were ever going to be down, it was right now. The last turn in the dirt road that bordered the long, winding popple stand always held a certain magic for me; on the left side were the popples and on the right, just a couple of feet higher and drier, were the birches. I always hunted the popples first because the birds I flushed or shot at and missed would almost always swing across the road and into the birches, where it was a lot more open. (Figuring this out gave me a highly exaggerated idea of my bird sense that I cherished for years. I guess I was on a level of intelligence with a three-month-old setter puppy; I have gotten somewhat smarter.)

Just before I turned the corner where my hunting would begin, I was cheerily greeted by a handsome tricolor setter, tinkling a small bell on his collar. I had known him for years, but my heart fell as I realized that Judge Landis either was about to enter my cover or had just finished hunting it. He must have seen me first, because he was leaning up against his yellow Packard and holding an apple in his hand; he tossed it over and I put it in my pocket.

The Judge as often as not hunted wearing his business suit, over which he'd pull a pair of farmer's bib overalls. I don't ever remember seeing him without a necktie. The little door on the side of the convertible was open—it was called a golf-club compartment—and I could see the leather shotgun cases.

"Good morning, sir," I said.

"And good morning to you," he replied with a generous smile. He was one of my hunting heroes and I suspect he knew it.

"I gather you are a fancier of *Philohela minor*," he said, "and you have been listening to all that nonsense from the loafers at the post office about the full moon and you are standing there wondering if I've left you any birds, right?"

"Yes, sir," I said, trying to keep Rufus from licking my face anymore.

"Well, sir," the Judge said, "we are now involved in a fine point of the law—unwritten, of course. We have two gentlemen arriving at the same place at about the same time for a similar purpose and we must adjudicate who has priority. Is that about the way you see it?"

"Yes, sir."

"Fine," he said. "Since we are agreed on that, we have to proceed. I'll grant that we have arrived simultaneously, since I have the advantage of a motor. May I ask how many years you have been gunning this cover? Eight, ten, twelve?"

"I'm only fourteen, sir," I said.

"Let me rephrase the question. How often have you hunted this cover?"

"Twice last year," I replied. "My father and I found some birds in it last fall when we were looking for a place to set mink traps."

"Did you get any mink?"

"Two, sir."

"Did you get any birds?"

"Three the first time, and only one the next."

"How many shells?" he asked, looking at my single-barrel 20-gauge.

"Almost half a box," I answered.

"These things take time, of course, and I notice that you aren't hunting with a dog. Rufus is a marvel on woodcock."

"So I've heard," I said.

"I'll tell you what," the Judge said after a bit of a pause, "there is usually far too much time wasted in useless court procedures when the basis of contention is purely common sense. I have always held that two just and honest men can usually settle their differences with both equity and amity, given a quiet moment to discuss them. May I make a suggestion?"

"Yes, sir," I said. And I knew what he was going to say and it was like a dream come true. I'm sure I was smiling as hard as I was trying not to.

"If you would be so kind as to do me two favors, I would greatly appreciate it."

"And what would they be, sir?" I asked him.

"Well, here I am with a new sixteen-gauge from England, a company by the name of Boss, and I can't wait to use it. On the other hand, I want to give Rufus a good workout since I'm sure we're going to be into birds, and I'll need some help. Would you mind using my old 20-gauge Parker? I think the two shots are an advantage over one, and between us I believe we could do justice to Rufus. We could sort of back each other up if we have to; hate to see a dog work hard and not have the reward of a retrieve. What do you say?"

I handed him my single-barrel, carefully opened, and he slid it into the golf-club compartment after he withdrew the two leather cases. I will remember the look and smell of the Boss as long as I live, and the fear that I would fall and scratch the Parker he'd put together and handed me. He made no condescending chatter about gun safety, merely said that the gun had an automatic safety and was bored pretty open in both barrels.

He noticed that I was walking a little gingerly into the alders, and he took a minute to point out that the gun was his bird gun, already had plenty of "good honest scratches," and one or two more wouldn't hurt it any.

Rufus was as good as I'd heard, and the loafers down at the post office were right, for once. The flight was in and the morning was such that I still, all these years later, sometimes wonder if I'd only imagined this or if it really happened. After I'd gone through my six or eight shells, the Judge put a couple of handfuls in my pockets and told me not to be nervous. We shot often side by side over a point, and the Judge claimed that most of his shooting was just insurance and that I may have been born just so I could handle his Parker. I think this was the first of many, but not enough, days when shooting had that magical aspect of being "perfect." I had never gunned with a person like the Judge—in truth, I had hardly gunned with anyone at all other than my father—I had never seen a bird dog like Rufus, nor had I ever before been into birds seemingly spaced the ideal time apart. I dreaded the moment when the Judge would pull out his railroad watch and then snap the cover down on the day of days.

Close to noon the Judge called in Rufus and snapped the leash on his collar, opened his gun and left it open across his arm. I did the same with the Parker and handed the Judge the two shells that had been in it. They were the last of the handfuls he had given me. "Better keep those," he said. "I don't believe there's a more empty feeling than having a gun over your arm and not a shell in your pocket."

On the walk back to the car the Judge chatted about this and that—just as if I were a grown-up friend of his—and something inside me changed; I could almost hear a click, the sort of sound the hour hand makes on a grandfather clock. A couple of hours ago I was just an ordinary boy, now I was something else; I wasn't sure what I was but I was something else—I was *thinking* differently than I ever had. I suddenly knew that someday I would be somebody like the Judge, that I would have my own Parker and my own Rufus, my own Packard—I could see it all happening, and I wasn't afraid of it as I had been before. It was like I was walking alongside someone I used to know; it was a little scary but in a nice kind of way, like seeing your reflection all broken up in the ripples of a lake.

At the car we watered Rufus, and the Judge put the guns up and slid them back into the little compartment. "I've got the time to drop you off close to home, if you'd like," he said. I said I'd like that very much, if it wasn't too much trouble. "No trouble at all," he said, tugging the bill of my corduroy cap down over my eyes a little—the way men will do—"we're friends, hunting partners, how could it be too much trouble?"

I tried to tell him how I felt, how much I'd enjoyed his allowing me to go along, but words didn't come easily to me then. He said he understood and that the pleasure was all his and he thanked me for helping him work Rufus. Then he asked me a strange question. He said, "What does hunting mean to you, besides shooting something to give to your mother?"

I couldn't begin to sort out all the things that were in my head— I don't think I've got them all sorted out yet—but he really didn't want to hear what I had to say; it was just that he wanted to answer his own question. He wasn't being rude, it was simply part of his manner.

"I think a lot about hunting, it's a complicated piece of business," he said. "But I remember one thing that came to me when I

was a little older than you are. I was out by myself, with one of my
father's good bird dogs—and one of his good guns. He didn't mind,
he believed that things are meant to be used. And while I was out, I
had what I like to think of as a T-H-O-U-G-H-T." (He spelled it out
and it sounded like it was all in capital letters.) "I haven't had too
many, so they're not all that hard to remember. I was hunting grouse,
and a young bird flew up in front of the dog and landed on a branch
of some kind of pine . . . tamarack, maybe. I'd missed three or four
and I hated to come home empty-handed, my father always had
something to say about *that*. I swung the gun up on that bird, and
then I put it down. That's when I had my *thought:* I thought that
here I was alone, doing the right thing—a thing I knew that many
men wouldn't blink an eye over—and I was in the most vulnerable of
moments—*when no one is looking*. I knew then that I'd turn out all
right. I knew then that I was an honest person. *That I could trust
myself*. What do you think of that?"

I thought about it without saying anything. The Judge didn't
really want an answer as much as he wanted an audience. He went on
about law being the civilizing structure and was quoting himself
when we came up to the lane that led to our farm. He stopped the car
and got out and walked a few steps with me while he told me that it
had been his pleasure to have had my company, and some other
things like that. No one had ever talked to me that way before in my
life, and as a matter of fact it was a good many years before I met another man with the natural good manners of the Judge. We shook
hands, made an indefinite date to meet, and he promised that if he
could he'd drop by the farm on his way gunning to see if I might be
free.

I was going to say that while I was doing my evening chores I
began thinking about the Judge trusting himself, but that wouldn't be
true—I've always thought about it, sometimes in the context of hunting but more often not. It got to be a joke between me and the Judge
in later years. We did meet gunning every so often, and true to his
word he would now and then stop by the farm to see if I could go—
my father respected him very much and would gladly take on some of
my work in order for me to spend a little time with what he called an
"educated person."

I was on vacation from college and, feeling homesick to chat
about dogs and shotguns, I went for the first time to the Judge's

home. A maid answered the door, and before she could even ask me to wait, the Judge had come out from a room on the hall and was shoving me into his study. The maid brought us tea and he asked about college and I asked about the bird covers and how Rufus II was coming along. Toward the end of the afternoon, when it was time to leave, I told the Judge that I might go on to study law. He smiled all over, knowing the answer to why before he asked the question, but I sidestepped the real answer and reminded him of the day we first gunned together and the story he told me about discovering that he was an honest man.

"I think I am, too," I said. "I'm not as sure as I think you were, but I'm pretty sure."

"I think I shall ask my wife to refer to me, in private of course, as Diogenes," he said.

We both smiled and I said goodbye.

We continued to see each other, not often of course, but enough so that "Diogenes" became a private joke between us—not a funny joke, really, but more a term of understanding, a basis of rank in a philosophical way. He was there when I foundered a bit in law school and he helped me find the strength to go on. But I think the strangest day was during my last Thanksgiving vacation. I'd come home and gone to see him, and he wasn't feeling well and asked me to do him a favor. "Of course," I said.

"Old Rufus the Deuce has been driving me crazy. Would you take one of the shotguns and stick him in the woods for an hour or so?"

I said I'd go right now if that was all right with him. I piled into the car and Rufus calmed down and went to sleep on the back seat. We drove back to a corner much like the one where years before I'd met the Judge, and I found a likely-looking cover and turned Rufus out while I put the old Parker together. A lot of things had changed, but one thing was as constant as truth and that was the sound of the fore-end clicking into place and the lock closing on the barrels. I opened the gun up and closed it again, with my eyes shut, just to hear the faint tinging the barrels made.

I looked at the gun I held and at Rufus II watching me with his cataract-heavy eyes. I can still remember how pure was the wave of happiness I felt standing there—where no one was looking—and saying, out loud to a young man who wouldn't ever be there again, "I gather you are a fancier of *Philohela minor*," and then, so I wouldn't forget it, I started to tell Rufus II the story of how I first met the Judge—because I liked the sound and the import of the words, especially when he got to the part about having a T-H-O-U-G-H-T and knowing he was an honest person.

A NOTE ABOUT THE EDITORS

ROBERT ELMAN is author of *The Hunter's Field Guide* and a number of other books and articles on outdoor subjects. He is an editor at Winchester Press. DAVID SEYBOLD has written for many magazines and is the co-editor of a book of fishing stories, *Waters Swift and Still.*

A NOTE ON THE TYPE

This book was set in a digitized version of Janson, a re-drawing of type cast from matrices long thought to have been made by the Dutchman Anton Janson, who was a practicing type founder in Leipzig during the years 1668–87. However, it has been conclusively dem-onstrated that these types are actually the work of Nicholas Kis (1650–1702), a Hungarian, who most probably learned his trade from the master Dutch type founder Dirk Voskens. The type is an excellent exam-ple of the influential and sturdy Dutch types that pre-vailed in England up to the time William Caslon developed his own incomparable designs from them.

Composed by American–Stratford Graphic Services, Inc., Brattleboro, Vermont.
Printed and bound by Fairfield Graphics, Fairfield, Pennsylvania.

Typography and binding design
by Dorothy Schmiderer